3-16 G
15.00

W9-CBE-594

Pick another
CHECKOUT LANE,
honey

{ SAVE **BIG** MONEY &
MAKE THE GROCERY AISLE
YOUR CATWALK! }

JOANIE DEMER & HEATHER WHEELER

THE *Krazy*
COUPON LADY®

Pick Another Checkout Lane, Honey
Save BIG Money and Make the Grocery Aisle Your Catwalk!
© 2011 Joanie Demer & Heather Wheeler

Address all inquiries to:
The Krazy Coupon Lady
permissions@thekrazycouponlady.com

PickAnotherCheckOutLaneHoney.com
TheKrazyCouponLady.com

ISBN: 978-0-615-52517-4

Library of Congress Control Number: 2011919059

Editors: Kinsey Lindgren and Ruth Dunbar
Cartoonist: Hugo Camacho
Graphic Designer: Darlene Dion Design

Printed in United States of America

Second Edition

For additional copies visit: PickAnotherCheckOutLaneHoney.com

Dedication

To our awesome kids, nothing brings us joy like you do, not even free detergent.

To our loving husbands, thanks for understanding
every time we disappear to the store for hours longer than promised.

To our parents, thanks for teaching us to work hard and be frugal, and for
never buying that pony we begged for after watching *Wild Hearts Can't be Broken*.

To our readers, thanks for your support and for checking TheKrazyCouponLady.com
more times in a day than you check your kid's diaper.

Oprah and Donald, when this coupon thing catches on and
you want a private lesson, have your people call our people
and we'll see if we can squeeze you onto our calendar.

CONTENTS:

From the Authors

Are we the only people touting coupons as an easy way to save money? Are we deep-pocketed VIPs straight from the Ivy League who have uncovered some exclusive secret? Are we scarily smart or especially eloquent? Nope, nope, nope. We're just two motivated, hard-working, stay-at-home moms with a knack for saving piles of cash, here to offer you some tried and true tips that will change the way you do just about everything. The two of us have saved thousands of dollars by using coupons, and we're ready to help you do the same for your family. We've got this down to a science: an addicting, rewarding, entertaining science. In this book we'll share with you our experiences: sometimes awful, sometimes embarrassing, often hilarious, so that you, too, can learn to enjoy paying mere pennies of the retail price on just about everything. We're bold, sassy, and ready to tell it like it is so you'll be prepared for the real deal. Ready? With our help, you're about to save a ton of money.

Keep in mind, anything worthwhile takes effort. Think of couponing a little like surfing. There's a definite learning curve, some new lingo to master, and a bit of practice before you're riding the waves like it's second nature. You never just jump on your board, catch a wave, and bust out a few "fat 360s". It takes some practice and a little work before you're enjoying the highs of those awesome rides. You'll never learn to surf waiting idly for the perfect wave to carry your lazy rump to shore. You've got to paddle hard and catch the waves as they come. And so it is with couponing. To learn, you've got to jump right in and be willing to work hard. Be patient with yourself as you learn the coupon lingo, find the coupons, and crunch the numbers. After just a few shopping trips you'll become competent, comfortable, and krazy as you enjoy the high from saving big. No need to be an expert math whiz or to spend every second of your free time with store ads and scissors. Our methods are simple and can be used by anyone willing to give it a whirl. If you have this book in hand, you're almost ready to go. First, simply commit to some steady paddling and a little hard work, and soon you'll find yourself walking the aisles confidently, smiling as cashiers and people in line behind you gasp in amazement as your total plummets. Before you know it, these couponing methods will come naturally to you, and you'll find yourself up at dawn, itching to go to the store for the next krazy bargain.

One word about the text—throughout this book, we will use "I" to refer to one of our particular experiences or to refer to experiences we've both had. With the exception of a couple of places where we refer to one of us in particular, the stories and savings we describe have typically happened to both of us. We decided to write as if we were one person because we want *Pick Another Checkout Lane, Honey* to be a down-to-earth, personal book that makes you feel as though you are learning from a friend and actually in the grocery store shopping with us.

If you apply what we teach you, you will easily save at least 50% off your entire grocery bill each month. If you're interested in getting more for less in all aspects of your shopping life, let's do this. Ready to ride this krazy couponing wave with us? Here we go. Visualize success. Picture yourself coupon-confident, with all the skills and tools you need, proudly shopping those grocery aisles…oh, and don't forget a pair of heels.

Frugally yours,

Heather and Joanie

Introduction

Why Couponing

is About to Change Your Life

Sometimes I wear high heels to the grocery store. I strut down the produce aisle and smile at the sharp clickety-clack they make on the cold, square tiles. My coupon binder weighs more than my firstborn (literally!), and it teeters precariously on my shopping cart. As I make my way through the grocery store, a sense of empowerment fills me. I feel comfortable and wise—at ease in this all too familiar place. I get closer to the checkout counter and an odd sort of excited anxiety swells within because I'm about to check out with a basketful of groceries and pay just a few dollars. The grocery store has become my arena! It's where I work my magic. It's where I save my family hundreds of dollars a month. It holds the secret to my success.

With coupons, miracles really *DO* happen! Like the time I purchased a year's worth of dishwasher detergent for the price of one box! Or the trip when the drugstore paid me $25 in rebates plus a free movie ticket for purchasing over $100 worth of name-brand products! And then there was the time I went shopping at the last minute for Halloween candy and realized I had left my wallet at home. With coupons, the $2.00 in change I scrounged from my car and an eight cent loan from a kind cashier, I toted over $20 of Halloween candy home with a smile on my face! And you know I paid that cashier back!

As a Krazy Coupon Lady, I've discovered how to slash my grocery budget by 70-80%. I never pay for toothpaste, body wash or deodorant, (and NO, I'm not smelly)! I never pay more than a dollar for a box of cereal. A quarter is all it costs for cake mix, shampoo, fruit snacks and pasta sauce. In fact, I sometimes go to the store and walk away with extra money in my pocket. That's right. I've made money shopping. Most recently on TLC's show, Extreme Couponing, I showed the world I could take a $600 grocery bill and walk out the door paying only $2. I had four basketfuls of food for only $2. It's all possible. I know because I do it every single time I go to the store. Okay, okay, if I'm being completely honest, I don't usually save 99%. That trip was extreme, even for me! It would be unrealistic for me to expect results like that every trip! But I'm completely proud and satisfied when my savings are right around 70%!

How do you pronounce "coupon"?
Koo-pon or Kyoo-pon
Based on results of our poll, half of us say koo-pon and the other half say kyoo-pon. Either pronunciation is correct!

I don't coupon because I'm poor. I do it so I can decide where to spend my money instead of letting retail prices decide for me. Couponing makes sense. Whether it's to pay off debt, make ends meet, save for a glam family vacation, or build a stockpile that will have your neighbors wondering if your new addiction is shoplifting, it's simply an improvement on life.

Because of coupons my husband and I have each started retirement accounts. Because of coupons my kids aren't dressed in strictly second-hand clothes! In fact, some days they look pretty cute. And this year we started saving for their educations. Because of coupons I'm lucky enough to have my dream Pottery Barn dining table that my husband NEVER would have allowed me to buy before I started using coupons (and "YES!" I did use a coupon to buy it!) Because of coupons my family remains debt-free, and my day-to-day life is conducted with greater ease and occasional indulgences, which we did not have when we were dropping $500 at the grocery store every month.

> *I used to hate the feeling of standing at the cash register as (beep after beep) my fate was decided. Now I love watching how high my bill goes before it plummets down the cliff of coupons and Catalinas. As I stand there, I know that I am in control, and that, miracle of miracles, I am more than happy to pay the bottom line. It's a reward for what I do daily. I tell the cash register what is an acceptable amount. I am not his victim. — Sarah*

Whatever your reasons for beginning, I'm here to guarantee that The Krazy Coupon Lady lifestyle will change your life. It'll change the way you shop, the way you think about being a consumer, the way you live. Once you go krazy, you're krazy for life. Every last Krazy Coupon Lady (or Guy!) will shop differently until she is ancient (and she will be living the good life thanks to a posh retirement made possible by dedicated couponification). After your eyes have been opened to the truth about paying retail price, after the cloak is lifted and you finally understand how ridiculous it is to shop any other way, you'll be hooked for good.

One Krazy Coupon Lady wrote in:

> *Couponing has absolutely CHANGED my life! We always were living paycheck to paycheck, and when we really sat down and looked at where our money was going, we found we were spending $1,400/month on food and other necessities! Yikes! In only six weeks of couponing, I was able to bring that cost down to only $90!!! WOW! I'm hoping my new hobby will allow us to feel a bit more relaxed about our finances. — Sarah Ray*

Don't worry. I'm no miser, applauding people for saving $0.30 on paper towels. I don't buy cases of soup I'll never use just so I can get $0.50 off. Maybe that's your perception of coupon ladies: eager to work hard for a few pennies or nickels. Though I think working to save every penny is respectable, that's not me. I work to find the big coupons, and I use them only when the item I'm buying goes on sale, making the final price mere pennies on the dollar.

Someone you know is likely clipping coupons already—a coupon lady. That's not enough; you're going to become a Krazy Coupon Lady. Don't just use your coupon on a full-priced product at the store. Get multiple coupons, wait for the product to go on sale, and stock up. The difference between a coupon lady and a Krazy Coupon Lady is *when* she uses her coupon. Often, I pay only sales tax because coupons allow me to get the item for free. In the upcoming chapters, I'm going to explain, step by step, how to do just that. Not converted yet? Read on!

I save an average of $600-800 per month from all my coupon shopping for my family. Over the period of a year, saving $800 per month totals almost $10,000. Talk about a pay raise! Take a second or two and think about what an extra ten grand could mean for you and your family. This isn't about saving a nickel here and there. We're talking about life-changing sums of money, financial security, and peace of mind...not to mention acquiring the audacious attitude and confidence of a Krazy Coupon Lady.

These results won't take you twenty years to achieve, either. You could be saving 80% at the grocery store within a few short weeks. Here is just one of the thousands of success stories from another Krazy Coupon Lady:

> *I am definitely a changed woman!! I used to spend soooo much money feeding my large family, but not anymore! I've been couponing for just over two months now, and I've finally reached the point where I've got such a large stockpile that I've cut my weekly grocery bill by more than half!! Now I only buy what's on sale and the things we really NEED that week (like produce, dairy, or other perishables). Yes, couponing does take a lot of work, but it's been WELL worth it! I love that I've not only been able to cut back significantly on my grocery budget, but that I also have a great food storage as well. THANKS Krazy Coupon Lady!! — Jennifer*

Another fellow Krazy Coupon Lady relates her savings success. Listen to what Julie in Knoxville, Tennessee had to say:

> *I've only been at this for two months now, but what a difference it has made. In two months alone, I've been able to purchase $750+ in groceries/supplies for under $350. That's only $175 a month, and that's mostly because I've been*

stockpiling at the same time; in the months to come I expect to spend less because we'll already have much of what we need. My husband was kind of iffy when he saw me putting my binder together and clipping inserts, but now he asks me how I did as soon as I come home from the store. And now, instead of awaiting "my doom" at the cash register, I'm all smiles when I sign that receipt. Thank you so much!

Becoming a Krazy Coupon Lady means more than just saving on your groceries. *Pick Another Checkout Lane, Honey* is a new attitude, a new way of life that will get you all the things you've been dreaming of, and I'm going to show you how you can do it. Once you're saving 80% on your monthly grocery budget, you will have a surplus that you can use to pay down debt or buy that new handbag or chaise you've been eyeing. My methods are so effective and, dare I say, "krazy", you just might do both.

At first, it might sound too good to be true. I still remember talking to my aunt on the phone after she had just returned from a shopping trip where she saved $600. I turned to my husband and said, "This has got to be a pyramid scheme." How wrong I was! Look at me now, preaching the coupon gospel to all who will listen.

Maybe your family budget is feeling tight or you've recently considered finding more work to supplement your income. Maybe your home is in bad need of repair or your car is on its last legs and you cringe at the idea of going in debt to fix them. Maybe you simply want to take those beautiful kids of yours on a greatly deserved family vacation. Wouldn't it be nice to remedy all of these concerns and save hundreds of dollars a month simply by shopping smarter? Whatever the reasons, you've turned to the right place! Coupons give you more financial freedom than you've ever dreamed possible.

Although couponing just for the savings is reason enough, a Krazy Coupon Lady does it for more. She treats couponing as one big party. You'll quickly feel the coupon buzz, and then you'll be hooked. I'll show you how to get hundreds of dollars in savings, a feeling a freedom, and a new found sense of empowerment all for only a couple of hours a week. It'll be your new favorite hobby. All the scrapbookers, golfers, gym rats, and tennis club gurus pay money for their hobbies, but your new hobby is about to pay YOU.

Just to make one thing clear, this isn't multi-level marketing. I'm not going to ask you for a penny. I'm not selling you a subscription to a website or Krazy Coupon Lady-brand coupons. I'm just here to teach you something new and, hopefully, help you stop running your finances into the ground. But in order to do so you've got to open up that mind of yours. A lot is about to change! Everything your mother taught you about shopping is wrong. (Sorry, Mom.) All your perceptions about coupons and coupon-ers are most likely incorrect. I know what you've been thinking, and I'm here to convince you there's a better way. Get ready to throw everything you thought you knew about coupons out the window! Keep reading and start saving!

Throw everything you thought you knew about couponing out the window.

Are you ready to keep an open mind? Are you ready to rock your grocery shopping world? Are you ready to learn how to take the reins of your family finances? Want to get soap, maxi-pads, salad dressing, barbecue sauce and more for absolutely FREE? How would you like to make money while shopping?

If you've answered yes to any of these questions then you're ready for coupons to make the difference. I'm here to give you all the inside tips you need, just like any great girlfriend would. And that's what we're about to be: girlfriends, or as I affectionately call us, "krazies." So grab your favorite pillow, curl up somewhere comfy with the last full-priced Diet Coke you'll ever buy, and get ready to throw out everything you know about grocery and retail shopping.

SECTION ONE

Making the Change

SOMETIMES IT'S THE SMALLEST DECISIONS
THAT CAN CHANGE YOUR LIFE FOREVER.

CHAPTER ONE

From Meltdown to Miracle:

RAINY DAY CRISIS MANAGEMENT

The premise of couponing is founded on the idea that change happens. Whether we create it ourselves or it inadvertently creeps up on us, it's always there, lurking right around the corner. Things occur in our lives over which we have little power. But the better prepared we are, the easier it will be to deal with whatever comes our way. John F. Kennedy, in his 1962 State of the Union Address, said, "The time to repair the roof is when the sun is shining."

The best time to prepare is now! What would happen if your family's income disappeared tomorrow? Do you worry about unforeseen financial burdens like a health crisis or an auto accident? Instead of fearing your financial future, prepare by summoning your fearless inner Krazy Coupon Lady. The sooner you start saving money and building your stockpile, the sooner you'll experience the security and peace of mind that comes from knowing you can handle anything that's headed your way.

• •

JOANIE'S STORY

My family rang in the New Year happily. We were optimistic about the future and had no reason to worry. I lived in a cute little house in the suburbs with my two beautiful children, my husband, and our little beagle, Sadie. I was a couponing whirlwind, creating a stockpile and slashing our family budget. In January we celebrated our daughter's first birthday. We had just paid off the hospital bills from her birth and some early medical problems, which were now resolved. Our only debt was our home, which we had owned for four years. It had been a bit stressful watching our equity disappear because of the plummeting market, but we didn't worry too much since we weren't planning on moving anytime soon.

Then suddenly, without warning, my husband lost his job. One day he had a job and the next he did not. And there we were, amidst all this peace and happiness, with absolutely no income. Immediately, we stopped all unnecessary expenditures and scrambled to put our house on the market. The thought of selling our first home, the place where I'd brought my babies home, made me physically sick. The equity we'd felt so excited about a few years earlier was gone, and we were heartbroken. Despite our sadness, we gratefully accepted an offer that would barely get us out above water, and we started to pack up. My husband met with a recruiter for the U.S. Coast Guard and started the process of joining the military. It was at that point we decided we had to sell our dog, Sadie. I can count on one hand the number of times I've seen my husband cry (not at our wedding or the birth of our kids, mind you), but when the new family walked out the door with our dog, he couldn't hold back his tears. We knew we still had much to be grateful for, but nevertheless, it was a devastating time for our family.

In the face of adversity, I stayed strong. I had not yet allowed myself to shed a tear or throw a pity party over the loss of a job, our dog, and our home. But all of that changed a few days later. My infant daughter started wheezing. We took her in to the doctor only to have an ambulance called immediately because she wasn't getting enough oxygen to her brain. They rushed her to the hospital where we spent the next twenty-four hours on the brink of being admitted to the pediatric intensive care unit. Thanks to many prayers, her condition began to improve the next day, and four days later, we took our healthy baby girl home. We were grateful that the situation hadn't been worse, but we still faced $15,000 in hospital bills. We had private insurance and received some assistance, but with a high deductible, we still owed almost $10,000 out of our (unemployed) pockets.

My daughter was released from the hospital two days before we sold our home. We frantically finished packing, threw everything onto a trailer and headed out. In the space of two months, my family lost our income, sold our house, sold our dog, incurred $15,000 in unexpected hospital bills, and moved in with my in-laws. To top it all off, our kids said goodbye to their daddy for two months while he went away to military boot camp. I was left dazed and alone with my two children, wondering what had happened to my life.

I'm not sharing this story for sympathy or to throw a pity party. I'm sharing this story to tell you how much security my stockpile provided and how my couponing skills and experience helped keep me from panicking during this time of vulnerability. One month after my husband returned from boot camp, our medical bills were entirely paid off. I stopped all unnecessary spending and lived off of our stockpile of groceries. My grocery expenses over four months totaled less than $150 for a family of four. I had a good stockpile of milk, cheese, chicken, and veggies in my freezer in addition to all my packaged foods. The money bought our perishables like fruit and bread, but you won't believe this: I continued to replenish my stockpile. I only bought things that were under a quarter or totally free. For four months, I didn't have to spend a penny on toilet paper, shampoo, diapers, wipes, crackers, snacks, candy, or baking staples.

Now that I know it's possible to live on so little, our family lives without fear of the un-known financial future. Whatever comes my way, I'm ready to handle it. *Krazy Coupon Ladies don't need to fear the future; because of their stockpiles and frugal habits, they are prepared for anything and enjoy feeling secure in the face of uncertainty.*

• • • • • • • • • • • • • • • • • • •

PREPARING FOR YOUR RAINY DAY

Some of you are probably interested in couponing because of an unexpected financial downturn in your life. Maybe you haven't had a chance to build your stockpile. Perhaps you have bills to pay and not enough income with which to pay them. Whoever you are and wherever you are on the financial spectrum, the time to start is NOW. Today. Seri-ously. You can cut your grocery bills in half by using The Krazy Coupon Lady's methods.

After you have developed your stockpile (usually within about three months), you will see your total grocery expenditures drop by 70-80%. Individual shopping trips may yield savings of over 90%.

Take a look at Amber's story:

Coupons changed my life before I ever started using them! Last year my husband had a "mid-life crisis" (at twenty-eight). I suddenly found myself a single mom to three kids. As if that were not hard enough, my youngest is medically fragile. She has had fifteen surgeries in two years and has spent a year's worth of days in the hospital. We owe more in medical debt than the value of our home, and the light of day seems far away sometimes.

I was in complete shock and was in a panic about how I was to provide for these kids, keep them in a house, with my unsteady income from my job as a photographer. And then a friend of mine showed up on my doorstep with a near laundry basket sized load of cleaning supplies and food. I tried to pay her for it and she simply said...Why? I got most of it for free. I thought for sure that she was trying to make me feel better, but I would later learn that she was serious.

I can remember coming home from my daughter's first open heart surgery. Our bank account was overdrawn, our credit cards were maxed out, and we had a few spoiled items in the fridge. We had nothing to feed our kids. I remember how I felt like a complete failure.

I have only been seriously stockpiling for 2-3 months now, but in that time, we have been able to keep our food budget to $50/week, and we are gradually chipping away at our debt. Moreover, my kids will never be hungry again. No matter how long we are hospitalized now, I know I can come home to a fully stocked freezer with meats and cheeses, cereal (brand name at that!), rice, and pastas in the perishables pantry...and I know that I can provide for them, even if I had bought nothing else...for at least a month.

I am so thankful for coupons. My husband is home now (thanks to some amazing prayer warriors), and we are enjoying date night—couponing together. Coupons have inspired me, lifted my spirits, provided for my family, and have helped my husband and me bond again. Coupons are so much more to me than a few bucks saved.

I hear hundreds of these stories every month: lives transformed by nothing more than strategic shopping with coupons. Financial problems can eat away at your security and your marriage. Those who learn quickly how to restructure their budgets and cash in on these huge savings are experiencing a total financial makeover. *No matter your situation, saving money by using coupons will relieve stress and allow you to breathe more easily.*

● ● ● ● ● ● ● ● ● ● ● ● ● ● ● ● ● ● ● ●

WHERE ARE MY BOOTSTRAPS?

Murphy's Law states, "Anything that can go wrong will go wrong." Although that's a bit pessimistic for my taste, we all face many unexpected bumps in the road. Perhaps we would do better to expect them. Times that require the greatest flexibility are those we cannot see coming. Save some money, build a stockpile, buy insurance, learn CPR, and always carry an Advil and extra tampon in your purse.

Nearly 170 years ago in 1841, the *Huron Reflector* newspaper printed this poem:

> *I never had a slice of bread,*
>
> *Particularly large and wide,*
>
> *That did not fall upon the floor,*
>
> *And always on the buttered side.*

I had to learn to smile and laugh at my sad predicament that year, just like I have to laugh when my toast drops buttered side down. I really have nothing to be upset about with my life or my toast. The most important things in my life—the people I love—are here with me now. But I know the importance of preparing for the future, and that's why you will find me in the store on any given day, continuing to build my stockpile for the next rainy day.

Terri shared the same feeling with me:

> *I started couponing a few months ago. At first it was just something fun to do with a few friends who were also into it. We were going along nicely, getting great deals and building a stockpile of personal care items and foods when my husband was laid off (his second layoff within eight months). Like a lot of people, we are underwater on our house, and there are no jobs out there in his industry. We are so grateful to have enough stored away only to have to purchase staple items like milk and bread on a weekly basis. Couponing has literally helped us survive this trying time. Even with our drastically reduced*

income, I am still able to take piles of change to the grocery store and continue building our stockpile. I will never stop couponing!!! Thankfully, we were prepared when a financial hardship came up. If it weren't for that, we'd probably be using credit cards to buy our groceries, putting us even further into debt.

Don't wait for a crisis to motivate you. Now is the perfect time to start couponing and building your stockpile of food and toiletries. Don't wait for a traumatic event to be your wake-up call or for a tragedy to motivate you to prepare. Don't put off for tomorrow what you can do today. Buy your umbrella before it starts pouring. Luck favors the prepared. How many more clichés do you need me to list before you're ready to climb on The Krazy Coupon Lady bandwagon?

MELTDOWN TO MIRACLE

FAQs:

What if I'm already standing in a downpour? What if my rainy day is here right now?

You can begin couponing with little to no cost, and you will see immediate results. If you have no money, you can find everything you need to get started—including coupons—without paying a cent. TheKrazyCouponLady.com is always free, and many Krazy Coupon Ladies get extra coupons from neighbors, family members, or convenience store owners before they toss them out. If you are behind on credit card payments, if you don't know where your next house payment is going to come from, if you are unemployed, now is the time to begin couponing.

How much do you suggest stockpiling?

I suggest: a two week supply of milk, eggs and bread; a one to two month supply of perishables that can be frozen, such as meat, cheese, berries, grapes, etc; six or more months of edible non-perishables, such as canned goods, drinks, packaged foods like applesauce, crackers, cereal, etc; and one to two years of non-perishables, such as laundry detergent, dishwasher detergent, cleaning supplies, toiletries, etc. Call me krazy, but I personally try to keep a one-year supply of all my food items. It is a decision that my family made together, and we have the room to do it. When possible, stockpile as much as you can use before the expiration date. The larger your stockpile, the less you will be buying each week for your family's immediate needs. Krazy Coupon ladies save money by buying things before they need them. I'll talk more about stockpiling in Chapter 9.

How long can you comfortably survive on your stockpile?

I could comfortably feed my family for about two months. The things we'd miss the most would be milk and eggs. I have dry milk powder, but it doesn't taste very good. I would start to add more beans to stretch my meat further, but I think we could almost get by without my husband noticing for two months. If I had access to fresh produce, milk, and eggs I could last comfortably for a full six months. Doesn't that security sound wonderful?

CHAPTER TWO

The Mental Makeover:

FROM SKEPTIC TO FANATIC

Now that you realize the powerful potential of coupons and you're ready to see that same magic work in your own life, let the fun begin! The first step to becoming a Krazy Coupon lady is a complete mental makeover. This might just be the hardest step of all, throwing away everything you thought you knew and replacing it with a brand new way of thinking. It's all about making that mental shift: changing the way you think about coupons and the way you approach shopping. If you're willing, everything you thought you knew about grocery shopping is about to go out the window. Go ahead and let go of those stubborn views and open your mind to something new—something that literally has the power to change your life. I'll help you avoid all the common pitfalls and set you up for huge savings success. Here are the first few things you need to do to make that mental shift in order to take control of your family budget and start saving big.

• •

SMASH THOSE STEREOTYPES

Years ago, before my own coupon conversion, I was the biggest skeptic of them all. I couldn't help but roll my eyes when I found out a friend of mine had begun to coupon. And before my eyes returned to their original position, a flood of images came rushing to my mind. I'm sure we've all had similar pictures pop into our heads when we hear the word "coupon". Suddenly, I was five again in my grandma's kitchen watching her slowly comb through her newspapers in her daisy dukes. Yes, my grandma wore daisy dukes! Her table was a newspaper mess, her scissors lost somewhere under all that mayhem, and yet there she sat congratulating herself for finding that $0.25 off toilet paper coupon. At that point the whole coupon thing didn't look so appealing to me. I carried that perception of coupons (along with a few others) with me for a couple of decades. Like the image of the exhausted looking mother of four you see standing in the line ahead of you: hair a mess, clothes disheveled, kids all over the place, ready to collapse, clutching her coupons as if they were her lifeline. Or my favorite, the dreaded bright pink accordion-style envelope so full that its bulging seams can barely contain the clipped coupons within—something you'd never dare get caught carrying in public.

Sound familiar? Well, throw all those pictures out and replace them with a new image: a sassy, hip, high-heel wearing woman proudly balancing her coupon binder on the handle of a shopping cart full of groceries that she'll pay just a few dollars for; a proactive, intelligent buyer who knows how and when to use those coupons to maximize savings and turn her own finances into freedom; a bargain shopper who dictates her own prices and only makes a purchase when she decides the price is right.

This isn't the new coupon lady of today just because I say it is. The statistics speak for themselves. Where we once thought only the poor and struggling were using coupons, today's story is much different. According to Nielson.com, a consumer research company, "More affluent households dominate coupon usage: 38% of 'super heavy' users and 41% of 'enthusiasts' come from households with incomes greater than $70,000. Households with income of $100,000 and up were the primary drivers of coupon growth in 2009." That statistic alone blows my little stereotypes out of the water. But the following statistic makes me feel even more proud to use a coupon. Research has shown that coupon usage is higher among the better educated. Coupons.com, a digital coupon distributor, goes on to say that "users of digital coupons are better educated than the general population overall, dispelling the perceived low-brow stigma of couponing." This just proves that those old images associated with the word "coupon" no longer apply. So go ahead and throw them out right now.

That's right! Crumple up that old picture and toss it right in the trash. Coupon users are smart, intelligent and have nothing to be ashamed of!

This is the new reality. This is the coupon lady (or man) of today. And whether you realize it or not, you fit right in. You're just what the coupon world needs—another savvy shopper ready to take the retail world on and show them what she's got; someone not afraid to roll up her sleeves and put in her time. This is what a Krazy Coupon Lady is. A powerful woman, coupon-binder in hand, changing her life because she can!

CHANGE WHAT YOU CAN CONTROL

Most of us can't control the price of groceries. We can't control the economy, we can't control the weather, we can't control our kids (!), and we don't always have total control over our monthly income. Good news: you can control the pants off of your budget! No more lamenting that the price of milk has skyrocketed or that you don't have a grocery store close to your home. Leave the negativity by the wayside and focus on what you CAN control. Make the change: get your coupons, learn the ropes, and get organized! Then YOU gain control, and you're in the driver's seat. Don't allow the grocery store to tell you what price you'll pay for that loaf of bread or box of cereal. You dictate the price. Does that freak you out? Let me say it again: you dictate the price. Relax! You don't need to start dickering about prices with your cashier in the checkout lane or start showing up with your chickens and butter churn ready to barter with your grocer. We dictate the prices because we *only* buy items when, one, they are on sale and, two, we have a coupon. Seriously. The primary trick we krazies know that you don't is that you have to save the coupons from your Sunday paper and *only* use them once the item has gone on sale. It's as simple as that. Soon you'll build a stockpile of food, all bought for a fraction of the retail price. You'll be prepared. You'll be powerful. You'll be ready to take advantage of any sale at any time. You'll be a sharp, thrifty Krazy Coupon Lady who soon has funds to put toward something more exciting than paper towels.

Krazy Coupon Ladies set their price
in a socially appropriate way.

THROW OUT THE THINGS
YOU THOUGHT YOU KNEW

Your mental makeover isn't quite complete without one last final sweep. Sure those stereotypes are gone, and you've already let go of some of those control issues, but now begins the real change. Go ahead, open your mind and throw out all those things you thought you knew, and get ready to replace them with the truth!

1. *I can't eat healthy, balanced meals with the kinds of foods the Krazy Coupon Ladies stockpile.*

Wrong! At first glance, you might think you can only find coupons for processed foods.

34

How do you think we Krazy Coupon Ladies stay so trim? Stuffing our frugal faces with mac and cheese by day and Twinkies by night? Come on, now. Of course, not. Many of the items we receive for free are processed foods: macaroni and cheese, granola bars, juice, cereals, etc. But we've also purchased many other items, such as cooking ingredients, spices, and baking staples like oats and sugar. We've even couponed milk, cheese, yogurt, eggs, carrots, bread, pork, chicken, and beef. Sometimes we can find completely free frozen veggies (great for stockpiling) or bagged salads for $0.50 or less. And it's even easier to be healthy when you have more wiggle room in the family budget. Don't worry; you can certainly continue to buy the items you want and mix and match them to fit into your family's diet. Plus, coupons follow American spending patterns, so you'll begin to notice deals on what is currently popular. These days, I can always find coupons for organic, diet and health foods. *Coupons can save you money on many healthy foods.*

2. *I've seen the coupons in the Sunday paper, and they aren't for things that I buy.*

Wrong! Be honest. Get your grocery list out. Are you going to buy any of these things anytime soon?

- Granola bars, breakfast bars, fruit snacks
- Canned or individual cups of fruit
- Canned soups, broth
- Breakfast cereal
- Condiments, salad dressing
- Yogurt and other dairy products
- Frozen dinners, rolls, pizza, veggies, desserts
- Foil, plastic bags and containers, trash bags
- Diapers, wipes, baby formula and supplies
- Dish soap, dishwasher detergent
- Juice
- Cake and brownie mixes
- Prepared side dishes
- Paper plates, napkins
- Candy
- Pet food and treats
- Batteries, light bulbs
- Make-up
- Medicine, vitamins
- Lotion, sunscreen

- Laundry detergent, fabric softener
- Soap, body wash, face wash
- Shampoo, conditioner, styling products
- Toothpaste, toothbrushes, mouthwash, whitening strips
- Surface cleaners: sanitary wipes, bathroom cleaners and more
- Medicine, vitamins
- Feminine hygiene products
- Shave gel, razors, deodorant

If someone isn't planning to buy at least one thing on that list, she is one starving, hairy, smelly nutcase. In addition to all the food items to buy with coupons, almost half of all the coupons you'll find in your local Sunday paper are for household items and cleaning supplies. These items are normally quite expensive, but thanks to our krazy couponing ways, we get them for close to free. The best part about getting a good deal on stuff like toiletries, cleaning products and plastic bags is they don't expire for ages. This means you can wait for a rock bottom (or free) price. Purchase two years' worth of dishwashing detergent when they're $0.50 each (after sale and coupon) instead of $5.99, and you'll be saving yourself almost $200 over the next two years just by stockpiling one product! *Your Sunday paper contains many valuable coupons for things you already buy all the time.*

3. *It's embarrassing to use coupons.*

Wrong! This is so false it pains my frugal little heart. Coupons are for everyone: guys or gals, living in tidy trailers or Trump towers. They're for any and all smart and savvy people who might like to do something with their money besides happily hand their hard-earned cash to a grocery store. Clipping coupons is becoming the chic way to shop, and you should never feel embarrassed to use them. The manufacturer reimburses the store for every cent of each coupon, plus a handling fee, so use them without shame. Sometimes I think I'm living in a bizarro world: a place where people are paying eight times what I pay for my groceries, and everyone calls them normal. Since when does senseless spending make you rational? Seems like we should be called the "sane coupon ladies". The crazy ones are those next to us in line paying $150 for a cartload of groceries. *People of every income level use coupons proudly, and you should never feel embarrassed to do the same.*

4. *It's not worth my time to shop at multiple stores, plus invest all the time it must take to clip and organize coupons.*

Wrong! Yes, using coupons takes some time. Anybody who tells you otherwise is lying and probably wants to steal your coupons. But it doesn't have to take over your life. You can limit your organizing time to about an hour a week and still experience serious savings. Sure, you'll spend more time at the grocery store once you're a Krazy Coupon Lady. Is saving obscene amounts of money worth a few hours? You can be the judge of that. I often think of my old economics teacher explaining the principle *there is no such thing as a free lunch.* She would have told me that free groceries aren't actually free, given the time it takes to clip coupons, travel to the store, and do the shopping. But in just a few short hours each week, you'll be reducing your spending by an average of $50-200. Though it may not technically be free, that will definitely buy a lot more than lunch. And even my economics teacher would agree with that, especially on her salary. *Couponing, like any solid investment, takes some time, but I think you'll find it's worth it.*

5. *Buying generic brand products at discount stores or bulk items at wholesale clubs will be cheaper than buying name brand products with coupons.*

Wrong! It's all about TIMING. I'll admit I used to think store brands were cheaper. I would clip my coupons, make my shopping list based on the meals I was cooking that week, and head to my grocery store. I would look at the coupon for $0.25 off Bounty paper towels, and then look at the price of the store's generic. It was always much cheaper to buy generic, so I would ditch my coupon and grab the store brand towels. I would always leave the store feeling bad for those poor souls who use coupons and don't save a dime. But I had it all wrong! A Krazy Coupon Lady doesn't make her list and buy what's on it regardless of the price. She waits until an item goes on sale and then she "stacks" that sale with a coupon. ("Stacking" means she adds a coupon on top of a manufacturer coupon and/or sale, so her savings start to "stack" up.) But I don't stop there. I take the opportunity to STOCK UP. Ever since I've become a certifiable Krazy Coupon Lady, I can't go into a wholesale club without cringing. Everything I used to buy every month or so now looks ridiculously overpriced. Things like razors, cereal, toilet paper, barbecue sauce, dish and laundry detergent...I could go on all day. The first time my wholesale club membership was up for renewal, I canceled it and used the money I saved to buy several newspaper subscriptions for coupons. Now all I miss about my old wholesale club is the cheap hot dog and soda combo. *Effective couponing is all about timing. Keep your coupons ready, and use them only with great sales so you can stockpile at prices much lower than the price of a generic item.*

6. *You shouldn't keep coupons for products you won't use.*

Wrong! Krazy Coupon Ladies keep them all. It takes a little longer to save and organize them all, but if you throw them out against my best advice, you'll regret it. Keeping and clipping everything allows you to take advantage of every krazy sale that comes along, and sometimes (watch out, this might blow your mind), you can actually make money. Check this out: at Walgreens a while back, Bayer Blood Glucose Meters were on sale for $25.00. There was a coupon for $25.00 off, which some short-sighted couponers may have tossed thinking they'd never use a blood glucose meter. But those of us who had clipped and organized every coupon were able to make money, because, when we bought one, we received a $10 Register Reward (a coupon that works like cash on your next order). That's $10 in my pocket. Plus, you will look like a saint when you donate the item to your favorite nursing home. Some may think this is silly, but that $10 earned can go toward things your family actually uses—like $10 worth of deodorant or baby wipes, and yes, we have coupons to use with those things too. When you clip and organize coupons for everything, you'll be ready to take advantage of incredible promotions sans regret.

7. *You can't save the big money if you don't live in an area with stores that double coupons.*

Wrong! Couponing is not just for people in a certain part of the country. Opportunities to double your coupons are great but not necessary. I have never shopped at a store that doubles coupons regularly, as many do, and I'm about as krazy as a coupon lady comes. Chances are that, as you begin learning your local store policies, you may find that a store in your area occasionally doubles coupons. For instance, K-Mart doubles coupons (up to $2.00 in value) on a fairly regular basis. If you're already trying to shop on a budget, the grocery store you currently shop may not be the store where you can save the most once you start using coupons. The best deals are often found at higher-end stores with specials such as store coupons; "spend $20, save $5 instantly" promotions; or weekly ads with special sales. *Krazy Coupon Ladies always save big, with or without stores that double coupons.*

8. *People who use coupons end up spending more money on products they didn't need in the first place.*

Wrong! When I first started couponing, I didn't see a HUGE drop in my monthly spending. I was spending close to the same amount of money, but I was buying six times the stuff. I was thrilled to be stockpiling items we used daily, like shampoo, conditioner, salad dressing, toothpaste and cereal. After the first few months of couponing I had a one-year supply of many non-perishable items. Even so, my husband began to get fed up as I continued bringing home carloads of toothpaste, soap and lotion. Of course, I was paying next to nothing, but I had become so consumed with shopping for these free toiletries, I neglected buying him much of anything to eat. "I can't eat shampoo!" was a complaint I heard more often than I care to admit. But once our stockpile was built up, suddenly my spending plummeted. I regularly spend about $150-$180 each month on groceries, toiletries, cleaning supplies, and produce for my family of four. Are you concerned with spending too much money, especially on things you may not use? If it's an item you don't already use routinely, make it your personal rule not to pay more than $0.10 for the item. *Krazy Coupon Ladies know how to save, which means they never spend money on things they won't use.*

Whew! Now that the myths are busted and you know the truth about couponing, are you ready to get started? Have you decided what to do with all the extra money you're about to save? Make room in your piggy bank and hold on tight. In the next year, you can save $10,000 on groceries, build a stockpile of food and toiletries that could feed a small army, all while increasing your financial security, assuring your peace of mind in an uncertain economy, and fostering new self-confidence and pride that might just leave you feeling so good you'll be wearing high heels to the grocery store.

It seems like so often people end up spending money on products they would never have bought before coupons, so how can they be saving money?

Because I know this does happen, I've dedicated an entire chapter to teaching you exactly when to use your coupons. As a Krazy Coupon Lady, I never buy a product simply because there's a coupon for it. I'm very careful to only buy products I know I'll use or donate. And I only use my coupons when those items are on sale. This ensures that I'm always getting an incredible price on anything I buy.

With today's record-high fuel prices, is it really that frugal to shop at multiple stores?

If you think about the many hundreds of dollars you can save each month, a slight increase in your gas bill is definitely a worthwhile investment. Since I'm saving about $600 dollars or more a month, the gas isn't even an issue. Think of couponing as your very own part-time job. But instead of making $20 an hour, you're making $200! If you're really worried about spending too much on fuel, consider only shopping at one store each week. Although you may not be able to build your stockpile as quickly, you can still experience total success!

Are there ever coupons for generic brands?

Yes! I've seen coupons for all sorts of brands. They're not as common as name brand coupons, but they do exist. Most recently I saw a peelie for Target brand diapers sitting right on the package. You won't normally find generic brand coupons in the Sunday coupon inserts; they're more likely to be printable coupons from a store's website or in-ad coupons in the store's weekly circular.

CHAPTER THREE

Revolutionize Your Routine:

DEVELOP YOUR SAVINGS STRATEGIES

The Mental Makeover is a good start, but it's not all you need to change in order to become a major coupon success. I'm sure you're still practicing some of those same ancient habits your mom taught you—habits that are crippling your budget whether you realize it or not. So get ready for some more revolutionizing! It's your routine this time that needs the makeover. You will not be able to shop the way you've been shopping if you want to start saving 70% at the grocery store. How does the old saying go? "If you keep doing what you're doing, you'll keep getting what you're getting." You've got to change your routine, mix it up a bit, and approach shopping in a whole new way.

* * * * * * * * * * * * * * * * * * * *

MAKE TIME

Ready for the honest truth? This will take work. There is no magic potion, no quick fix, no snap-your-fingers-to-a-zippy-tune-and-make-a-wish. Of course, you're going to spend more time than you're used to preparing to shop and actually shopping. But you'll also save more money. I could say that just buying this book and eating some pie will save you thousands, but that would be a big, tasty lie that would get you nowhere. The truth is that you'll need to allocate one to two hours per week to clip and organize coupons and plan shopping trips with the coupon match-ups you'll find at TheKrazyCouponLady.com.

How valuable is your time? If it takes an hour a week to save $800 per month, $200 per hour is absolutely worth my time. The only time I remember effortlessly making money was on each of my birthdays, and my Grandma told me it was because I was very special. Just about everything of value must be earned, and this is no different. While this will take time, you'll find that you really enjoy couponing. The rush you get from saving obscene amounts of money is unlike anything else (although I haven't tried shoplifting, drag racing, or illegal drugs....) Besides the huge savings and the exhilarating high, living frugally is fun. I take pride in knowing that I'm teaching my children to be resourceful and smart shoppers. A few months ago, a question came up while I was giving a news interview. Someone from the control room asked, "Are your kids embarrassed to shop with you and your coupons?" I responded that my kids are a little young to be embarrassed by anything, including the free chocolate chip cookies smeared all over their faces, but the real answer is ABSOLUTELY NOT. They love to help me with my coupons. Together, we excitedly watch the total drop by hundreds of dollars at checkout. When they ask for a treat at the store and I say "No", they inevitably ask, "Do you have a coupon?" They will not remember a time when they had a mother who didn't shop this way. I hope someday I'll be signing them up for their own multiple newspaper subscriptions to be delivered to their college dorms so they can stock up on items for all of their roommates. *Krazy Coupon Ladies set aside a reasonable amount of time each week to organize their coupons and plan their trips. This time is an investment you'll find well worth it.*

• • • • • • • • • • • • • • • • • • •

LEARN TO SAY "NO"

Once I was shopping a particularly good sale, stocking up on toiletries during a "double coupon" event at a local store. As I recall, I bought about sixty items that day, spending about $5 and saving several hundred. (I told you it was a particularly good sale!) As the kind cashier rang me up, we talked (as we most always do) about my huge savings. The cashier told me how much fun she had watching all of the Krazy Coupon Ladies come through and get these amazing deals. I asked whether or not she partook of any of the deals herself, especially since she's already at the store. She told me she "just didn't have the time to coupon." As we chatted, I gave her my best sales pitch, but she insisted that between her job and her family, she just did not have the time to drive around to different stores cashing in on these great deals.

Her refusal to reallocate her time baffles me. How can you not make getting free stuff a priority? "Oh, I think I'll pay for my toothpaste....I don't have time to cut out a tiny piece of paper and get it for free." Of course, there are many people (especially parents) who feel totally burnt out and stretched to their limits. The last thing I want to do is add one more thing to the things-mothers-should-do-or-else-feel-guilty-for-not-having-done list. Ooooh, I hate that list.

You are already good enough just how you are. If you decide not to use coupons, that's okay. If you really feel you just don't have the time, you don't need to feel guilty for paying $3 for jam or $4 for cereal. It is your prerogative to allocate your time as you wish. Don't let anyone pressure you into adding this "coupon craze" on your to-do list against your will. As women, we often take on more than we can handle due to feelings of obligation. We're all on an endless quest to do more and be more. There is nothing wrong with taking time to stop—look in the mirror and tell ourselves we are already good enough.

But with couponing, I am confident that any person can fit this into his or her schedule if they want. For me, it means sometimes staying up past my children's bedtime so that I can run to the store while they are tucked sweetly into their beds. For others, it may mean waking up at the crack of dawn to shop before you head to work, and it often requires loading up your kids for a firsthand lesson on economics and social interaction. Or for some it may be saying "NO" to any one of the many things that pop up in your everyday life. Do not be afraid to say "No" to things for which you really don't have time. If you decide to invest one to two hours a week to save your family money, it may take some creativity, but you can find ways to fit couponing into your schedule.

● ●

SAVE TIME BY CHANGING THE WAY YOU SHOP

Once you decide to make the time, you will find that couponing can actually save you time in the long run. Remember, in order to become a Krazy Coupon Lady, you must change the way you shop. I can't tell you how often I used to find myself at the grocery store at 4:00 p.m. on a weekday afternoon, grabbing all the necessary ingredients to prepare dinner for my family. With hungry mouths to feed in an hour or two, I'd usually rush around the store, buying whatever I needed regardless of price. I'd often come home with stuff for dinner that night and anything else that caught my eye while at the store. I rationalized my impulsive, expensive ways by remembering food is a need, not a want. Food, shelter, and clothing, right? (I've spent years trying to convince my husband that shopping for clothes is a need, but I digress.)

Krazy Coupon Ladies get their afternoons back. I *never* run to the store to find something to make for dinner. Thanks to my stockpile, I can just step into my garage and shop off my own shelves. I know the foods I use most often for my family, and I make sure I have plenty on hand at all times. No more wasted time, fuel, and patience making a last-minute run to the store; no more impulse buys, no more fighting rush hour on the way home. And most importantly, the groceries on my shelves at home were purchased at prices far below retail. I often feed my family of four on just a few dollars, including the fresh fruit and a salad. *As you change the way you shop, you will no longer need to make a last-minute run to the grocery store. Krazy Coupon Ladies save time, money, and patience as they build their stockpiles and reclaim their afternoons.*

● ●

CHANGE WHERE YOU SHOP

Where you shop can make a huge difference in your savings. There are six main categories of stores to consider when choosing the best places to shop:

   1. Supercenters: Shop for your groceries, garden hose, camping tent, school clothes, and new tires all under one roof. Supercenters like to be your one-stop shop. They generally distribute weekly circulars, have regular sale cycles and run limited promotions. The best thing about them? They often match competitor prices, allowing you to do all your coupon shopping in one place. *Examples: Target, Walmart, and Kmart.*

2. Drugstores: Shop for diapers, beauty products, lotions, and sunscreens at drugstores. Drugstores usually have a few aisles of food, too. Regular prices are high, but drugstores have some of the most competitive weekly ads around. A Krazy Coupon Lady saves big money, but how would you like to make money while shopping? Participate in drugstore rebate programs, and get paid to shop. Each week items are offered cheap or "free after rebate". Add a coupon to one of these "freebates", and it becomes a "moneymaker." *Examples: CVS, Walgreens, and Rite Aid.*

GROCERY STORES:

3. No-Frills: I grew up shopping the "no-frills" stores, touted as the everyday low price leaders. Here, you'll find shrink-wrapped palates of groceries stacked up to the thirty-foot ceilings. What you won't find is a weekly ad or advertised sale. These no-frills stores are simple: keep costs low and pass along savings to the customer. Without any coupons, this is the cheapest place to shop. If you like to bag your own groceries and save money by buying generics, you've probably already been trolling these aisles. These stores will accept your coupons and can be a good place to shop. Most shoppers only achieve between 20-25% overall grocery savings by shopping solely at a no-frills store. Examples: WinCo, Aldi.

4. High-End: These supermarkets are often on every corner and are the place you've been using for your late-afternoon shopping runs or for that hot loaf of French bread. You wouldn't do all your shopping here because sometimes prices are even higher than the drugstores. The aisles are clean and wide, the organic section is expansive, and the natural cheeses and olives are tempting. You read the store's large and colorful weekly ad and listen to the radio and television ads, salivating as you hear about all of its gourmet salads and marbled meats for the grill. Everyday prices are sky-high, but sales and gimmicks touting, "Spend $30, receive $15 off your next order" make this the place to stack your coupons with sales and score big. *Examples: Kroger, Safeway, Publix, Shop Rite and Albertsons.*

5. Wholesale Clubs: Free samples are all that's free at the local wholesale club. Seeming as large as the Superdome, warehouse clubs are the best place to go if you're in the market for a five-pound can of creamed corn. Yearly membership is required to be a patron, usually $40-50 annually. Wholesale clubs can be a good place to shop, but only if you are meticulously careful. I don't necessarily recommend wholesale clubs because they're dangerous! An impulse buy at the grocery store might cost you $3.50, but at a wholesale club, you'll be hard pressed to find an item under $10.00. Many wholesale clubs do not accept manufacturer coupons. Wholesale clubs do tend to consistently have the best prices on milk and eggs. *Examples: Costco, Sam's Club, and BJ's.*

6. Natural Foods: This category includes totally organic grocers, co-ops, natural foods stores, or specialty diet stores. These stores often have the highest prices of all. Fewer of the items in these stores will have coupons, and shopping like The Krazy Coupon Lady at a natural foods store will never get you a cartload of groceries for under $20, but you can still find big savings. If you're shopping at a natural foods store, you've already made the decision to pay more money to get a premium product. By watching for sales and stacking coupons, you can see a percentage of savings on your monthly grocery budget. Even if you only save 10% on a monthly grocery budget of $500, that's still $50 in your pocket. *Example: Whole Foods and Trader Joes.*

Got it? Those are the categories. Your new best friend is the local high-end grocery store. Drugstores and supercenters are the next best thing! If you're like most Krazy Coupon Ladies, once you get started, you'll only visit the "no-frills" stores, wholesale clubs, and natural food stores occasionally. Depending on the stores in your area, you may primarily shop at a supercenter or even a great drugstore. But typically high-end grocery stores will now be your bread and butter, literally. Start watching their weekly ads. Look for sales and promotions, such as "Buy 5, Save $5" or "Spend $25, Save

"$10", "Buy One Get One Free" offers, and in-ad store coupons. Get ready to set up camp in the high-end's backyard, and watch the savings pour in.

• • • • • • • • • • • • • • • • • • •

CHANGE THE WAY YOU COOK

I used to make a weekly dinner menu and then shop for the foods on my list. Of course, I'd forget to buy something, so I'd end up running back to the store almost daily for 1-2 items. Now I plan my meals around the foods I have in my stockpile or around items that might be on sale. Recently, my local store had an incredible sale on pork, making it nearly free. I spent the week researching and sharing new pork recipes with my readers. I had never prepared a lot of pork, but I enjoy trying new things. We managed to spice up our lives, while saving a significant amount of money, just by adjusting our eating habits for an exceptional deal. New foods are challenging and fun. I thoroughly enjoy cooking and menu-planning around my stockpile. It's like finally having someone around to answer the eternal question: "What should I make for dinner?" I open my garage or look in the fridge, and something new calls out to me. I often used to find myself in a cooking rut; nothing sounded good, and I cooked out of obligation. Even now, sometimes I just don't feel like cooking, but I like having all the food on hand to try something new. *Couponing adds an exciting flexibility and versatility to your diet.*

• • • • • • • • • • • • • • • • • • •

FIND YOUR BALANCE

Warning: anything this rewarding and fun is going to be addicting. Once you start couponing, it can be difficult to stop. When you walk out the automatic doors with your first full cart of groceries for under $20, you're going to feel that rush, that coupon "high", and you'll want to do it again as soon as possible. Soon you'll nod in agreement when your fellow Krazy Coupon Ladies call coupons a drug. Krazy Coupon Lady reader, Amber, wrote in:

> *When I first started couponing, I went nuts! The thought never occurred to me that these sales could happen more than once in a lifetime. After about a*

month of overdoing it, I was totally burnt out. Now, I realize that most sales will be back, and I am able to pace myself and remember that couponing is a marathon, not a sprint. I have found a great couponing routine that works for my family and me. I am not running to the grocery store hourly, and I am still able to save 70% each month on my grocery bill.

When I first started couponing, I was so excited about all the money I was saving that I thought I needed to cash in on EVERY deal at EVERY store. I was shopping at five stores each week: Albertsons, Walgreens, Walmart, Target, and, occasionally, Kmart. All five, every week. Ridiculous, right? Obviously, it didn't take long before I was completely burnt out. Plus, sometimes my kids would spot the big red bull's-eye and burst into tears.

You might be a Krazy Coupon Lady if...
an afternoon errand turns into a 4 hour
coupon extravaganza & you still want more!

We can almost guarantee that most beginning Krazy Coupon Ladies will get "carried away". Your husband will joke about the other man in your life—your checker—who sees you more than he does. He'll get frustrated by all the free shampoo you bring home and will try to remind you that he can't eat shampoo. He might even try to verify that you are legitimately buying all of this stuff and not just stuffing it in your purse and high-tailing it out of the store. Rest assured that as soon as you have your stock-pile built up, and about the time you can't take any more harassment from your husband, you won't need to go to the store as often. The ten trips per week will dwindle to five and then to two, and soon life will be back to normal, except with way more room in your budget. *As you get started, find a workable balance with your couponing and resist the temptation to let it take over your life.*

● ● ● ● ● ● ● ● ● ● ● ● ● ● ● ● ● ●

SET YOUR PACE

The Coupon Race isn't a sprint. There is no need to dash to every store as fast as you can in an effort to beat other coupon moms. Couponing is not a big conspiracy that's going to be shut down as soon as the stores find out. Your worst enemy will be yourself if you take on too much and become burned out. Set a pace you can maintain.

If you're a coupon novice, just starting out, we'll refer to you as a "coupon virgin". It's best for coupon virgins to learn one store at a time. You will be way too overwhelmed if you are trying to learn every store policy all at once. Decide on one store where you would like to get krazy, and start there.

Remember that good sales come around all the time. When I was a coupon virgin, I didn't realize that the prices I was seeing were not once in a lifetime sales. The industry standard for coupon and sale cycles is three to four months. Instead of buying a two-year supply of salad dressing, just buy enough to get your family by for three to four months. An obvious exception to this rule is for items without an expiration date, like body wash, toilet paper, and shampoo. *Start slowly, and find a pace you can maintain. Remember that this is not the only time you'll be able to take advantage of great deals.*

START TODAY

There you have it. Are you feeling up for the challenge? Are you ready to jump on board the train of the coupon revolution? Don't set this book down for a week or a month or worse. No excuses. You can absolutely make this work, and you have me to guide you through it. If you're feeling overwhelmed by all of this, grab a friend or two, and make it a party. Make learning, clipping, and shopping a group effort. If your friends aren't interested, just wait a month or so. When you start building your stockpile, they'll come back around asking for your secrets.

- It's time to grow a spine and seize the day.

- It's time to throw everything you know about grocery shopping out the window.

- No more running to the store at 3:00 p.m. everyday to buy what you need for dinner.

- No more making one list every week to buy ingredients for the five meals you are going to cook, regardless of price.

- No more enormous monthly shopping trip where you spend who-knows-how-much and cringe in horror when you hear the total.

- No more running to the store because you are out of toothpaste and Q-tips.

Say goodbye to those days.

Here's what you need to know...

- You will be going to the store a lot, and you will most likely develop a close relationship with certain stores and the people who work there.

- You will have a one-year supply of toothpaste, soap, razors, and disinfectant wipes (among other things) before you can blink.

- Before you know it, you'll be saving between 50-90% at the grocery store!

FAQs:

How much time will it really take to clip my coupons?

It's up to you. On any given Sunday, there may be one to four coupon inserts in your local newspaper, sometimes more. Holiday weekend papers carry no inserts at all. I average one hour each week clipping and organizing my coupons. We'll show you how to coupon in Chapter 10 and teach you two different methods with two different time constraints, so you can choose the method that best fits your needs. One method requires more time up front and is easier to use, while the other requires less initial work because you file the coupons without even clipping.

Do you really refuse to pay retail? What percentage off retail do you typically save?

Yes, I really refuse to pay retail most of the time. I always refuse to pay retail in order to build my stockpile. My stockpile is comprised of items I purchase for around 25% of retail value or less (in other words, at least 75% off). I've seen a coupon for just about everything, but even so, I often buy bread, produce, and milk without coupons. I like to think I'm still refusing to pay retail because I know my price points. For example, I will not pay over $0.98 per pound on most fruits: peaches, grapes, strawberries, pears—you name it. If bread is too expensive, I make my own. When eggs are pricey, I'm tempted to get a chicken coop and some hens. Of course, then I come to my senses. No offense if you have a chicken coop. Maybe you could trade me your eggs for some of my extra coupons?

How do I get multiple coupons?

I discuss this in great detail in Chapter 4, but the two main ways to get multiple coupons are to (1) subscribe to multiple copies of your local Sunday paper and (2) print coupons directly from the Printable Coupon Database on **TheKrazyCouponLady.com**.

What if I hate grocery shopping?
Will this ever work for me?

The other day a friend called and asked me to teach his wife to coupon. When I spoke with her about it, she turned to me, exhausted, and said that between her new (and fourth) baby and her bitter hatred of grocery shopping, couponing would never work for her. Although she has yet to jump in the coupon game, under the right conditions (such as her husband watching the kids a few nights a week so she can learn, prepare, and shop) she could quickly become a happy and successful Krazy Coupon Lady.

If you hate the grocery store, don't despair. I used to hate grocery shopping too, but coupon shopping is nothing like the mindless aisle-weaving you've done before! It's a game, a challenge, and the best natural high since exercise—without all the fatigue and body odor.

Give it a try, and you just might find yourself hooked after your very first trip.

Do you altogether refuse to shop at Wholesale clubs? Don't they sometimes have better deals?

I don't refuse to shop anywhere. Sometimes I do purchase fresh fruits, dairy, meats and non food/drug items from my wholesale club. But I generally do not shop at wholesale clubs. As a reminder, although wholesale clubs often release coupon booklets, most do not accept manufacturer coupons of any kind. Generally speaking, wholesale club prices are much higher than the prices we find at our local grocery stores where manufacturer coupons are accepted.

You might be a Krazy Coupon Lady if...
you check your suitcase so you can
carry-on your coupon binder.

SECTION TWO

Starting the Stash

START BY DOING WHAT'S NECESSARY;
THEN DO WHAT'S POSSIBLE;
AND SUDDENLY YOU ARE DOING THE IMPOSSIBLE.

CHAPTER FOUR

Coupon Fetish:

STARTING YOUR COUPON COLLECTION

I used to dream of a closet bigger than my master bedroom—sleek wooden hangers, mirrors, track lighting, and a wall of designer shoes. The shoes were perfectly organized by color and occasion. (In the dream, of course, I have special "occasions" to attend.) The closet dream has been replaced. My head is now filled with coupons, sleekly organized by category, filling page after page of an enormous binder, covering nearly every product in all sorts of brands. This krazy collection of little cut-out pieces of paper brings my life excitement and gives me a sense of empowerment, not just in my dream but in real life. Who would have ever guessed a coupon had such power?

The Federal Trade Commission estimates that 3,000 companies distribute nearly 330 billion coupons each year. It's not just grumpy penny-pinchers using them, either. Some 77% of American households use about 8 billion coupons to save $4.7 billion at grocery stores, reports the Nielson Company. So how can you get your piece of that pie?

You're about to learn how to get your hot little hands on the newest, hippest currency. Remember, a coupon lady clips only the coupons she will use that week, but a Krazy Coupon Lady *keeps every last one*. You'll thank me later. There are many different types of coupons. Use them all! The bigger your coupon stash, the better your savings will be. This chapter will teach you about the different types of coupons and how they all contribute to your coupon closet. I like to think my coupons are like a hot fudge brownie sundae.

● ●

NEWSPAPER COUPONS—
THE BROWNIE OF MY SUNDAE

The best way to accumulate coupons is riding around every Sunday morning in a messenger bag over the shoulder of your thirteen-year-old paperboy. In that bag you'll find the greatest volume of coupons for all sorts of products. With each new Sunday you'll uncover a better coupon, a new item to try, and experience a whole realm of jittery excitement as you turn the pages.

The Sunday newspaper contains valuable freestanding coupon inserts from a variety of manufacturers and marketing companies. Each week the paper will include at least one coupon insert, except on holiday weekends. A paper may often have two to three inserts and sometimes as many as five. Procter & Gamble (PG) inserts come out once a month, while Smart Source (SS) and Red Plum (RP) marketing companies have inserts that come out nearly every week. Now that you're ready to become a Krazy Coupon Lady, you'll need several copies of these Sunday inserts. This is the key to huge savings. There's no way around it. You must get your hands on several inserts.

Here's how to get them:

- Subscribe to multiple copies of the Sunday paper in your area. You should be able to do this for $1.00 or less per paper, per week. Call your paper's circulation department and ask what specials they offer for people who would like multiple Sunday papers. Also ask whether their paper carries Smart Source, Red Plum, and Procter & Gamble coupon inserts. Usually, the largest paper in your area will distribute the most coupon inserts. Many papers offer a Sunday-only subscription, or at least a weekend-only subscription, at a lower price than the full week subscription. Do not pay over $2.00 per week for a subscription because you can usually buy the paper from a newspaper stand for less. I get six copies of the Sunday paper and recommend subscribing to at least four, if possible. Four to six subscriptions should only cost $16-$25 per month. Since you'll soon save an average of $600-$800 per month, the investment is clearly worth it.

- Ask your family members, neighbors, or co-workers to save their coupon inserts for you. After the rumors spread about your new hobby of extreme couponing, the topic will begin to come up naturally—because you'll always be talking about your savings! Perhaps when you find a rock-bottom price on dish soap, you could buy enough to share with a neighbor or your fellow employees at work. Sharing provides the perfect opportunity to mention, "If you want more free stuff, just save your coupon inserts for me, and these baskets of free goodies will keep appearing." You might have a dozen weekly inserts before you know it.

> **Tip:** Don't use the coupons the week you get them. I carry about three months' worth of coupons around in my coupon binder. The coupons are organized by category or date, and they only come out of the binder when I find a great sale or they expire. Coupons don't need to be used immediately.

- Buy off the stand. Many grocery stores and supercenters sell Sunday papers all week long, typically for $1.50 to $2.00 per paper. Some Dollar Stores even carry the Sunday edition of the paper and sell it for a buck! This option is nice because you can decide how many papers you want to buy, based on the coupons that are inside each week. Before you pay for your papers, be sure to look through each copy to ensure it has the right amount of coupon inserts. You don't want to get home and realize you were shorted.

- Talk to the managers of your local convenience stores, grocery stores, hotels or coffee shops that sell newspapers and ask what they do with the extra papers they don't sell. Many shop owners will love to have you take the extras off their hands so they don't have to worry about recycling them. The key is to make their lives easier, not harder. Have good, clear communication and always show up when you say you will. Make sure to take the complete copies of the papers and sort out your inserts at home. Just pop in, grab your stack of free papers, thank them, and go.

You might be a Krazy Coupon Lady if...
your idea of date night is casing
neighborhood dumpsters and recycling centers.

- If you're feeling brave, consider leaving your pride in the car and rummaging through a community recycling bin. I've known many savvy ladies who have a regular dumpster where they know they can grab a stack of old Sunday papers each week. Recently on TLC's show, Extreme Couponing, I did just that, and I was amazed at how many inserts are just casually thrown out. Before you begin, make sure to get permission from the site owner or manager; most are more than happy to let you take the discarded papers! Give it a try. You might be equally surprised! Now *that's* krazy!

• • • • • • • • • • • • • • • • • • •

BUYING COUPONS ONLINE

At first this may sound strange, but you can actually buy pre-clipped coupons online. Pre-clipped coupons are an easy option if six newspaper subscriptions aren't in your budget, or if you think you don't have time to clip or file all those coupons. Pre-clipped coupons are also great if you're looking to supplement or jumpstart your collection.

Coupon sellers have access to hundreds of coupon inserts, and they've established home businesses to clip and sell these coupons on a number of different websites. Coupons generally sell for a handling fee of $0.05-$0.20 each, and their values range around ten times that much. Buying pre-clipped newspaper manufacturer coupons online is an effective way to build your stockpile quickly.

Watch your local sales closely, and buy coupons that will "stack" with a store sale. Never pay money for coupons unless they'll definitely save you more than you paid. When you see a sale price at your store and find a set of coupons online that will create a good stock-up price, that's the time to buy. To be successful, you'll have to stay ahead on your store's upcoming deals. Find out your favorite supermarket's sale schedule. The first day the store releases its ad (usually Sunday or Wednesday), find the coupons you want to buy and purchase them quickly so they'll arrive before the sale price ends. With a little planning, purchasing coupons online is fun and easy.

Even after you have multiple subscriptions to the paper and you're super-organized, buying coupons online is a great supplemental tool. When I see an especially good sale, I love to buy twenty extra coupons online to build up my stockpile for that item. For example: I often buy $1.00/1 toilet paper coupons because I know the four-packs often go on sale at my local store for 10/$10. I pay as low as $0.10 per coupon, so I'll get twenty coupons for $2.00, total. When I take my coupons to the store, I bring home twenty 4-packs of toilet paper for a final price of $0.10 (plus tax) per pack. That could be written as under $0.03 per roll, and with around 450 sheets per roll, the cost per wipe is so low you won't need to be stingy with your bum. And if you find your two-year old threw an entire roll into the toilet, you might not kill him.

Be careful when buying items that expire. Always check expiration dates on the products before buying bulk quantities of coupons online to make sure you don't over-stockpile. Just the other week, I found a great sale on tuna. After the sale price, store promo and manufacturer coupon, the final price was only $0.10 each. Before I hit the computer to search for coupons, I visited the store to check the expiration dates of the tuna in stock. Luckily, the tuna didn't expire for two years, so I ordered forty coupons for about $4.00 including shipping! Later that week, I received my coupons in the mail, purchased forty pouches of tuna and shared them with some very grateful family members. Staying on top of your expiration dates is necessary in order to be a successful Krazy Coupon Lady.

● ●

COUPON CLIPPING WEBSITES

Websites such as TheCouponClippers.com or CouponsThingsbyDede.com offer coupons for around $0.07-$0.40 per coupon. Just google "coupon clipping service" and you'll find a plethora of other sites doing the same thing! They sometimes have clearance coupons for as low as a penny! The price they charge is generally about 10-15% of the coupon's value. These websites clearly state you are paying for the time and handling of the coupon so as not to breach the legal verbiage on the coupon that reads "may not be transferred".

Phew! Now you know all about newspaper coupons and the many ways to get your

Special Ordering

Sometimes a store will sell out of the item before your coupons arrive in the mail. One strategy to avoid this problem: ask your store whether it will special-order items for you so you can pick them up on a designated day before the end of the sale period. Here are a few tips on how to do this most effectively:

- After you order your coupons, head to the store to talk to the manager. I always try to place my "special orders" through the same person. Make sure you're doing your best to place your order with a store manager. The last thing you need is some punk teenager (said with all the love in the world—I love punk teenagers, especially when they're my checkers!) who will forget to order it, order the wrong thing, or accidentally put my order out on the shelf when it arrives.

- Write down the name of the manager who helped you, and write down the day and time he or she said you could come get it.

- Don't wait for a phone call. Managers are busy and will rarely remember to call you, even if they say they will. Just head to the store once your coupons arrive and when you know your product will be there.

- If you know stores in your area that are high traffic spots for coupon ladies looking for the same product, try not to place your special order at that krazy store. If possible, choose a

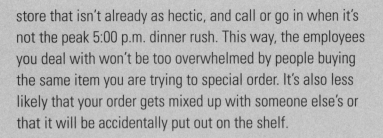

store that isn't already as hectic, and call or go in when it's not the peak 5:00 p.m. dinner rush. This way, the employees you deal with won't be too overwhelmed by people buying the same item you are trying to special order. It's also less likely that your order gets mixed up with someone else's or that it will be accidentally put out on the shelf.

- Pre-paying for the items when they're not in the store constitutes fraud. Don't do it. However, you can legally have items ordered in and held if the stores are willing. Special ordering can be a lifesaver! I have only had a problem, once, when a store employee accidentally put my order out on the shelf, and it sold before I got in. The process is usually smooth and easy. Store managers are happy to sell you product in bulk and appreciate that you're not clearing them out to do so.

- Don't feel bad about placing a special order if the store is willing. Manufacturers reimburse the store for the coupon's worth (plus a handling fee to more than cover shipping!) so the stores aren't losing money on you—they're making it!

hands on them, including: subscribing to multiple copies of the Sunday newspaper, buying clipped coupons online, and maybe even dumpster diving at your recycling center! Remember, newspaper manufacturer coupons are the brownie in my "hot coupon sundae". They are dense, consistent, and a substantial part of my coupon collection. Just like making a brownie, acquiring or clipping these coupons takes maybe forty-five minutes of work. But these coupons only make up 60% of the coupons I redeem. Before I became The Krazy Coupon Lady, I was unaware of all the other sources for great coupons. I was just eating plain old brownie, without even knowing what I was missing.

● ● ● ● ● ● ● ● ● ● ● ● ● ● ● ●

PRINTABLE COUPONS & ECOUPONS: THE ICE CREAM

Coupons printed or loaded directly from the Internet (I call them "printable coupons or eCoupons") make up 30% of my total coupon spending. These coupons are the vanilla ice cream scoop melting on my brownie. Printable coupons or eCoupons only take a few seconds to acquire; a quick click (or should I say scoop) of the mouse, and out they come.

PRINTABLE COUPONS

Printable coupons were first distributed in the 1990s; people could easily print them at home and redeem the coupons at their local grocers. They disappeared for a while in 2003 because many fraudulent coupons were distributed and sold on the Internet. (This is why I recommend only purchasing from the coupon clipping sites.) Hundreds of stores unknowingly accepted these coupons and lost thousands of dollars. In response, many stores stopped accepting ALL printed coupons. Slowly, over the past seven years, nearly all stores are again accepting printable coupons, but not without some hesitation and a few stringent policies to ensure legitimacy.

Where do I find printable coupons?

One of the best features of **TheKrazyCouponLady.com** is the comprehensive list of current printable coupons. It's the most user-friendly list of its kind, organized and alphabetized by product name. It's never been easier to find all the great, high-value coupons ready to print right from your home computer. The Krazy Coupon Lady printable coupon database includes coupons from individual manufacturer sites (such as Dove or Nestle), larger marketing sites (like coupons.com or smartsource.com) and even social networking sites (like facebook). The Krazy Coupon Lady's printable coupon database is your one-stop shop for free printable coupons straight from the Internet. Read more about how to navigate **TheKrazyCouponLady.com** in Chapter 14.

Coupons included on the database look like this.

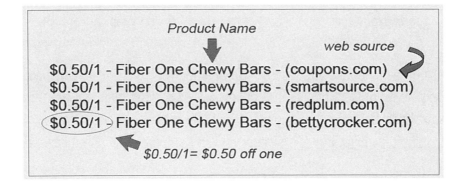

How do I print them?

Many of the coupon websites require that you download their software before you print coupons. This is a onetime step and is completely safe. Follow the simple instructions, and soon you'll be on to printing some of the best coupons out there. Companies like coupons.com, smartsource.com and redplum.com offer hundreds of printable coupons, and each site requires a software download. You'll only need to download once, and rest assured, these companies are VERY legitimate and safe.

How do I know when to print?

Now that you know where to find printable coupons, you may wonder, "Should I print all these coupons now or wait until I need them?"

Here are a few things to take into consideration:

(1) Many coupon offers have a print limit. Once that limit is reached, the campaign is over, and the coupons will no longer be available to print.

(2) Consider the likelihood that you will buy the product for this particular coupon. When you find a printable coupon, ask yourself: "Will I be disappointed if I come back to print it and the offer is no longer available?" If the answer is yes, print it right away.

(3) "Will this coupon save me money on something I buy regularly?" If the answer is yes, print it right away. Often, if you wait until the product is on sale, the coupon will no longer be available to print. Many printable coupons expire thirty days from the day you print, so keep this in mind when deciding whether to give the printer the green light.

People often ask, "Are these printable coupons worth all the ink it takes to print?" Well, only if you redeem the coupons. If you won't use them, don't print them. And remember, Krazy Coupon Ladies don't pay retail price for ink or paper, either!

How many can I print?

After deciding that a certain coupon is definitely worth printing, how many can you get? Most coupon sites have set a limit of 2 coupons per computer. If you want to stock up on diapers using the $3.00 Huggies printable coupon, you'll need a strategy. The best way to get more than 2 copies of a printable coupon is to gain ac-

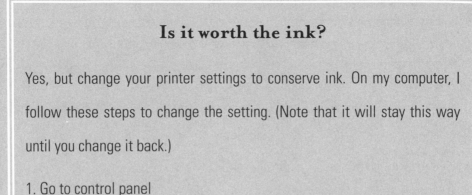

Is it worth the ink?

Yes, but change your printer settings to conserve ink. On my computer, I follow these steps to change the setting. (Note that it will stay this way until you change it back.)

1. Go to control panel

2. Click on devices and printers

3. Select which printer you want to adjust

4. Right click on the selected printer and select *"Printing Preferences"*

5. Click on the tab *"Main"*, then select *"Fast"* under *"Print Quality"* and check the box next to *"Grayscale"*

cess to more than one computer. If you have 2 computers in your home, you will be able to print a total of 4 coupons, 2 from each computer. You'll only need a single printer, though—even if you turn your bonus room into a computer lab just for all the coupon savings!

eCoupons

Save on ink, and avoid a clipping cramp by loading electronic coupons (eCoupons) straight to your store loyalty card. eCoupons are the newest wave of coupons to hit the market. They are manufacturer coupons and cannot be used in conjunction with other manufacturer coupons, though you may usually "stack" eCoupons with store coupons. There are many sites that distribute eCoupons, such as Cellfire, PGeSAVER, Shortcuts, SavingStar and Upromise. Find links to all your eCoupon sources on TheKrazyCouponLady.com. Load them from your home computer, or download them while at the store using your smartphone.

There are two kinds of eCoupons:

1. **Save to Card Coupons:** these are the most common way to save at the grocery store with eCoupons. Load coupons to your supermarket loyalty card by going to your store's website or one of the eCoupon websites listed above. Then, during checkout, swipe your store card or enter your phone number at the register and see the savings automatically deducted on your receipt.

2. **Mobile Coupons:** Target is leading the way with this type of eCoupon. Sign up at Target.com to receive a text message containing Target store coupons and a barcode image that may be scanned at checkout! Hand your cellphone over to the cashier, who will scan the image and register the savings when you purchase the items!

There you go; everything you need to know about printable and eCoupons. Combine these with newspaper coupons, and that makes up about 90% of my coupon collection. As great as this is, my sundae just wouldn't be as delicious without a few essential toppings.

● ●

CATALINA "YOUR BUCKS" COUPONS: THE HOT FUDGE

Uh oh! I've gone into such detail on newspaper, printable, and eCoupons that this brownie sundae of ours is half-melted; but that's just the way we like it, right? And face it, moms, when was the last time you ate warm toast or finished your cereal before it was soggy? We're used to getting dragged away from what we're doing by all the forces of family and nature combining against us. So, back to the ice cream analogy. Keep the artificially sweetened fruit topping to yourself—my favorite part of my sundae is the hot fudge. I like to let it slide down the edges of the bowl so I can scrape it off the bottom...delicious. Just like hot fudge is the best part of a sundae, my favorite coupons are called "Your Bucks" or "Catalinas".

Never heard of a Catalina? Next time you're at the grocery store, look for a little grey machine connected to the laser scanner at your checkout stand. These smart little machines print out coupons based on the items you buy. Catalina machines are present in over 23,000 stores in 200 different grocery chains.

You've probably thrown away or left these long receipt-like coupons at the checkout many times before. I used to throw these coupons out without a single glance. Little did I know I was throwing away money. Ever since my husband saw how much I could save with these Catalinas, he has made sure never to leave them behind at the register. After one trip in particular, he came home with a whole handful of Catalinas. I was surprised and asked him if those had all been dispensed after just one transaction. He said, "Oh, no. I found these on the ground." It made me laugh, but it's the perfect example of how valuable those simple pieces of paper are. Who needs flowers, when you've got a husband bringing you coupons?

HISTORY OF THE CATALINA

Catalina is a giant of a company that collects information through store loyalty cards on more than 90 million households in nine countries. (Not bad for a company founded in 1984 by five friends while sailing to Catalina Island off the Southern California coast.) Catalina's massive data collection computers access info on more than 250 million transactions every week. Sound a little too much like big brother? Relax. They don't track you by your name; instead each customer is identified by a 40-character number. When I swipe my store loyalty card, the Catalina machine knows the shopping habits associated with my card, and the machine prints out a relevant ad or coupon. In an article by *The Wall Street Journal* we read an example of how these smart machines work:

GlaxoSmithKline PLC [the manufacturer] has distributed ads for its Tums antacid to target shoppers around holidays like the Fourth of July and Thanksgiving, when they tend to eat more heavily. Catalina serves up the ads [and sometimes coupons] to shoppers who have bought Tums in the past. Glaxo found that 60% of shoppers shown the ads come back and buy Tums.

Catalina coupons are redeemed at a rate of over 6%, much higher than the overall newspaper coupon redemption rate of about 1%. Because of the higher redemption rate, manufacturers pay more to put out a Catalina coupon and, in turn, often put out high dollar value savings!

TYPES OF CATALINAS

Nearly all Catalina (also called "Your Bucks") coupons must be redeemed at the store where they printed out or at another location of the same grocery chain. There is only one exception, which I'll show you below. Here are the four types of Catalina coupons:

1. **Store coupons:** *E.g.: Save $2 off purchase of any fresh "store brand" meat.*

This coupon is considered a store coupon and can only be redeemed at the same store (or another location of the same chain). These may be used in conjunction with other manufacturer coupons. Other examples of these store Catalinas might be:

$3 off your next produce purchase of $10 or more

$3 off your next purchase of any chicken product

$10 off your next in-store purchase of $60 or more (Exclusions such as dairy, tobacco, or lottery may apply.)

2. "Courtesy of" Manufacturer coupon: *E.g.: Save $5 off your next shopping order courtesy of General Mills.*

These Catalina manufacturer coupons are good on your next shopping order of $5 or more. You'll receive this Catalina by purchasing a minimum dollar amount of specific products. For example, the store's weekly sales circular might say something like, "Spend $25 on participating products and receive $5 off your next order courtesy of Procter & Gamble." Another way to qualify to receive this kind of Catalina is by purchasing a certain number of specific products. For example, "Buy 2 containers of peanut butter and receive $2 off your next shopping order courtesy of Skippy Naturals Peanut Butter."

These Catalinas can be used in conjunction with other manufacturer coupons on a future purchase. These Catalinas may only be redeemed at the store where they printed out or at another location of the same chain. These "courtesy of" manufacturer Catalinas can be used on almost any purchase. You can use your $2 Catalina from Skippy on a loaf of bread or your $5 Catalina from Proctor & Gamble on a couple of pounds of ground beef. Catalina coupon exclusions may include dairy, tobacco, lottery items, etc. Other examples of these Catalinas might be:

$3 off your next shopping order courtesy of Post Cereals

$10 off your next shopping order courtesy of ConAgra foods

3. Product-specific manufacturer coupon: *E.g.: Save $2.00 on any Listerine product. Redeem at Walgreens.*

Surprisingly enough, the Catalinas that name a single product and say "redeem at

Walgreens" (or another store) are actually the only Catalinas that may be used at other stores, including Walmart. You must check your individual store policy, but many stores that accept competitor coupons will accept these product-specific manufacturer coupons. Here are a few other examples of these store Catalina coupons:

Free Sobe LifeWater. Redeem at Safeway.

Save $1.00 on any Cottonelle Aloe and E toilet paper. Redeem at Kroger.

Save $4.00 on any one Airwick Freshmatic. Redeem at Albertsons.

4. Catalina Advertisements: some Catalinas are just product ads or previews of upcoming promos. These are the ONLY Catalinas you're allowed to throw away!

> When a store promo requires a minimum purchase to receive a Catalina coupon, the minimum purchase amount is almost always *before* coupons and tax. If the minimum purchase is $20 and you spend $19.97, you won't get a Catalina. But if your total is $20.01 before tax and then you use coupons to bring your total down another ten dollars, you *will* receive a Catalina.

WHAT DETERMINES THE CATALINAS THAT PRINT AFTER MY CHECKOUT?

Some Catalina "Your Bucks" print consistently for all shoppers, and others are generated based on your individual purchase history, as the *Wall Street Journal* explained with the Tums example. Catalina advertises some of its "Your Bucks" offers on their website, www.CouponNetwork.com. You can find out about others in store circulars and, of course, on **TheKrazyCouponLady.com**.

HOW TO RECOGNIZE A CATALINA OFFER

Catalinas often provide a straight dollar amount off your next purchase. These coupons usually print in conjunction with a store promotion, reading something like: "Spend

$25 on any combination of these 50 participating products and receive a Catalina good for $10 off your next shopping order." Other examples of advertised Catalinas:

Buy two Degree Deodorant, receive $2.99 off your next shopping order.

Buy 5 select juices, receive $5 off your next shopping order.

These coupons are usually valid for about two to four weeks after the issue date. Krazy Coupon Ladies know how to maximize these Catalina savings. In the above-mentioned instance, "Spend $25 on participating products and receive $10 off your next shopping order", I could buy $100 worth of products. But instead of buying them in one transaction, I buy them $25 worth of groceries at a time. After my first transaction, I use my "$10 off" Catalina to offset the cost of my next transaction. Then another Catalina prints and I repeat the process. I am rolling the Catalina from one transaction to the next. I end up getting $40 off of $100 worth of products!

> Rolling Catalinas: this refers to the practice of separating your purchase into multiple transactions in order to use register Catalina coupons from your first transaction to pay for your second transaction. Another Catalina prints from the second transaction that pays for the third transaction and so on.

Catalina coupons only comprise 5% of the coupons I have on hand, but they definitely provide more than 5% of my total savings. As you begin scoping out the best stores for coupons in your area, keep an eye out for stores that run promos like "Spend $30, get $15 off your next order." These are just fancy words for a Catalina promo. "On your next order" is code for Catalina! When you "roll" your Catalinas, a "Spend $30, save $15" promo translates to 50% savings before you even use a coupon. This is where it starts getting fun.

A Krazy Coupon Lady steps up to the register and buys just over $30 of groceries and toiletries. Then she hands the cashier her stack of coupons totaling $14 worth of sav-

Catalinas often go by different names at different stores. At Walgreens, for example, they are called Register Rewards. The coupon looks just the same, but it goes by a different name. The store policies surrounding Catalinas also vary.

For example, at Walgreens, you cannot "roll" Register Rewards from one transaction to the next for the same product. Walgreens' promos often run like this: Buy 1 shave gel, get a $1 Register Reward. If you want to buy three shave gels, here's how you can do it:

Option A: Buy all three together in one transaction and receive one Register Reward coupon for $1 off your next shopping order.

Option B: Buy one shave gel, then receive one Register Reward for $1 off your next shopping order. Buy the second shave gel and use your $1 RR to pay for the shave gel. NO new Register Reward will print.

Option C: Buy each shave gel one at a time and Do NOT roll your Register Rewards. When all is said and done, you will have three shave gels, which you had to pay for, and three $1 off Register Rewards.

Option C is the smartest choice for Krazy Coupon Ladies who save their coupons to maximize their savings. The following week, when Walgreens runs a Register Rewards promo on Breyers ice cream, you can use your three $1 off Register Rewards from the shave gel to pay for the ice cream and still receive new ice cream register rewards. You *can* "roll" the Register Rewards, just not on the same promotion.

ings. So she only pays $16 plus tax and then receives a Catalina coupon for $15 off her next order. Lather, rinse, repeat! This Krazy Coupon Lady has two more stacks of groceries each totaling just over $30 before coupons! She smiles sweetly and tells the woman getting in line behind her, "Pick another checkout lane, honey," and waits patiently as her cashier rings through the next $30 of groceries. She hands over another stack of coupons totaling $14 worth of savings, and in addition a $15 Catalina coupon and now her total due will be only $1.00 plus tax on the original $30 purchase. That's easily going to be over 90% savings.

Now that we've covered Catalinas, we've discussed 95% of the coupons that most Krazy Coupon Ladies redeem AND we've got a pretty good looking sundae sitting right before us. We could gobble that sundae up (ignoring calories) and call it good. But it's a sundae, and that means it's time to get fancy. How about the whipped cream, nuts, and the cherry on top? Okay, we may have lost a few of the peanut allergy folks with that one, but stick with this analogy because there are a few more types of coupons that could really spice up your life: blinkies, tear pads, and peelies. I know they sound like awkward college nicknames, but they could save you big bucks.

• •

BLINKIES: THE WHIPPED CREAM

Have you seen those black plastic boxes with a blinking red light that hang on the shelf and dispense coupons? I wish I'd overheard the conversation when they were invented: "What are you gonna call these things?" Surely I would have laughed aloud when someone said, "Just call it a blinkie!" Or how about the fact that someone came up with those adhesive coupons that peel right off the front of a product and decided to call them "peelies"? We all would have laughed at such a corny coinage. Certainly the blinkie mastermind must have had a better name planned for these little coupons—something a little swankier, like "Catalina." But alas, there's no swanky name, just goofy sounding ones that accurately portray exactly where you can find these coupons.

SmartSource Coupon Machines, otherwise known as "blinkies," may have a ridiculous name, but they also have a high redemption rate. The SmartSource coupon brochure reports redemption at 17% by AC Nielsen/Market Decisions. And with over a billion coupons dispensed each year, that means a whole lot of successfully redeemed coupons. The redemption rate is high because many customers take a blinkie coupon, grab the coordinating product, and redeem it immediately upon checkout. And though we might take blinkies out of the store to put in our binders, we don't take the coupons home if we don't intend to use them. SmartSource Coupon Machines are meant to increase impulse buying, launch a new product, or even kickoff a counterattack against a competitor's new product. By now you know that Krazy Coupon Ladies do NOT impulse buy, but we utilize every coupon opportunity to its fullest.

Blinkies are manufacturer coupons. The specific coupons and their values vary by location. If you find a blinkie in California, don't expect your auntie in Texas to always find the same great deal in her area. Although blinkie coupons appear in all sorts of different places, they can be used at any store; you don't have to use them at the store where you found them or even at a store that displays the SmartSource coupon machines. See what I'm saying? You can use them *anywhere*. The blinkie machine is there to disperse manufacturer coupons. The manufacturer is happy to have you take as many as you'll reasonably use! If I see a good coupon in a blinkie machine, I'll often take five of them and place them in my coupon binder. I end up using them maybe two-thirds of the time. Don't flip out...but...sometimes I take them, and then they expire before I can use them. As long as you're not strutting down the aisles, clearing every machine and taking coupons you aren't reasonably likely to use, you're not breaking blinkie etiquette.

Keep in mind that blinkie machines spit out one coupon at a time in about twenty-second intervals. Luckily, blinkie machines make excellent babysitters for children and even better special ops assignments for teenagers and husbands. Give the order, detail how many coupons you want, and let your troops loose in the minefield of grocery aisle blinkies. The point is that blinkies are free coupons. Don't take them and use them as collage-style gift wrap, but if you think you'll use them, check the expiration date and take a few to add to your stash.

●　●　●　●　●　●　●　●　●　●　●　●　●　●　●　●　●

TEARPADS: THE NUTS

Tearpads are just like blinkies, but (wait for it...) you tear them off a pad instead of pulling them out of a blinkie machine. Just like blinkies, tearpads hang in the aisle right next to a product. It's just a pad of coupons stuck together like a stack of Post-it notes. Tearpad etiquette is exactly like blinkie etiquette: take as many as you reasonably believe you will use. Never take the entire pad. Krazy Coupon Ladies don't use tearpad coupons on every trip, but keep your eyes open. You never know what deal you could stumble onto.

● ● ● ● ● ● ● ● ● ● ● ● ● ● ● ● ● ● ● ●

PEELIES: THE CHERRY ON TOP

"Pull a peelie, get a dealie, head on home and make a mealie." Peelies are in-your face manufacturer coupons, trying to get you to buy the brand with the peelie as opposed to its competitor. Like blinkies, peelies vary by region. Watch the expiration dates, as some stores continue to carry products with expired peelies. The big secret when it comes to maximizing the savings of a peelie coupon is this: sometimes it's okay to actually remove a peelie coupon and use it on another product! Always, always, always read the fine print. For example, a package of string cheese (24-count) had a "$2.00 off" peelie. But when I read the fine print, the coupon was valid on any package of string cheese six-count or larger. So I peeled off five of the coupons, immediately picked up five smaller packages of string cheese marked at $2.78, and voilá!—a great deal. Please remember, these are manufacturer coupons that cannot be stacked with another manufacturer coupon from your binder. Learn the rules and read the fine print so you know all your options.

And now we have a magnificent brownie sundae and a handle on various types of coupons. Remember, everything listed above is a manufacturer coupon. No two of these types of coupons may be used together on one product. The only exception to this rule is the Catalina coupons such as, "$10 off your next purchase, courtesy of Post Cereals". These outright value-off coupons can be used with other manufacturer coupons. A sample transaction might go like this:

> Buy 10 boxes of Cheerios at $2.00 each. Use 10 $0.50 off manufacturer coupons. Your subtotal is now $15.00. Hand over your "$10 off" Catalina, bringing you total to $5.00 plus sales tax. Now you're cereal is only $0.50 per box.

In review: Subscribe to multiple copies of the Sunday paper, as many as you dare. Even if your spouse has to pull out a wheelbarrow to haul them in, your savings will be worth it. Print coupons online and download eCoupons to your store loyalty card. Don't forget to ask your cashier for all those Catalinas you see printing. And never forget to keep your eyes peeled for blinkies, tearpads, and peelies at the grocery store. These are all your manufacturer coupons! Now, on to store coupons!

You might be a Krazy Coupon Lady if. . .

Your husband has to get out a wheelbarrow
to bring in all your Sunday papers.

STORE COUPONS

Many stores have their own store coupons, which you'll be able to find in a few different places. First, stores often publish these coupons in their weekly sale circulars. So before you throw away your store ads, browse through them for coupons. These ads are often (but not always) available in the store. Second, you may be able to find store coupons on the store's website. Third, watch the coupons in your Sunday inserts closely. Some coupons may contain a Target or other store's logo and say "store coupon". Finally, check out **TheKrazyCouponLady.com** where you'll find printable store coupons on my "print coupons" page and others on my "newspaper coupons" database! Just remember, as long as it doesn't say "manufacturer coupon" at the top, it is a store coupon.

A store coupon is basically a discount or price break from the store. The store sacrifices a bit of its price margin to entice you to buy. Note that with manufacturer coupons, stores are reimbursed fully for the coupon's value, but reimbursement usually doesn't take place with store coupons.

"Stacking" (using more than one coupon on the same product) is a fabulous way to save money. Nearly all stores allow you to use a store and a manufacturer coupon on one product. Here is an example of how stacking coupons can result in tremendous savings:

Aveeno Baby Products, regular price: $3.50

$2.00/1 any Aveeno product (printable manufacturer coupon)

$1.00/1 Aveeno Baby product (store coupon)

Final Price: $0.50

Both store and manufacturer coupons are essential to your coupon collection. Together they make for some amazing deals. But in order to use them correctly, you've got to know how to read them! Abiding by the wording on a coupon is imperative. So here's a quick lesson on verbiage.

• • • • • • • • • • • • • • • • • • • •

VERBIAGE

One Coupon per Purchase

Sometimes the verbiage on the manufacturer coupons can be confusing. Often a coupon reads "one coupon per purchase"; this means one manufacturer coupon per purchase of any one item. Many coupon virgins (and some uneducated checkers) think that "purchase" means "transaction". This is not true. "One coupon per purchase" means *per item purchased.* If you have five bottles of shampoo, that is five purchases, even if you pay for them all in the same transaction. You can use five "$0.50 off one" coupons, one for each product. One coupon per purchase is the manufacturer's way of telling you that you cannot use two manufacturer coupons on one item. The cash register is smart, and it will remember how many items you purchased. If you try to use six coupons on five bottles of shampoo the cash register will make an angry beep at the sixth coupon and prompt the cashier to refuse the coupon.

You can almost always use one manufacturer coupon per item. There is only one exception. If you have shampoo coupons that say "Save $1.00 off 2", and you want to buy 5 bottles of shampoo, you cannot use five coupons. When a coupon's value says save on two, or on three, you can only use one manufacturer coupon on every two or three items, respectively.

One Coupon per Transaction

Unlike the common verbiage stating that you can only use one coupon per purchase, if you see a limit that states "one coupon per transaction", this coupon means business. You cannot use more than one coupon that has a limit "per transaction" in one shopping order, even if you buy multiple products. If you want to buy 2 products and you have 2 coupons, you'll need to buy 1, use 1 coupon, pay the cashier and then do a separate transaction for your second product, use a second coupon and pay the cashier again. Not very many manufacturer coupons have this wording; you're more likely to find this on your store coupons.

4 Like Coupons per Shopping Trip

A newer addition to the standard coupon verbiage, which can be found on all Proctor & Gamble coupons is, "Limit 4 like coupons in same shopping trip". If you have five "$0.50 off one" Herbal Essences shampoo coupons, and you want to buy 5 bottles, you won't be able to do so in one shopping trip. Like the coupon states, you can only use four coupons per shopping trip, commonly defined as: making your purchase, leaving the store, and coming back again later. If you want to redeem more than four identical coupons, you'll have to come back and shop again during the week. Companies who put limits on their coupons want to allow you to stock up on their products but not wipe out a whole shelf.

Now that you know exactly how to get your hands on all these hot little coupons and you know how to read them, let the coupon collecting begin. You'll soon start noticing coupons everywhere for almost everything. In the Sunday paper, at the checkout counter, in an ad, on a product, in an aisle, on a website....they're everywhere. Pick them up, cut them out, tear them off and, most importantly, save them all. Soon you'll have a mountain of coupons, and in no time your nice little stash will enable to you to start saving big.

FAQs:

Do you save money by printing coupons? Even after paying for all that ink and paper?

Absolutely. The average coupon value is over $1.00 and you can usually print three coupons to a page. Remember to print in grayscale, and your savings should exceed your printing costs by a huge margin! TheKrazyCouponLady.com shares deals and coupons on ink and paper, too! I'm always watching for a deal on the things I need and use.

Do you really take the peelies off the packaging? Isn't that dishonest?

Krazy Coupon Ladies have high ethical standards and don't participate in dishonest or fraudulent couponing. Manufacturers want you to use their coupons to buy their products. If all you're doing is removing one peelie and using it to buy another size of the product (that the coupon does not exclude), you are doing just what the manufacturer intended when they printed the coupon. The coupon is only stuck on the product as a temptation meant to increase impulse buying. Removing peelies may make you squirm at first. The loud ripping sound doesn't help you do it covertly in the store, either. Follow you heart, and if it makes you feel like a creep, don't do it. That just leaves more peelies for me.

Can I be a Krazy Coupon Lady and just get one copy of the Sunday paper?

Mmmm, well….uh…sorta. You can be a successful coupon lady, and you can save money, but you won't see the huge $500 per month or more savings without multiple copies of your Sunday paper. If you choose to supplement with newspaper coupons purchased online or if you live alone and eat very little, then maybe you could be a Krazy Coupon Lady with only one copy. Get creative. You don't necessarily need five subscriptions if you can find friends and family willing to give you their inserts.

Is getting all those Sunday papers wasteful?

Throw away papers or throw away money—the choice is yours. But you can actually find good things to do with your Sunday papers. Some Krazy Coupon Ladies donate to animal shelters. You may even have neighbors that would like to read a copy of the Sunday Paper. There's nothing wrong with getting your papers, swiping the inserts, and then sharing the newspapers with neighbors or family members. Please bear in mind it is illegal (and classless) to remove coupon inserts from newspapers which you do not purchase.

CHAPTER FIVE

The Coupon Process:

FROM CREATION TO CLEARINGHOUSE

Coupons are just ads. They're valuable, but, in essence, they're still just tiny billboards advertising a product. It's a simple concept: reduce the price of the item with a coupon; entice consumers to buy, and beat your competitors; create name and brand recognition; and capture new customers who would not otherwise try your product. The idea is simple but effective and quite ingenious. Wanna know who came up with it?

• • • • • • • • • • • • • • • • • • • •

HISTORY OF COUPONS

Believe it or not, the first coupon was created in 1894. A drugstore owner named Asa Candler bought the formula for Coca-Cola for $2,300. The massive success of the soft drink today is attributed to Candler's innovative marketing, the first of which was...you guessed it...the coupon. Mr. Candler used handwritten tickets that entitled customers to a free bottle of Coca-Cola. Eventually, the drink became a national icon, and Candler became the mayor of Atlanta—all proof that good things come from coupons.

"Mommy, where do coupons come from?"

". . .when a manufacturer loves his product very, VERY much. . ."

The next year, Mr. C.W. Post created a coupon for a penny off his new health cereal—Grape-Nuts. Coupons (and apparently Grape-Nuts) are over a century old! The twentieth century brought the Great Depression and it was then, in the 1930s, that coupons became a staple in many American homes. Coupons allowed families to afford food for their children when it had never been more important to be a penny pincher. In the 1940s, supermarkets replaced neighborhood grocers, and coupons made the leap. The 1950s saw more than the emergence of cute poodle skirts; the first clearinghouse for sorting and redeeming coupons was created in Chicago. In the 1960s, half of American households were clipping coupons. By 1975, some 35 billion coupons were being distributed in the U.S., and 65% of households were using them. Internet printable coupons and online discount codes began to be distributed in the 1990s. And now, in the new millennium, Krazy Coupon Ladies have hit the streets (and the aisles) and thousands of coupon-clipping moms are taking a turn toward the extreme. These new couponing methods are so innovative that I think Asa Candler would be proud!

• • • • • • • • • • • • • • • • • • •

COUPON BEGINNINGS

What motivates a manufacturer to release a coupon, and who determines the value of that coupon? Some manufacturers such as General Mills or Proctor and Gamble release coupons on a regular basis. Coupons are nearly always available from their family brands including: Yoplait, Crest, Nature Valley or Tide. These manufacturers use coupons day in and day out to promote their products over their competitors'.

Other manufacturers use coupons on a case by case basis. When a manufacturer changes an existing product, launches a new product, or just needs a little boost, it releases a coupon to undercut its competitors. In order to release a coupon, either in the Sunday circulars or online, most manufacturers turn to massive coupon distribution companies for help. Companies like Coupons, Inc.; SmartSource; and RedPlum create and distribute coupons for the manufacturer's product. The purpose of a coupon is to increase sales—period. It works just about every time, tried and true.

Though the last few years have shown a dramatic rise in coupon use, coupon redemption rates are still sitting at around 1%. There's your call-to-action, coupon ladies! We can do better than 1%! These manufacturers went to all the trouble of creating and distributing these little slips of paper; the least we can do is redeem them right up!

• • • • • • • • • • • • • • • • • • •

COUPONS BEYOND CHECKOUT:
THE REIMBURSEMENT PROCESS

My two-year-old absolutely loves to hold coupons for me in his sweaty little fists as I peruse the shopping aisles. He loves to hand over the coupons to the cashier so they can "go beep". I love that he often gets to watch me shop with only coupons and the change from my purse! But after the cashier scans those sweaty, crumpled, beloved coupons, where do they go?

After I pay, the cashier places the coupons right into her drawer. At the end of her shift, when it's time to count out her till, she will likely be required to count the coupon values and add them to her total drawer count. The total of the cash and coupon value in her drawer will be calculated to ensure the drawer is accurate. The store manager will collect the week's manufacturer coupons and put them in a pouch to mail to the store's headquarters or straight to a coupon clearinghouse.

Where do coupons go when they die?

Peanut Butter
Coupon funeral.
Jelly was inconsolable.

Here's where the real work begins. Clearinghouses are huge centers where coupon values are scanned and totaled so that stores may receive reimbursement checks from the manufacturer. The redemption process requires a great deal of tedious labor, so it's no surprise that the nation's largest coupon marketer began outsourcing in 1962 by building its first processing facility outside the United States. Over 90% of clearinghouses are located in Mexico. Take a glance at your coupons. How many coupon remit addresses are located in El Paso or Del Rio? Coupons are often sent to such locations in the southwestern United States before being shipped out-of-country to the clearinghouse. Though mostly a practice of years past, some coupons are even sorted by paid U.S. state prisoners. These processing centers are responsible for sorting through literally millions of coupons every year. As you can imagine, the variance in size, printing, material, and all the wrinkles in the paper make it necessary to do much of this sorting by hand. Coupons are first sorted by manufacturer. Then coupons from one manufacturer are placed on a conveyer belt, and a large scanner scans each UPC Bar Code and totals the value of all those coupons. Clearinghouse workers have to ensure that each coupon is counted. Coupons that are damaged will be sorted out and totaled by hand. Once the clearinghouse has separated and determined the total value of the coupons, it sends the coupons and the invoice with the total due in reimbursement to the manufacturer. Lastly, the manufacturer pays the store back for the amount of the coupon's value, plus shipping and handling.

Manufacturers ask stores to provide "proof of purchase" for nearly all types of coupons. Stores must submit supplier information, product purchase receipts, and product movement reports. Manufacturers want to make sure that the retailer's customers have redeemed the coupons and that the store is not just cutting Sunday Newspaper coupons and submitting them as though redeemed by customers.

Manufacturer coupons provide for a handling fee, usually around $0.08, which is simply an additional fee the grocer receives for the trouble of accepting a coupon. If a small grocery store handles, sorts, totals, and invoices the manufacturer on its own, that store keeps the handling fee in addition to the coupon value as reimbursed by the manufacturer. If a store uses a clearinghouse as addressed above, the clearinghouse cost is covered by the handling fee, and the store is reimbursed for the coupon's face value. Some larger grocery stores still get a portion of the handling fee back from the clearinghouse. This whole redemption process takes about a month.

The misconception that stores lose out when consumers use coupons has now been put to rest. We all win. Coupons really are like cash. The stores get fully reimbursed, while you and I get cheap stuff! Never feel like a sub-class shopper for paying with coupons. And certainly don't allow yourself to be treated like one! Now that you understand why coupons were created, and you know exactly how stores are reimbursed for every penny of the coupon's value, you can pull the coupons from your wallet and proudly use them just like cash! So keep clipping, and shop with confidence!

FAQs:

Do stores love coupons or hate them?

Most stores really don't mind. Coupons require more work, but that's why they have the $0.08 handling fee. Some stores like coupons and some don't, but either way, feel confident knowing that stores are reimbursed for the value of every manufacturer coupon you use. You should never be embarrassed to use legitimate coupons.

Are manufacturers going to stop distributing coupons when they realize that we're getting things for free?

No Way! One of the most important things to remember is that manufacturers use coupons as a way to build their customer base; it's a form of advertising. (Remember—tiny billboards!) Of all the coupons released, only about 1% of them are being redeemed. That's a lot of unused coupons that the manufacturer was willing to print.

If a manufacturer releases a "$0.50 off" coupon, and you use it on a product that's on sale 2/$1.00 (thus getting the item for free), the manufacturer doesn't feel any differently toward you than the customer who redeemed the same coupon on the item at its regular everyday price of $1.09. When you get something for free, your savings is usually coming from more than one source. In the above instance the store is giving you a discounted price ($0.59 savings) and the manufacturer gave you the coupon ($0.50 savings). You got the product for free; neither the store nor the manufacturer lost a full $1.09.

CHAPTER SIX

Playing Fair:

WHAT YOU SHOULD KNOW ABOUT COUPON FRAUD

You know the old saying about how one bad apple spoils the whole bunch? It's truer than ever when it comes to couponing. Almost every Krazy Coupon Lady (including me!) can tell you a story of a mistake she made before she knew better. You're already a step ahead! After reading this book, you're going to be ten times more informed than I ever was as a coupon virgin. Why all the admonitions not to misuse the information I'm giving you in this book? Why devote an entire chapter to placing my hand on my hip, tapping my foot, and shaking my finger at you? Coupon fraud is a serious and, unfortunately, all too common offense. A prison sentence of three to five years is not an uncommon penality given to someone convicted of coupon fraud, nor are the financial penalties of well over $200,000. As of this date, the most severe penalties for individuals convicted of coupon fraud include a prison sentence of 17 years and a financial penalty of five million dollars. With consequences like that, who would ever dare mess around with something as innocuous as a little coupon? Coupon fraud is no joke and is not to be taken lightly.

There are a few different ways to commit coupon fraud. Some are intentional and many are unintentional. Remember, knowledge is power. Krazy Coupon Ladies need to be knowledgeable about what to do and what not to do.

• •

FRAUDULENT COUPONS

In the past, fear of counterfeit has sometimes caused stores to stop accepting coupons altogether. Security measures are increasing, and new bar codes are reducing instances of fraud. There has been such a huge consumer demand for retailers who will accept coupons that nearly all stores now accept them. Even still, it's important to understand why stores may be wary to do so.

The Coupon Information Corporation, a non-profit organization made up of manufacturers fighting coupon fraud, says:

> *Counterfeit coupons have cost manufacturers millions of dollars and have created numerous costs and challenges for retailers and other industry participants. These counterfeits have ranged from amateurish home-made ones to high quality, professional examples virtually identical to those printed by the industry. Unfortunately, even the amateurish coupons are often accepted for redemption, creating liabilities for a variety of industry participants. Once a counterfeit is accepted, someone, whether it is a manufacturer or a retailer, is going to have to pay for it.*

> *Counterfeiters have forced retailers to be more aggressive in reviewing coupons at the checkout lane. The increase in front end security procedures has created consumer discomfort, increased costs, and longer lines.*

Yikes. Checkout sounds like airport security when the CIC talks about it! Understanding the reason for the increasingly slow checkout and the longer lines can help us be more patient. There will always be criminals exploiting opportunities to make a buck, so get used to the skepticism and security on coupons.

There are several ways to commit coupon fraud including barcode decoding, using expired coupons, photocopying and, worst of all, creating fake coupons. By being aware of all the potential risks, you'll be able to avoid handing over a fraudulant coupon at the register and you'll understand the need for diligent inspections!

MANUFACTURING YOUR OWN COUPONS

The most well known way to commit coupon fraud, and the best coupon-induced way to get thrown in the clink, is to create your own fraudulent coupons. Come on now, any takers? Are you good on photoshop or paint? Is this sounding appealing to anyone? I highly doubt that any one of us is considering entering into the crime ring of creating fraudulent coupons.

You might be a little too krazy if...
you thought making or selling your
homemade coupons was a good idea.

Selling counterfeit coupons is a serious crime and the most likely culprit for the 17 year prison sentence I mentioned above. The problem with coupon fraud for the rest of us isn't about creating them; it's about accidentally purchasing or redeeming them. We need to learn how to spot an illegitimate coupon before we ever think about using it! We'll delve deeper into how to spot the signs of a fraudulent coupon later in the chapter, but for now, remember that we do not ever attempt to purchase coupons that could possibly be fakes, and we never purchase printable coupons.

BARCODE DECODING

Attempting to use a coupon for any item for which it was not intended is considered barcode decoding. Some individuals will disobey the verbiage on the coupon and attempt to trick the cash register into accepting a coupon that doesn't match the product. Manufacturers have fought back against this practice with the new GS1 barcode. These new barcodes pack more information into a more compact, linear space. Traditional UPC barcodes would often scan at the register for a wider variety of items than they should have. Now, with the recent rollout of the GS1 barcodes as an industry standard, your coupons are coded to the exact product, in most cases. This new barcode system is really great for honest couponers everywhere because it will reduce some of the all too prevalent coupon fraud. But, regardless of the technology, the bottom line for coupon shoppers is: you must only use your coupons for items specified by the verbiage on the coupon—period.

USE OF EXPIRED COUPONS

Some people try to redeem their coupons after they have expired. The register should beep, rejecting your expired coupon automatically. But an unaware cashier might simply override the beep and pass it through. This, too, is dishonest and considered a form of fraud. There are a few stores left that accept expired coupons, but you can bet your local store isn't one of them. Military members shopping at overseas commissaries may use expired coupons for up to six months past their expiration date. Visit **TheKrazyCouponLady.com** and find out how to send in your expired coupons each month to be distributed between my many adopted bases.

PHOTOCOPYING COUPONS

Photocopying printable coupons is an all too common rookie mistake, but it is just as illegal as creating your own. If you want more than the usual print limit of 2 coupons, the best way to accumulate them is to ask family and friends to print and mail them to you. Remember that you can print two coupons per computer, not per printer. If your family has a desktop and a laptop, that means you can print 4 of each coupon.

Since photocopying printable coupons is fraudulent and a huge no-no, how can one tell the difference between a stack of ten identical coupons printed from 5 computers versus one printable coupon which has been photocopied? Most printable coupons will have an individual code found under the bar code in the top right corner. The last few digits will be different on every coupon. This helps cashiers weed out photocopied coupons or other invalid reproductions. Make sure to point out this barcode to your cashier if she ever calls your coupons into question.

There you go. Your coupon commandments: Thou shalt not photocopy coupons. Thou shalt not use expired coupons or use coupons for any product which is not explicitly allowed in the verbiage on the coupon. And lastly, thou shalt not be stupid enough to create your own coupons or to support someone who's creating them by purchasing homemade coupons online. Next, read the strategies that cashiers use to spot a fake coupon and learn how to use those same strategies at home!

• • • • • • • • • • • • • • • • • • • •

THE RED FLAGS

To help everyone stay honest and to make sure none of your children ends up as property of the state 'cause mom's in the slammer, here's the lowdown on how to spot a legitimate coupon and how to weed out a fake. *Things your cashier might look at when scrutinizing your coupons in the checkout lane:*

- **Expiration Date:** Your cashier may check for unusually long expiration periods or dates that appear to have been altered. Valid printable coupons often have short expiration periods, usually 30-90 days.

- **Easily Scannable Barcode:** Proper printable coupons use technology that creates clear barcodes. Your cashier will look for barcodes that are unusually fuzzy or appear to have been altered.

- **Legal Language:** Manufacturers include legal language to protect against fraud and/or misredemption. Words such as "coupons are not to be altered, copied, transferred, purchased, sold, etc." are included on most printable coupons.

- **Instructions for the retailer:** Your cashier may look for a mailing address and directions on reimbursement.

- **Unusually high dollar value.** If the brand usually puts out coupons between $0.25 and $1.00 and you find one for $4.00 off, that should raise a red flag.

These are general guidelines. As always, there are exceptions to every rule. Stores usually reserve the right to refuse any coupon, so sometimes we're just out of luck at checkout. The best way to ensure that your coupons will be accepted is to perform the same examination before you ever leave home. If you find a coupon that raises more than one of these red flags, be a skeptic. One of the first tests I perform on a printable coupon is to find the source of the coupon. If I can reach the coupon from the manufacturer's home page, I know it is legitimate. Rest assured, when you find a coupon on **TheKrazyCouponLady.com**, I have run it through the ringer to assure its validity. I've done the grunt work so you can print and save without the worry.

• •

SLOW CHECKOUT LANES AND AIRPORT SECURITY

When I named this book *Pick Another Checkout Lane, Honey*, it was no joke. When shopping with coupons, you will be much slower than the average shopper. A responsible cashier who makes sure to check each of your coupons is slower still. Learn more about how to choose the best cashier in Chapter 12.

Think of the line at airport security. Is it slow? Yes. Similarly, is the meticulous scrutiny of your coupons an inconvenience? Yes. Is there profiling going on? Maybe. Cashiers are becoming more vigilant about reading the fine print on a coupon, and all of the honest couponers have to be patient as they do this. They are (understandably) trying to protect their stores from losing money. I used to get easily irritated at a cashier who felt over-entitled to scan my coupons with her eyes, close her lane, turn on her blinking light, and ask for a manager to come pat me down and read me my rights. (Okay, so they never patted me down—what would they be looking for, anyway? What does an accused fraudulent couponmaker carry on her person? A printing press?) Now I am grateful for thorough cashiers. Just like when a store clerk asks for ID when I pay by credit card *for my own protection*, I thank the checkers who are thoroughly examining my coupons.

On a recent shopping trip, when I handed the checker my stack of coupons, she exhaled a big annoyed breath and started to read the coupons over. She informed me she'd have to call over a manager to do an override (because of the number of coupons I was using). I had expected nothing less; this particular store always requires a management override. I thanked her for taking the extra time to make sure my coupons were valid, and I told her how grateful I was that her store recently began accepting printable coupons after a few years of denying them due to an outbreak of fraud. I went on to explain that cashiers like her would make it possible for coupon moms like me to continue to use coupons. Words can't describe the look she then gave me. She rolled her eyes and looked perfectly perturbed. At that moment, the manager walked up, and after my coupons were all cleared, I left without pressing the issue, but it makes me laugh to think about her reaction. She must have been so accustomed to shoppers being annoyed by the slow and excruciating examination process that she made me out to be the worst of all. She thought I was feeding her a bunch of sarcasm, when I was trying to pay a genuine compliment. Meticulous employees getting out their figurative magnifying glass to check each coupon ensure that their stores will not lose money on the coupons we use.

I cannot control how others interpret my words or actions. I can only make certain I act with the right intent. I always try to say, "Thank you" to a cashier who is particularly thorough. The more meticulous the cashiers, the fewer fraudulent misuses will get past them. If stores are getting scammed, they'll be less likely to accept coupons in the future, and then everyone will lose. If your cashier doesn't look at your coupons, she's not looking at anyone else's either. Let's make it clear that we want store employees to be reading all the fine print.

Again, when your cashier is being slower than molasses and scanning each and every printable coupon as if searching for a secret watermark treasure map, have patience. A few slimeballs ruin it for everyone. Remember to think of it like airport security—a necessary inconvenience but one that ensures a happy ending!

FAQs:

What if my cashier accuses me of photocopying my coupons?

The easiest solution is to point out the individual barcode numbers in the upper right-hand corner found on many printable coupons. If you find that a particular store consistently has a problem with your coupons, don't clip your coupons until you're at the checkout. This way the cashier can look at the url source and the date and time-stamp. This should help prove that your coupons are valid and not photocopied.

What happens if I use a coupon and later find out it was fraudulent?

Consider calling your store's manager, apologizing, and giving him or her a heads-up that you found the coupon to be fraudulent. This way the store can avoid accepting these fraudulent coupons in the future.

What if my valid coupon won't scan?

This could happen for a few reasons. First, if your printer is from the Stone Age, you may not get a clear barcode. Second, some coupons from manufacturer's sites print in a different format from the norm, and their barcodes may not always scan. You can explain to your cashier where you found your coupon and that it is valid, and that cashier should manually enter the coupon in the computer. Be aware that some stores maintain a policy to deny any coupon that does not scan.

What if my coupon has many of the "red flag" indicators of a fraudulent coupon, but I still think it's legitimate?

The best place to check the validity of a coupon is to find its source. If it comes from a manufacturer site or from a huge marketing company like coupons.com or smarsource.com, it is a legitimate coupon. Feel free to send suspicious coupons to The Krazy Coupon Lady for verification. Rest assured, printable coupons posted on **TheKrazyCouponLady.com** will have been through a rigorous verification process.

Why does The Krazy Coupon Lady advocate buying coupons if the coupons clearly state: "void if transferred"?

I wouldn't jump off a cliff just because everyone else was doing it, but I will buy coupons online. The manufacturer puts out a coupon to sell products and by transferring coupons, the redemption rate has never been higher. Be very careful that you never buy fraudulent coupons. But other than that, in my expert opinion, there's nothing wrong with paying someone for his or her time in clipping and mailing you coupons.

What is barcode decoding?

Barcode decoding is the practice of misusing coupons for products for which they are not intended. Decoders learn how to trick the cash register so the coupons will be accepted as long as the cashier doesn't read the wording on the coupon. Barcode decoding is dishonest, fraudulent, and illegal.

CHAPTER SEVEN

My Other Baby:

HOW TO BUILD
YOUR COUPON BINDER

Once you get the coupons, deciding how to organize them will make or break your couponing experience. There are many theories on how best to organize your coupons. But I'm about to introduce you to the most efficient method out there. First, let me remind you of one thing: you are not a standard coupon lady. The standard coupon lady has an envelope or a small plastic accordion file where she keeps her coupons. She only clips and files the coupons she thinks she needs, and once she's at the store, she's constantly realizing she left valuable coupons out or back at home. Her method is too small, too unorganized, and too outdated. You are a Krazy Coupon Lady. Hence, one small envelope is much too insignificant for your needs. You need something larger, grander, more organized, and much more accessible—something you can tote around; something that can hold your constantly growing coupon stash; something that you're just plain proud to show off! And I've got just the solution. You are about to be introduced to your new baby. Let the drum roll begin! And now, a new challenger for the "Thousand-Dollar-Savings-in-a-Month Fight", weighing in at 12 lbs 9 oz (I told you it weighed more than my firstborn), the rookie heavyweight contender—organized, enormous, heavy, bicep-buildinnnnnggggg...the incredible Krazy Coupon Lady Binder!!!!

Honestly, I've tried all the other ways. The Krazy Coupon Lady binder system is the best way to organize your coupons—bar none. I'm so confident you're going to love it, so confident you won't be able to live without it, so confident you'll want to kiss me for showing it to you that I'll give you a money-back guarantee. That's right! Just four monthly installments of $19.99, plus shipping and handling, and this incredible system with all its secrets…RRRRRRR…WAIT! Remember how I told you I'm not a salesperson, and I said I wouldn't try to sell you any information? Well, that's why this binder system is FREE. I'm not withholding info or forcing you to fork over extra money to get my tried-and-true tips. I've learned for myself what works, and I'm ready to share the info to help you start saving. Ready?

You might be a
Krazy Coupon Lady if. . .

You catch your husband checking out another
woman's coupon binder, but he assures you,
"yours is better looking than hers."

There are a two different ways to organize your coupon binder. Both have perks, and both have drawbacks. The important thing to remember is that each takes a bit of time. The good news is that 50% of Krazy Coupon Ladies report that they spend less than 2 hours a week organizing coupons. That might sound a bit daunting at first. But think about it. That's one evening of easy organizing while watching the finale of The

Bachelor. Then you're done for the entire week and don't have to think about it again. So ultimately, your choice boils down to where you want to spend your time. Regardless of which system you choose, begin by separating the pages of your inserts. Here's how you do it:

First, take the inserts out of all your newspapers. If you have six subscriptions, go through all of the papers and pull out every insert for the week. Then separate the inserts by company. Put all the SmartSource inserts together, put all the RedPlum inserts together, put all the Procter & Gamble inserts together, etc. Choose one group to start with and set the others aside. Go through your first stack of inserts and tear all the pages at the seam until you're left with a bunch of single, unattached pages. Next, clear off the table and spread the pages of the insert out one by one. Then follow up by grouping all like pages together. Soon you're left with several stacks of matching insert pages. If your P&G insert was twelve pages, you'll have twelve stacks, six pages in each stack (because you get 6 copies of the Sunday paper). I like to staple each set of pages together. At this point, throw away any ad pages without coupons. There are usually a few pages full of ads toward the back. To spot them, look for something targeting the over-eighty crowd, such as a model wearing seersucker clamdiggers, polka dot muu-muus, or orthopedic shoes in your choice of five colors. Mark my words, eventually these ads will start to target the younger generations, but for now it's muu-muus and collector plates.

Now it's time to choose one of two different organizing methods: organizing unclipped coupons by date or clipped coupons by category. I know, I know—choosing teams brings a painful flashback to high school PE, but this is an important decision! Team one spends less time up front and more time right before shopping. Team two spends more time up front and gets to shop hassle free. I'll outline both methods so you can decide which works best for your time and organization strategies.

● ●

METHOD #1: ORGANIZE BY DATE

The basics: file pages of coupon inserts by date, with no clipping.

Supplies:

- 200 clear 8 ½ x 11 sheet protectors

- 4-5 inch binder

- Tabbed Page Dividers

- Scissors

- 3-ring pencil holder (to hold your scissors)

This method involves less work up front because you spend less time clipping. Once you've separated, sorted, and stapled your ads (as described above), get out a sharpie and write the date on each set of pages; this will be the date of the corresponding Sunday newspaper. (Tip: find an empty space in the corner to write the date, as you do NOT want to write across your coupons.) Next, place them in 8 ½ x 11 sheet protectors and file them in your binder with the most recent ones in the back. Use tabbed page dividers to separate each week, and be sure to label the divider with the date. Ta-dah! When I outline deals on **TheKrazyCouponLady.com**, I'll always tell you the date of the coupon. If your binder is organized by date, this info will allow you to flip right to the page you need, find your coupon and clip it right before you use it. With this method, you don't clip the coupon until you know you're going to use it. Pros: very little time up front. Cons: more time getting ready to go before each individual shopping trip. This makes for the heaviest binder of them all...this is my twelve-pounder!

For this method to work, you and your binder need to be best friends on very familiar terms. Flip through it regularly to see which coupons are nearing their expiration dates. Consider flagging pages with coupons that you want to use before they expire.

METHOD #2: ORGANIZE BY CATEGORY

The basics: clip the coupons when you get them and file them by category.

Supplies:

- 38 8 ½ x 11 sheet protectors

- 3-4 inch binder

- 65-75 clear plastic baseball card holders (found at most supercenters, toy stores, or sports memorabilia collector stores)

You will spend an average of forty-five to sixty minutes each week clipping your coupons with this method. If you have multiple copies of the paper, your process will begin just as in method #1. Separate all the pages of your inserts, stack and staple them together. Now, instead of writing the date, you're ready to get out your scissors. You'll be cutting through a stack of six pages at once. The time it takes to clip all the coupons will vary each week, depending on how many inserts you receive on any given Sunday.

Once the coupons are clipped, organize them by category. This is the method most Krazy Coupon Ladies prefer because it takes less last-minute planning before a shopping trip. The categories coordinate with your shopping aisles, and there are one or more categories for each aisle in the store. I love having my coupons organized this way instead of by date. I can go to the grocery store without having planned a specific coupon trip; I just flip through the pages as I shop each aisle. Below are the tested and proven categories I suggest.

Table of Contents:

You might be a Krazy Coupon Lady if. . .

Your binder rides in a cart and your baby walks.

At **TheKrazyCouponLady.com**, you'll find a free download of these binder tabs, ready to print. After you've printed those thirty-seven pages, insert them into the sheet protectors and put them in your binder. Next, insert one baseball card holder sheet behind each category. You'll end up with many sheets of baseball card holders in the *refrigerated, freezer, medicine*, and *surface cleaners* sections and only one sheet in the produce and PB&J sections. You'll find that sometimes your coupons fit nicely into the baseball card holder while other times you'll have to fold them to fit. Regardless, it's a helpful way to keep pre-clipped coupons right at your fingertips. It's easy to shop spontaneously, browse the clearance sections, or get an unadvertised deal because the coupons are easily organized by category. I love having one clear sheet protector as my very first page, before the Table of Contents. As I shop, I pull coupons from their sleeves and place them in the front pocket until I make it to checkout. You could accomplish the same thing with an envelope or even stuffing them into your bra.

The best part of this method is I don't get frazzled clipping at the grocery store. I'm cool, confident, and my pre-clipped coupons are ready to rock! The maintenance is easy, too! Simply pull out the expired coupons to make room for the new ones. My husband is my expired coupon cop. Every week, he goes through my binder and tosses the expired coupons. It's an easy task to delegate—almost as good as the blinkie machine babysitter. The drawback to this method is the additional time it takes to clip everything at the beginning of each week.

In either binder, keep a few blank sleeves to hold store-specific coupons like "$5 off $25 purchase at Rite Aid", or a Catalina coupon for "$10 off your next purchase at Albertsons". You'll want to make sure to have room in your binder for drugstore coupons. (I'll share more about specific stores in Chapter 19.) Just make sure you have a few empty sleeves on hand so you don't lose these precious bits of paper.

> A note of caution: Please put your name and contact information on your coupon binder. I can't tell you how many heart-wrenching stories I've heard from Krazy Coupon Ladies who have lost or left their binders at the store only never to be reunited! My binder is like my third child; sometimes I give it more attention than my other children, and you already know it weighs enough! I would be heartbroken to lose it. Never underestimate the kindness of a stranger who might return your binder to you if there's a name and number to call.

There you have it—two pretty simple and straightforward organizing options. The choice is up to you, so pick whichever method you want. Remember, there isn't a right way or a wrong way. Just find what works for you and perfect it. In a poll of Krazy Coupon Lady readers, those who clipped and organized by category outnumbered those organizing by date by about four to one. If you're on the fence about which method is right for you, you may just want to take the advice of the majority. If you can't stand the thought of clipping all those coupons or worry that you won't have the time, go with the no-clip organizing by date. The trick is to stay organized and make sure you like the method you use. If you dread organizing, you won't use your coupons effectively, and this glorious operation will needlessly fail. Whichever method you choose, make sure that your binder is easy to transport. Nothing is worse than showing up at the store with just a few coupons and running into an unadvertised or clearance sale of which you can't take full advantage!

Once you get the hang of this, it will be smooth sailing. Just choose the method that sounds most appealing to you and suits your lifestyle. If you give it a try for a few months and find it isn't working for you, switch it up and go another route. We're all different, so one method won't work for everyone. Despite the time it takes to organize, remember that it's "mindless" time, so you can easily do it while you watch a movie with your family. You might even try getting several clipping helpers in on the fun around the table. No need to wait for valuable naptime or a chance to focus (which we all know may never come). However you organize, just make sure it works for you.

Where do I file printable coupons if I organize by date?

If you file by date, buy a few baseball card holders to keep at the front of your binder. As you print coupons from the Internet, clip them and slip them into a baseball card holder right away.

When you organize by category, do you clip every coupon?

No. Sometimes one Sunday insert page has six coupons, all attached; all belonging in the same section (such as oral care); and all expiring on the same date. In this case, don't bother cutting them all apart. Just grab an extra 8.5 X 11 sheet protector and throw in the entire section of coupons. Every coupon doesn't need to be pre-clipped as long as it's in its correct category so you'll know where to find it.

When you organize by date, do you really need 36 categories?

I've found this way to be the easiest and most effective, but you can certainly change the system to suit your preference. You could put laundry, dish soap and cleaning supplies into one category, or you could combine soap, hair care, and lotion into one category. The categories I have listed are broken down this way to follow the manner in which most stores arrange their products. In many stores you will find that the lotion is by the beauty products and the soap and hair care are in an entirely different part of the store. Try these categories and see what you think. It will be easy to adjust them and customize as you gain more experience.

Now that I've built my binder, I am paranoid I will lose her (yes, it's a "her" and, yes, she has a name). Can I take out an insurance policy on my binder?

While I think insurance may be going a bit overboard even for this Krazy Coupon Lady, I would suggest finding a permanent place in your binder to add your name and phone number. This will just take a minute and will help a Good Samaritan return a lost binder to its rightful owner.

CHAPTER EIGHT

Beat the Joneses!

BUILD A STOCKPILE THAT WILL PUT YOUR NEIGHBORS TO SHAME

With the introduction of TLC's Extreme Couponing to the nation, the shock at seeing garages lined with shelves of cereal boxes, endless rows of canned goods, and towers of toilet paper has left many people wondering, "Why?" Questioning the rationale behind such behavior has become a discussion at the forefront of couponing. But I'm here to convince you that the only way to coupon is through stockpiling. I have said it before, and I will say it again: *I would not coupon if I couldn't get multiple items at one time!* Couponing without stockpiling is like cooking without eating—like painting your living room with a makeup brush. It's like trying to mow your lawn with scissors or water your garden with a baby bottle. You can, but it's inconvenient and really not worth the time, especially when there's a better way. To really take advantage of the benefits of couponing and save big, you must jump on the bandwagon of stockpiling and embrace it with both arms!

Like I told you, my grandmother has always clipped coupons the old-fashioned way. She pulls the coupon inserts from her Sunday paper and clips the coupons she wants. During the following week, she uses those coupons, just like the manufacturer hopes she will. Grandma is a coupon lady, but I'm a Krazy Coupon Lady. Grandma saves a quarter here and there, or a dollar, if she's lucky, but I save hundreds each week. What's the difference? Because we Krazy Coupon Ladies get multiple copies of the Sunday paper, we also get multiple products at rock bottom prices! Here's an example. Since I get six copies of the paper, I also get six Skippy peanut butter coupons and file them away. Then, when the peanut butter goes on sale and ends up being free after the coupon, I just stockpiled a six-month supply.

So what exactly is a stockpile? A *stockpile* is the stash of food and toiletries that you collect over time. Your stockpile might be in your garage, your basement, your pantry, anywhere you can store your extra food. During a recent move, my stockpile even spent some time in a storage unit. It doesn't matter where you keep it; the important thing is that you have it.

• • • • • • • • • • • • • • • • • • •

WHY CREATE A STOCKPILE?

To Save Money (and have more cash to spend however you want!) Spend a little now to save a lot later. I stockpile for the extra zeros it adds to my bank account balance. To pay for your children's education, to pay off debt, to donate to your favorite charity, to hire a cleaning lady, or for the cruise you've been eyeing but can't quite justify yet... whatever it's for, saving hundreds of dollars per month lets you do whatever you want with the extra cash. Believe me, you can't afford NOT to stockpile.

To save big money, you have to buy in multiples. Need an example?

Mandarin Oranges are on sale for $1.00.

I have a "$1.00 off 2" manufacturer coupon and my store is doubling coupons up to a dollar in value.

I can get two cans of free mandarins with one (doubled) coupon, so all I pay is any applicable sales tax.

If I only have one coupon, I'll buy two cans for free, pay the sales tax, and walk out of the store happy. That evening, my family will cheerfully eat both cans of oranges and say, "Wow! Good job saving two dollars!" The following week, I'll make a grocery list and realize we need mandarin oranges. I'll go to the store, this time without any coupons and without the sale price, and buy two more cans of oranges at $1.39 each.

See what happened? If you don't stockpile, you only save $2.00 once. End of story. Getting two cans of free mandarin oranges is not worth the time and effort it takes to clip and organize the coupon in the first place. Think BIG. You need more than one copy of the coupon. Honestly, I like to have at least four copies…sometimes more! If I had four copies of that same "$1.00/2" mandarin oranges, I could have scored 8 free cans of mandarin oranges instead of just 2. The more copies of each coupon you have, the faster you'll create your stockpile, and the more money you'll save long-term.

It may sound counter-intuitive that buying and accumulating all this stuff is going to save you money, but soon you'll be a believer. When shopping with coupons, you'll be able to start building your stockpile without spending any more than you're already spending right now. In fact, you might even start spending less right from the start, even while you're packing tons of food and toiletries away for later. Within a few months, you can see overall savings of 60-80%, and your stockpile can be created entirely by items purchased for around 25% of the retail price (in other words, 75% off).

You'll be amazed at the amount of money you can save through the simple strategy of stockpiling, but there are other equally important reasons. Stock up when products are free or at rock-bottom prices, and avoid running to the store at 8 p.m. when you realize it's your toddler's bedtime, and there's not a single diaper in the house (true story). Stock up so you have the freedom to cook whatever you like, whenever you like, even if it's the middle of the night. Stock up so that no matter what comes your way, you have nothing to fear because you are completely prepared.

• • • • • • • • • • • • • • • • •

IN CASE OF CATASTROPHE

No one likes to think about it, but disasters do happen, and unless you've been living in a bubble you know exactly what I'm talking about. Hurricanes, tornados, droughts, earthquakes, floods, tsunamis, wars—they all occur, even to people who once watched the news comfortably from their couches and said, "Poor folks; hope they're okay. Glad something like that will never happen to me." A few shelves in your pantry and a few more shelving units in the garage with non-perishable food will go a long way in the event of a big emergency. I'm no paranoid, end-of-the-world naysayer, but I'll be darned if I'm going to let that crazy guy with the "end-is-near" sign out on the street corner get the last laugh when I don't have enough food on hand in an emergency. If an earthquake comes along and we're stuck, I'd like to be able to break out a picnic for my neighbors that will last us all a few weeks until the helicopters airlift us outta there (assuming my house is still standing and we're all above sea level). Maybe I'd just sell toilet paper for $10 a roll…I'd be rich!

But seriously, Krazy Coupon Ladies are strong and independent. We want to be totally self-sufficient. We hope we can help others, but we certainly won't be counting on anyone else to take care of us in a time of crisis. Recent disasters are good reminders that we need to be able to depend on ourselves if infrastructure fails and the government is unable to help everyone quickly.

According to FEMA, in the case of a major disaster, government aid will not be available to a mass group of people for approximately 3 days after the disaster. If you or a loved one has a life-threatening injury, hopefully, you are attended to by a professional. But for everyone else who is displaced from homes or isolated for whatever reason, having emergency food, water, light, warmth and a few comforts will go a long way! The peace of knowing you are prepared for whatever may come is just about priceless!

●　●　●　●　●　●　●　●　●　●　●　●　●　●　●　●　●　●　●

IN CASE FOOD PRICES BEGIN TO FLUCTUATE

There are many unpredictable problems that can affect the price and availability of food. If a new bacterium emerges and kills crops, if an illness sickens or kills livestock, if the demand for fruits and veggies skyrockets and their prices get insanely high, whatever happens, you won't regret having food on hand.

The price of corn has doubled in the past six months, and the price of wheat has doubled since the middle of 2010. The United Nations is projecting that the global price of food will increase by another 30 percent by the end of 2011. And according to ABC, food prices are surging: "Over the past 12 months, eggs are up 33 percent, beef is up 13 percent, chocolate is at a 17-year high." Rising chocolate prices? Forget the earthquakes, this is a catastrophe!

With statistics like these you never know what might affect the price of food and how high the prices might get. We've already seen a huge price increase in dairy. So nowadays, when a two-pound block of Tillamook cheese goes on sale for $3.99, or even $4.99, I buy a cartload and stuff my freezer full! When you're prepared, there's no need to panic. You'll easily be able to live off much of your stockpile and shop around the inflation.

• • • • • • • • • • • • • • • • • • •

IN CASE GAS PRICES GO THROUGH THE ROOF

Sound familiar? This hits home all too well in today's world. According to ABC, "More than half of Americans say record-high gasoline prices are causing them financial hardship, and three in ten say it is a 'serious' hardship, up significantly in the last few years." In the last three years gas prices have risen dramatically; in some areas it's over $4.00 per gallon. Although this increase is enough to put a dent in your budget, think of what higher gas prices do to the price of food. It's obvious that they are directly correlated. The more it costs to transport groceries, the more you'll have to pay to get them. The shipping and oil industries are often unpredictable, so it's comforting to have a stockpile. If truckers go on strike, if gasoline prices quadruple, you can insulate yourself from the effects by having a stockpile. It's nice to think that if gas prices jumped to $15 per gallon tomorrow, I wouldn't have to drive to the store twice a week for overpriced cereal. I could just walk out to my garage and congratulate myself for stocking up when boxes of cereal were $0.50 each.

• • • • • • • • • • • • • • • • • • •

IN CASE OF JOB LOSS

In any economy, job security is always relative. By the end of 2010 the United States saw its highest rate of unemployment in almost 30 years. If you lose your job, or someone you depend on is out of work, a stockpile of food will take care of your family's first need. You will be able to save money, keep making your mortgage payment, fly to job interviews, and keep your head above water instead of spending your savings to feed your family.

While many people are losing their jobs, many more are experiencing pay cuts. Maybe you still have a job but your hours have been cut. Perhaps you work for commission and have watched your paychecks shrink in recent months. Whatever your individual case may be, millions of employed Americans are adjusting to pay cuts. Could your family survive a 20% pay cut? Before I started couponing, a 20% decrease in monthly income would have crippled our family. Now, we would still notice the difference, but we have enough food in our stockpile so that we could cut our grocery spending to make room in the budget for other necessities.

● ● ● ● ● ● ● ● ● ● ● ● ● ● ● ● ● ●

FOR THE SPONTANEOUS COOK INSIDE YOU

On a happier note, having a stockpile allows you to cook what you want whenever you want. Say goodbye to those last minute, frazzled trips to the store because you're out of eggs. At 11:00 at night, when the urge hits me to whip up a red velvet cake for the neighborhood association meeting in the morning, (or a double batch of chocolate chip cookie dough to binge on in secret,) I'm glad I have the ingredients on hand in my perfectly stocked cupboards. It's nice to know everything I need is right at my fingertips!

● ● ● ● ● ● ● ● ● ● ● ● ● ● ● ● ● ●

FOR PEACE OF MIND

Essentially, creating a stockpile is all about peace of mind. Krazy Coupon Lady, Britanie wrote,

> I used to hate grocery shopping. I thought it was silly to spend so much money on items that were consumable. A year ago I was challenged to live a week on what I had to eat in my home, no grocery shopping, and there was no warning,

no last minute run to the store to stock up. My family survived; we got creative with meals, and we snacked less. We ran out of a few things, like flour. And I decided right then that it was time to improve on my food storage. Couponing has allowed me to do that. It has given me the ability to be prepared, at a price I could afford. In January of this year I was laid off from my job. This would've been a much scarier prospect if we had not been prepared. Our grocery budget was already down to a very affordable level. We were able to live on what we had already accumulated and continue to grow our supply. I coupon shop for peace of mind.

What price can you put on peace of mind? Telling fear and anxiety to hit the road and knowing you're prepared for the future is one of the best feelings in the world. Luckily, The Krazy Coupon Lady is about to teach you to do it without spending an extra cent. Just a few hours of time each week and you'll be hooked on the safest ephedra-free drug around: couponing!

●　●　●　●　●　●　●　●　●　●　●　●　●　●　●　●

FOR OUTDOING YOUR NEIGHBORS, OF COURSE!

And the last and most important reason to create a life-sustaining, budget saving supply of food? To out-stockpile your friends and neighbors, of course! While others are lowering their garage doors to hide their messes, you'll be "accidentally" leaving yours up to showcase your sleek rows of cans, stacks of cereal, and, if you're like me, a label for every category. Don't forget to keep your cans dusted! You don't want anything unsightly when you parade your friends into your house via the garage just so you can hear them gasp in awe.

And even if you aren't quite as competitive as I am, it feels pretty great to know that, in a pinch, you're in a position to help those around you. If my neighbor's husband loses his job, or if my daughter's teacher gets a serious illness, or if anyone I know is in need, I can provide meals or toilet paper or whatever else for, literally, pennies. And when you help someone with a box or two of supplies, they don't have to feel bad accepting it because you can tell them you got it all for mere pennies!

You might be a Krazy Coupon Lady if...
while your neighbors lower their garage doors
you leave yours open to showcase your stockpile.

We needn't dwell on all the "what if's", but wouldn't it make you feel better to know that you have food on hand to feed your family? What if you could keep them nourished and clean for three months? What about six months? It's why they call me "krazy"; I have a stockpile to last a whole year, and the best part is that I created this one-year stockpile in six months, all without increasing my grocery budget by a cent!

•   •   •   •   •   •   •   •   •   •   •   •   •   •   •   •   •   •

STOCKPILING PITFALLS

IS IT POSSIBLE TO BUY TOO MUCH?

You bet it is! Now that you're all hyped-up with visions of barricaded stacks of food that cost you next to nothing, let me offer a few points of caution. With the accessibility and ease of buying forty coupons online, it's easy to over-stockpile. The natural coupon high can sometimes lead us astray in this regard. Be careful not to buy more than you can use before the product expires. Diligently check expiration dates, and learn how much your family can consume each month. If you overbuy, keep an eye on those approaching expiration dates. When you realize you won't be able to use something before it expires, quickly donate your extras to a food bank at least a month or two before the "sell by" date. And never EVER stock up on a new product without trying it first. I mean it.

MEN AND KOTEX

A single (male) Krazy Coupon Guy bought a bunch of Kotex pads when they were free, just because he could. He came on The Krazy Coupon Lady website to confess and present his over-buying dilemma. We brainstormed ideas for alternate Kotex uses: washing windows, band-aids for serious trauma, wiping the dip stick after checking the oil. He turned his free Kotex into a success, but stocking up on a product, even if it's free or dirt-cheap, can sometimes be a mistake.

HIGH-FIBER CALAMITY

A few years ago, when both of my children were in diapers, I learned first-hand why buying too much is a bad idea. My kids' favorite breakfast was instant oatmeal, and they *each* ate two packets every morning! Breakfast was often the biggest meal of their day because they were at such busy ages and were on the go all the time. So when I saw a Quaker sale coming up at my local grocery store, I gathered up an extra 40 Quaker coupons (in addition to the coupons I already had from my newspaper subscriptions). The following week I bought two cases: forty-eight boxes of Quaker High Fiber Instant Oatmeal in Maple and Brown Sugar—their favorite flavor! The oatmeal was only $0.25 per box! I was certain this would last my children for at least three months. I was excited to try the "high fiber" variety. We hadn't used it before, but it sounded healthy.

How many of you wise parents have predicted the end of this story? My babies loved the oatmeal, gobbling it up happily. Twelve hours later, I received a fragrant first hand lesson in what fiber does to a small body's digestive system. Thankfully, I was also stocked up on diapers and wipes. It was a disaster, and the worst part was I kept feeding it to them. Are you wondering why I didn't immediately stop? Well, because I am stubborn! I figured that maybe their little bodies would adjust to all that good fiber and learn to cope with it. I also started adding bananas in hopes of counteracting some of the effects—all to no avail. Now I was left with a case and a half of high fiber instant oatmeal that we'd never use. Did I mention that I don't like oatmeal? I ended up giving away the surplus, but the bottom line is, I had spent close to regular price for the boxes we used—all for the oatmeal that my kids loved so much but that didn't love them back. Plus, then I had to start watching diaper sales again to make up for all those extra changes. Is it a good idea to stock up on an unfamiliar product just because it is free or cheap? NO! Always sample the product before buying in massive quantities.

Buy Slowly

One last reason not to overbuy: stores' sale patterns are cyclical, and you usually see similar sales run a few times per year. This means that a few times per year you'll see the same deal on Kellogg's cereal: on sale for $2.49 per box, with a Catalina coupon printing for every 5 boxes you purchase. Because of the repetition of sales, there is no need to buy the whole shelf-load of cereal and pile it into your garage. Not only is shelf-clearing totally taboo amongst coupon ladies, but it's just not necessary. Usually purchasing a 3-6 month supply of a product is a good guideline when you're wondering how much to stockpile. Trust me, if you buy 100 boxes of cereal all from one sale, your family will be tired of the one variety in a few months, and you'll be forced to give the 70+ extra boxes away to your neighbors!

•   •   •   •   •   •   •   •   •   •   •   •   •   •   •   •   •

STOCKPILING TIPS

Bigger is not always Better

The only way to save the big bucks is to *buy in large quantities with a coupon when a product is on sale*. Stockpiling is buying a lot at once, but not necessarily jumbo-sized products. Because of coupons, you'll have many opportunities to stockpile greater quantities of small containers instead of fewer large items. For example, I might buy four 16-ounce jars of peanut butter instead of the big 64-ounce tub. I still look at the price per ounce, but when you add coupons into the mix it makes the smaller items the cheapest. Here's an example.

Store Prices:

64 oz peanut butter is $6.98 ($0.11 per ounce)

16 oz peanut butter is $2.00 ($0.125 per ounce) With a coupon for $1.00/1 peanut butter, look what happens to the price per ounce.

Final Prices after coupon:

64 oz peanut butter: now $5.98 after coupon = $0.09 per ounce

16 oz peanut butter: now $1.00 after coupon = $0.06 per ounce

See what I mean? The smaller container of peanut butter started out with a higher price per ounce at retail cost, but once you factor in your coupons, the smaller size is a much better deal. Don't be fooled by those jumbo sizes. With coupons, the smaller size is the way to go.

FIND THE SPACE

One of the biggest discouragements people have when it comes to stockpiling is trying to figure out where to store it. So often I hear "But I just don't have the room. There's nowhere to put it." This is one of the biggest reasons keeping people from implementing the practice of stockpiling, even though they understand the benefits. In a recent poll of over 1200 Krazy Coupon Ladies, we asked, "Where do you store your stockpile?" The number one answer, by a large margin, was simply "Everywhere." How true that is! Although shelves in basements and garages are the most popular places to store food, many people store their stockpile in extra bedrooms, under beds, in random closets throughout their house, and in their laundry rooms. We even had a couple of people say they store their stockpile in their gun cabinet!   Whatever works!

There is no one way to store your stockpile. We each have unique challenges and have to find what works for us. I'm often asked, after doing an interview in New York City, "How can I make this work when living in a studio apartment in Manhattan?" I always reply to start by stockpiling small products with a large sales margin: namely, things like razors. Five blade razors retail for over $13, and my stock up price is around $1.00. If you buy 8 razors and remove them all from their packaging, you can squeeze them into one gallon Ziploc bag. This is one of many examples that goes to show, if you're concerned about space, don't start by stockpiling 12 cases of paper towels. Think about starting with small things and then working up to larger items once you can clear some space. With a little reorganization and some creativity you can make stockpiling work!

KEEP IT REASONABLE

Remember that your stockpile is a tool to help you save money! The stockpile allows you to buy more when it costs less, thereby avoiding expensive last minute purchases. If you go overboard and barricade yourself into your home, you've missed the mark. Make sure that you are in control of your stockpile, not the other way around. I've been asked, "Can a stockpile become too big?" My answer is, "YES!—but there is no universal number, such as over 100 boxes of cereal, or over 50 bottles of shampoo." Your stockpile becomes a problem the minute you loose track of what you have. Regardless of where you decide to store your stockpile, make sure it's in an easy place to rotate and watch closely. If you cannot rotate, you're going to end up with expired food. Keep an inventory. Make a monthly chore of sorting through your stash. Do something to ensure that all the products you worked so hard to purchase on a dime get used responsibly.

Creating a stockpile makes good financial sense, even if you do make a few oatmeal blunders along the way. Buying multiple products at rock bottom prices really is the secret behind The Krazy Coupon Lady's success. Stockpiling is what allows you to

save hundreds of dollars a month. But, as I've discussed, there are many more reasons, other than just saving money, to give stockpiling some serious consideration.
Even if you're unable to store a year's supply like I do, stockpiling makes sense in any
degree. Start small and soon you'll discover how having a few extras on hand saves
you so much more than just money.

FAQs:

What if I don't have room for a stockpile?
What if I'm living in an apartment?

Everyone's situation will vary. Whatever your circumstances, make stockpiling a priority. If you live in a tiny apartment take a look at your closet and see if there's a place you could make room for a shelf or two. You may need to get creative, looking high in the closet, under the bed, maybe behind the entertainment center. Consider putting in extra shelving or buying free-standing storage units. Don't wait until you have enough room for a one-year supply of food. Just start where you can and reap the savings.

What if I live in a 1-2 person household?
I don't use that much food.

Everyone eats! Even if you live alone you can benefit from a stock-pile. Find the items you eat most often. Maybe it's peanut butter or cream of chicken soup. Maybe it's pickles and potato chips; I'm not here to judge. Whether you generally cook for one or ten, there are some foods you use more than others, and you can save big money. Figure out what you usually buy. When those items go on sale and you have coupons for them, buy a six month supply.

How am I going to save money and buy more food at the same time?

I know, right? You'll see what I mean once you get started. For example, right now—without coupons—let's say you typically buy $10 worth of cereal every two weeks. You get two to three boxes of your favorite cereal and gobble it up. When you start couponing and find boxes of cereal for $1 each or less, you'll come home with 8 boxes. Did you buy more cereal than you used to? Yes. Did you spend less than you used to? Yes.

How do you make sure nothing expires?

Your own food rotation system will vary according to your needs, but you'll soon figure out what works best for your situation. When I restock my shelves, I make sure the oldest package, box or can goes in the front and the newest in the back. It's helpful to write the expiration date on the outside of the package in the large bold print so you can easily spot it when you're throwing together dinner. When you notice expiration dates approaching quickly, you can donate to friends, neighbors or a food bank before the "sell-by" date.

You might be a *Krazy Coupon Lady* if...
you hate shopping without your husband because
you can't carry your coupon binder on your own.

CHAPTER NINE

Sticker Sleuth:

HOW TO SPOT THOSE
ROCK BOTTOM PRICES

People ask me all the time, "How do you know when you've found a 'rock bottom' price?" As a coupon virgin, you may find it difficult to tell the difference between a "meh, just-okay" bargain and a screaming deal. When I first started couponing, I discovered toothpaste for $1.00 per tube. I was used to paying at least $2.50, so I thought I had hit the jackpot. Of course, I bought a bunch of them. Little did I know that Krazy Coupon Ladies buy toothpaste for less than a quarter all the time! Look, if you're completely out of toothpaste and your breath stinks, $1.00 for a tube is great to get you by, but this is not the price to use for stocking up. Be patient. It takes a few trips around the couponing block to figure out what's a good price and what's not. But once you've got it down, you'll never overpay again!

● ● ● ● ● ● ● ● ● ● ● ● ● ● ● ● ●

PRICE LIST

If you're having trouble spotting a good price, consider making a price list! It's just as it sounds, a list of the products you commonly buy in one column with the corresponding retail prices recorded in another. This comes in handy when trying to filter through the store ads. Just because a store puts up an oversized sign shouting that a product is on sale doesn't mean they've really marked it down. Believe me, all of those bright yellow tags down the aisles can be deceiving. By carefully recording retail prices you can determine whether a sale is hot or not.

The quickest way to develop your price list is to take it to the store where you normally shop (before you begin couponing) and record the prices of items you regularly purchase. Keep it as reference in your coupon binder. As a general rule, if you find a deal that is 75% less than retail, that's a great stockpile price.

As you create your price list, be sure to write down sizes and quantities along with the price. Only listing the price would be a shame. Often we spot those amazing deals by understanding the price per ounce or price per quantity. After you've made your record it's important to go home and start crunching those numbers. Next time you're at the store you'll know exactly what deal is best without having to do long division on your palm in the middle of the aisle! It'll be right there recorded in your notebook!

•   •   •   •   •   •   •   •   •   •   •   •   •   •   •   •   •   •

THE KRAZY COUPON LADY PRICE LIST

Because I love you so much, and because I know how hard it can be to determine what a great price really is, I've created my very own Krazy Coupon Lady Price List. It's big and it's grand, because that's how I do it. Check this out before you go shopping or before you decide to make a purchase. Or keep it as an easy reference in your binder so it's never out of reach. It will help you determine whether the price is right! I've found these prices all over the western United States. But remember, prices do vary slightly by region, so try not to be too frustrated if my prices don't exactly match yours.

I tracked my best purchases for an entire calendar year in order to create this price list. Some of the prices I found were so amazingly low, I saw them only once or maybe twice in the span of that year. These are the "krazy prices". When you find a price similar to one of the krazy prices, I suggest stocking up with enough to last your family 6 months to one year. These are prices that are so great, I don't expect you to see them very often!

During the year, I found other fantastic deals, too, many of which repeated about

3 to 5 times per year. These prices are what you'll see in the "decent stock up prices" column. These price are still gonna be really enviable! These aren't your average sale minus coupon prices. When you see a price similar to my "decent stock up prices" column, I suggest you stock up a 3 to 6 month supply of that product for your family!

Use my stock up prices loosely as a guideline. Because I cannot physically come shop in every city, I cannot make a price list specific to each region. Regions with regular double coupons may see prices that are even lower than my price list. Regions without any double coupons may notice that they never see prices quite so low. Remember, if you find a great product that your family uses for half the price you used to pay, you should buy that item, even if it's at a higher cost than I suggest on my stock up price list! The only thing you may be wary of is if the item is significantly higher than the "decent stock up price" from the list. If you've only been couponing for a few months and aren't quite sure about the price, don't buy much more than a 3-month supply. You may be likely to find a similar deal, or even a better deal, in the next 3 months.

Without further ado, here is the list that will answer your most burning question: "To buy or not to buy?"

Product	3 month price	6 month price
Produce		
Apples	$0.79/ lb	$0.50/ lb
Avocado	$0.50 each	$0.35 each
Bananas	$0.40/ lb	$0.25/ lb
Broccoli crowns	$0.69/ lb	$0.50/ lb
Cantaloupe	$1.25 each	$0.99 each
Cauliflower	$0.69/ lb	$0.50/ lb
Carrots, baby	$0.99/ lb	$0.85/ lb
Cilantro	$0.50/ bunch	$0.35/ bunch
Corn on the Cob	$0.20 each	$0.13 each
Cucumbers	$0.50 each	$0.35 each
Grapes, seedless	$0.89/lb	$0.79/lb
Lemons	$0.30 each	$0.20 each
Lettuce	$0.95/ head	$0.75/ head
Limes, key	$0.10 each	$0.05 each
Limes	$0.30 each	$0.20 each
Onions, yellow	$0.39/ lb	$0.25/ lb
Oranges, navel	$0.75/ lb	$0.50/ lb
Peaches	$0.95/ lb	$0.69/ lb
Pears	$0.95/ lb	$0.69/ lb
Peppers, bell	$0.50 each	$0.35 each
Potatoes, russet 5lb bag	$1.00 each	$0.75 each
Raspberries	$1.99/ 6 oz	$1.49/ 6 oz
Spinach, 9 oz bag	$0.50 each	$0.25 each
Strawberries	$1.00/ lb	$0.88/ lb
Tomatoes	$0.89/ lb	$0.69/ lb
Watermelon, seedless, whole	$5.00 each	$3.50 each
Salty Snacks		
Crackers	$0.75/ box	$0.50/ box
Nuts, mixed	$2.50/ lb	$2.00/ lb
Pistachios, 8oz	$2.00/ bag	$1.50/ bag
Pita chips	$1.00/ bag	$0.75/ bag
Popcorn, microwave 3pk.	$0.50/ box	$0.25/ box
Potato Chips, 5+oz	$0.75/ bag	$0.50/ bag
Rice cakes, mini	$0.65/ bag	$0.45/ bag
Tortilla chips, 9+oz	$0.95/ bag	$0.75/ bag

Product	3 month price	6 month price
Refrigerated		
Cookie dough, ready to bake	$0.95/ pkg	$0.75/ pkg
Creamer, 1 pint	$0.75 each	$0.50 each
Crescent rolls, ready to bake (6ct)	$0.50 each	$0.35 each
Deli meat	$3.00/ lb	$2.00/ lb
Eggs, dozen	$0.95/ carton	$0.75/ carton
Hummus	$1.25 each	$1.00 each
Orange juice, 48oz+	$1.00/ carton	$0.75/ carton
Whipping cream, 1/2 pint	$1.00/ carton	$0.75/ carton
Yogurt/ Dairy		
Butter	$2.00/lb	$1.50/ lb
Cheese, block or shredded	$2.00/ lb	$1.50/ lb
Cheese, cream 8oz	$0.75/ block	$0.50/ block
Cheese, string	$0.20 each	$0.10 each
Cottage cheese, 16oz	$1.25 each	$1.00 each
Milk, gallon	$2.00/ carton	$1.75/ carton
Sour cream, 16oz	$1.00 each	$0.85 each
Yogurt, regular	$0.30 each	$0.20 each
Yogurt, Greek	$0.45 each	$0.30 each
Freezer		
Fries/ hash browns	$0.90/ bag	$0.75/ bag
Frozen dinners	$0.80 each	$0.60 each
Ice cream, 1.5 qt	$1.99/ carton	$1.50/ carton
Juice concentrate, 12oz	$0.95/ can	$0.75/ can
Pie, whole	$2.50 each	$1.99 each
Pizza	$2.50 each	$2.00 each
Pocket sandwiches, 2ct	$1.35/ box	$1.10/ box
Vegetables, bagged 10oz+	$0.65/ bag	$0.45/ bag
Candy/ Sweets		
Bagged candy, 10oz+	$0.65/ bag	$0.45/ bag
Candy bars	$0.20 each	$0.10 each
Gum, 12+ pk	$0.25/ pack	$0.15/ pack
Mints	$0.35/ pack	$0.25/ pack

Product	3 month price	6 month price
Granola Bars/ Fruit Snacks		
Energy bars	$0.50 each	$0.25 each
Fruit Snacks	$0.50/ box	$0.35/ box
Granola bars, 6pk+	$0.65/ box	$0.50/ box
Peanut Butter & Jelly		
Jelly, grape 18oz+	$1.00/ jar	$0.75/ jar
Peanut butter, 16oz	$0.75/ jar	$0.45/ jar
Preserves, 18oz+	$1.25/ jar	$1.00/ jar
Fruit		
Applesauce, 48oz	$1.25/ can	$1.00/ can
Cranberries, sweetened & dried	$1.00/ 6oz	$0.75/ 6oz
Cranberry sauce	$0.45/ can	$0.25/ can
Mandarin oranges, 11oz	$0.40/ can	$0.25/ can
Peaches/ Pears, 29oz	$1.00/ can	$0.75/ can
Pineapple, canned	$0.75/ can	$0.50/ can
Raisins, 12oz+	$1.25/ bag	$1.00/ bag
Vegetables		
Beans, canned 15oz	$0.45/ can	$0.30/ can
Corn/ Green beans, 15oz+	$0.35/ can	$0.25/ can
Pumpkin, 16 oz	$0.65/ can	$0.45/ can
Salsa, 16oz	$0.65/ jar	$0.45/ jar
Tomatoes, diced 16oz	$0.45/ can	$0.35/ can
Tuna	$0.35/ can	$0.25/ can
Pasta		
Lasagna noodles, 16oz	$1.00/ box	$0.75/ box
Pasta (rotini, elbow, penne)	$0.15/ box	Free
Spaghetti/ Alfredo sauce	$0.50/ jar	$0.25/ jar
Soup		
Broth, 32oz	$0.65/ carton	$0.45/ carton
Condensed, "cream of" soups	$0.35/ can	$0.20/ can
Soup, ready 16oz+	$0.50/ can	$0.35/ can

Product	3 month price	6 month price
Baby		
Baby food, jar	$0.35/ jar	$0.25/ jar
Diapers (name brand)	$0.15/ diaper	$0.10/ diaper
Diaper cream	$0.50/ tube	$0.35/ tube
Wipes, 72ct+	$0.50/ tub	$0.25/ tub
Reynolds Ziploc		
Bags, gallon 25ct	$0.50/ box	$0.35/ box
Bags, quart 25ct	$0.50/ box	$0.35/ box
Bags, sandwich 100ct	$0.99/ box	$0.75/ box
Foil, 75ft+	$1.10/ box	$0.90/ box
Plastic containers, 2 ct	$0.95/ pkg	$0.75/ pkg
Plastic wrap, 100 yds+	$0.95/ box	$0.75/ box
Wax/ parchment paper	$0.95/ box	$0.75/ box
Paper Products		
Facial tissue, 100ct+	$0.45/ box	$0.30/ box
Napkins	$0.75/ pkg	$0.50/ pkg
Paper plates	$0.75/ pkg	$0.50/ pkg
Paper towels	$0.40/ roll	$0.30/ roll
Toilet paper, double ply	$0.20/ roll	$0.13/ roll
Utensils, disposable	$0.75/ pkg	$0.50/ pkg
Surface Cleaners		
All purpose spray	$0.45/ bottle	$0.30/ bottle
Bathroom spray	$0.50/ bottle	$0.35/ bottle
Disinfecting wipes	$0.50/ canister	$0.35/ canister
Glass spray	$0.50/ bottle	$0.35/ bottle
Toilet cleaner	$0.45/ bottle	$0.35/ bottle
Laundry		
Bleach	$0.75/ bottle	$0.50/ bottle
Detergent, 32+ load	$0.99/ bottle	$0.75/ bottle
Fabric softener	$0.99/ bottle	$0.75/ bottle
Dish Washing		
Dishwasher tabs	$0.75/ box	$0.50/ box

Product	3 month price	6 month price
Soup mix, dry (e.g. Onion Soup mix)	$0.33/ envelope	$0.20/ envelope
Baking		
Brownie/ Cake mix	$0.25 each	$0.13 each
Chocolate Chips, 16oz	$0.65/ bag	$0.45/ bag
Coconut milk	$0.99/ can	$0.85/ can
Cooking non-stick spray	$0.65/ can	$0.45/ can
Evaporated milk	$0.50/ can	$0.25/ can
Flour, 5 lb	$1.25 each	$0.99 each
Frosting, ready made	$0.50/ can	$0.35/ can
Gelatin	$0.15/ box	$0.08/ box
Marshmallows	$0.65/ bag	$0.45/ bag
Nuts, baking (e.g. Walnuts)	$2.99/ lb	$2.50/ lb
Oil, Canola, 48oz	$1.00/ bottle	$0.75/ bottle
Oil, Olive, 16oz+	$2.99/ bottle	$2.50/ bottle
Pudding, instant	$0.20/ box	$0.15/ box
Sugar, brown or powdered, 2lb	$1.00/ bag	$0.85/ bag
Sugar, white 5lb	$1.15/ bag	$1.00/ bag
Sweetened, condensed milk	$0.75/ can	$0.50/ can
Vinegar, white, 32oz	$0.50/ bottle	$0.35/ bottle
Yeast, 3 strip	$0.45/ pkg	$0.25/ pkg
Breakfast		
Cereal	$0.75/ box	$0.25/ box
Oats, 42 oz	$0.75 each	$0.25 each
Pancake/ waffle mix, 25oz+	$1.00/ box	$0.75/ box
Toaster pastries, 6 ct	$0.75/ box	$0.50/ box
Syrup, 24oz	$0.95/ bottle	$0.75/ bottle
Prepared Sides & Rice		
Macaroni and cheese	$0.45/ box	$0.30/ box
Pasta, seasoned dry mix	$0.50/ box	$0.35/ box
Potatoes, boxed	$0.45/ box	$0.25/ box
Rice, seasoned dry mix	$0.50/ box	$0.35/ box
Rice, white	$0.60/lb	$0.40/ lb
Stuffing mix	$0.45/ box	$0.30/ box

Product	3 month price	6 month price
Liquid soap, 20oz	$0.65/ bottle	$0.45/ bottle
Miscellaneous (batteries, school supplies)		
Batteries, AA or AAA	$0.25 per battery	$0.10 per battery
Light bulbs, CFL	$0.50/ bulb	$0.25/ bulb
Light bulbs, regular	$0.25/ bulb	Free
Paper, printing	$1.00/ ream	Free, after rebate
Tape, clear	$0.20/ roll	Free
Air Fresheners/ Candles		
Air freshener spray	$0.45/ can	$0.30/ can
Candle, small	$0.50 each	$0.25 each
Reed diffusers	$1.00 each	$0.75 each
Cold/ Allergy Medicine		
Allergy medicine, adult	$3.50/ box	$2.50/ box
Allergy medicine, children's liquid	$0.95/ bottle	$0.50/ bottle
Cold medicine, liquid, tablets	$0.75/ box	$0.50/ box
Pain relievers, 24ct	$0.75/ bottle	$0.50/ bottle
First Aid		
Bandages	$0.50/ box	$0.35/ box
First Aid travel kit	$0.40 each	$0.25 each
Ointment	$0.75/ tube	$0.50/ tube
Beauty		
Eye shadow	$0.40 each	$0.25 each
Foundation, liquid	$3.50/ bottle	$2.75/ bottle
Lip balm	$0.25 each	Free
Mascara	$0.75/ tube	$0.50/ tube
Nail files	$0.25 each	Free
Nail polish	$0.20 each	$0.05 each
Oral Care		
Floss	$0.25 each	Free
Mouthwash	$0.50/ bottle	$0.35/ bottle

Product	3 month price	6 month price
Condiments/ Salad Dressing		
BBQ Sauce	$0.15/ bottle	Free
Ketchup, 24oz	$0.50/ bottle	$0.25/ bottle
Mayonnaise, 32oz	$0.99/ bottle	$0.75/ bottle
Mustard	$0.35/ bottle	$0.10/ bottle
Salad dressing, 16oz	$0.50/ bottle	$0.25/ bottle
Soy Sauce, 5oz	$0.45/ bottle	$0.25/ bottle
Drinks		
Hot cocoa mix, 8 pouches	$0.45/ box	$0.25/ box
Juice, 100% pure, 64oz	$1.00 each	$0.75 each
Juice, cocktail 64oz	$0.85 each	$0.65 each
Soda, 2 liter (name brand)	$0.75/ bottle	$0.45/ bottle
Sport drink mix	$0.65/ bottle	$0.45/ bottle
Sport drinks, 32oz	$0.45/ bottle	$0.25/ bottle
Tea, bagged	$0.75/ box	$0.45/ box
Water, 16oz	$0.35/ bottle	$0.20/ bottle
Meat/ Poultry		
Bacon	$2.00/ lb	$1.50/ lb
Beef, ground 85%	$1.89/ lb	$1.69/ lb
Beef, ground 90%+	$2.20/ lb	$1.99/ lb
Chicken breasts, bone-in	$0.99/lb	$0.79/lb
Chicken breasts, boneless skinless	$1.99/lb	$1.69/ lb
Chicken thighs & drumsticks	$0.99/ lb	$0.79/ lb
Chicken, whole fryer	$0.89/lb	$0.69/ lb
Hot dogs	$0.75/ pkg	$0.45/ pkg
Pork chops, boneless	$1.75/ lb	$1.49/ lb
Pork loin, boneless	$1.75/ lb	$1.49/ lb
Pork roast	$1.75/ lb	$1.49/ lb
Roast, chuck	$2.25/ lb	$1.99/lb
Sausage	$1.89/ lb	$1.50/ lb
Steak, top sirloin	$4.50/ lb	$3.99/lb
Salmon, filleted	$4.00/lb	$3.50/ lb

Product	3 month price	6 month price
Toothpaste	$0.25 each	Free
Toothbrush	$0.25 each	Free
Whitening strips	$5.00/ box	$3.50/ box
Soap & Body Wash		
Face wash	$1.75 each	$0.99 each
Men's body wash	$0.50 each	$0.25 each
Soap, bar	$0.45/ 2pk	Free
Women's body wash	$0.75/ bottle	$0.50/ bottle
Hair Care		
Shampoo	$0.50/ bottle	$0.25/ bottle
Conditioner	$0.50/ bottle	$0.25/ bottle
Hair spray	$0.65/ bottle	$0.50/ bottle
Hair color	$1.50/ box	$0.99/ box
Mousse, stylers	$0.75 each	$0.50 each
Ponytail elastics	$0.75/ 12 ct+	$0.25/ 12 ct.+
Lotion		
Body lotion, 8oz+	$0.50/ bottle	$0.35/ bottle
Shaving & Deodorant		
Deodorant, men's	$0.45 each	$0.25 each
Deodorant, women's	$0.65 each	$0.45 each
Razor, men's	$0.85 each	$0.50 each
Razor, women's	$0.95 each	$0.70 each
Shaving cream	$0.45/ can	$0.25/ can
Feminine Hygiene		
Lubricant	$0.75/ bottle	$0.50/ bottle
Pads	$0.25/ pkg	Free
Pregnancy tests, 2 ct	$5.00/ box	$3.50/ box
Tampons	$0.95/ box	$0.75/ box

DAIRY, MEAT & PRODUCE

Even though a price list is super-important, when it comes to knowing when to buy, finding deals on perishable foods (whose prices don't fluctuate as greatly as shelf-stable food) can present a unique challenge. One of the most frequent questions I hear is, "How do I save on dairy, meat, and produce?" It's not often that you see huge promotional events or stacks of coupons for these products. But with a few tips from The Krazy Coupon Lady, you can be sure that you're never overspending when it comes to these necessities.

DAIRY:

Believe it or not, dairy coupons do exist. You can usually find coupons for yogurt, butter and cheese. On a good day, you might even find some for milk and eggs, as well. Keep a lookout for Catalina promos that offer a free gallon of milk with the purchase of cereals or cookies. And look for peelie coupons on shredded and sliced cheeses as well as milk coupons on boxes of cereal.

When dairy products near an expiration date, retailers often mark them down by up to 50%. Look for discount stickers on the individual products. Markdowns usually occur in the evening or early hours at grocery stores, so you have a greater chance of finding them if you shop early in the morning or late at night. Maybe the milkman is a vampire; I don't know. Ask your local store when dairy markdowns happen, and plan to be there.

Don't be afraid to shop around for the lowest price on dairy products. In addition to grocery stores, remember to check your local convenience and drugstores where staples like milk and eggs may be slightly cheaper.

Never underestimate how much dairy you can stockpile! When you find a krazy price on milk, cheese, butter, or yogurt, consider buying multiples and freezing the extras. Yogurt cups and sealed packages of butter and cheese can go straight into the freezer. For milk, you'll want to take out a few inches before freezing to leave room for expansion.

Most importantly, don't sweat it! Take a hint from the milk and "chill". While you should certainly do your best to use coupons and find the lowest price on dairy products, don't expect to save 90% on milk and cheese! Paying full price for a pound of butter or a gallon of milk is no reason to give up lactose all together. Buy a pint of ice cream to reset your priorities!

MEAT:

Don't be afraid of the butcher block at your local grocery store. And don't be afraid to buy meat that's on sale. Talk to your butcher and ask whether he's got any specials on meat. Invariably, he'll have something that is approaching the sell-by date and its price is greatly reduced. Just make sure you either cook it or throw it in the freezer when you get home. We've all seen those big orange "$1 off" or "$2 off" stickers on meat at the grocery store. My secret? Find the smallest package with the largest value off sticker. This week I saw lots of orange stickers on the meat so I went over to peruse. My best find was a small package of breakfast steaks. The largest breakfast steak package was priced at $4.79 and the smallest at $1.92, and they all had the same $1.00 off sticker. Buy the smaller package to get the better deal. I bought the small package with three small steaks for $0.92! So with prepackaged meat, watch for those orange discount stickers. The best price per ounce will come from the smaller sized package.

Another great tip is to buy meat in bulk. Find the best price per pound, and buy a family size portion. Then take the meat home, divide it into portions for your family, and freeze some of it for future use. Staying away from the "extra, extra-diet-lean" ground beef is also a helpful way to save. After you cook it up, make sure to drain the fat, and then rinse your ground meat with hot water (use a colander if the holes aren't too big) and all that extra fat goes right down the drain. If you want to get even more value out of your ground meats, consider adding beans to your cooked ground beef or turkey to stretch it farther. I like to add black beans, kidneys, or pintos to my Mexican dishes in order to stretch the meat. I think it's really yummy, and it allows us to make a dish, like taco salad, with half the ground beef I would normally use.

Produce:

Produce is another one of those tricky necessities that we have to have. Plus, it's my kids' favorite treat! So how do you save here? The first rule of thumb is to always buy fruits and vegetables when they are in season. Stay away from buying 10 pounds of strawberries in January. Make your apricot jam in early summer. Get your corn on the cob in August. And don't even think about buying Clementines unless your house is decked for the holidays! Sure, some produce, like fresh broccoli is grown year-round, and the price may not fluctuate with the seasons; the important thing is to pay attention to produce prices, and don't pay a premium price for out-of-season produce. When you do find a krazy price, consider buying extra! Can it or freeze it for later use. This is a great way to implement the smart sense of stockpiling! My favorites for canning are peaches, pears and homemade salsa. I love to freeze blueberries, strawberries, grapes and bell peppers. Not into canning? Here's another tip.

Believe it or not, by weighing your produce before purchasing it you can save 10%. Those funny looking scales are there for a reason, so use them! Even for those of you who, like me, have severe "scale-o-phobia", weighing produce is an anxiety free, savvy shopping practice! Start with weighing individually priced produce like lettuce, avocados, berries, grapefruit, kiwis, lemons, peppers, and pineapple, which are priced per item instead of per pound. It's also smart to weigh bagged produce. When you're purchasing a 3 lb bag of carrots, the processor, who originally placed the carrots in the bag, is supposed to fill the bag with at least 3 lbs of carrots. The weight of the bag should be the minimum 3 lbs, though you'll find, once you visit the scale, that's not always the case. Each bag of carrots has a slightly different weight. On my last trip to the store, I found a bag that rang in at about 3.3 pounds, so I got 10% more product for free just for taking, literally, 60 seconds at the scale.

Surprisingly enough, you can even find coupons for produce. Recently, I've seen in-store coupons for bagged salads, cherry tomatoes, avocados and Driscoll's berries. Peelies and tear pads sometimes feature "Buy this item, save on produce" (usually, Save $1.00 on fresh fruit when you buy cereal boxes, Save $0.20 on lettuce when you buy salad dressing, or save $0.50 on bananas when you buy Nilla Wafers).

With these few tips on dairy, meat, and produce you'll know exactly when to buy and when to walk away! Saving money, even on the necessities, is realistic. So don't fret. You can still have your bowl of fruit in the morning, a nice steak for dinner, and a tall glass of milk with your cookies without having to worry about anything but calories!

● ● ● ● ● ● ● ● ● ● ● ● ● ● ● ● ● ●

HOW TO BE A SALES PSYCHIC

Wouldn't it be nice if you could accurately predict what is most likely to be on sale in the next coming months? There's no way, right? You'd have to be some kind of crazy psychic carrying a crystal ball and wearing a scarf wrapped around your head. And then still there's no guarantee you'd get it right! WRONG! It's true that sales generally cycle every three months, but on a grander scale, monthly sales tend to follow a trend.

For example, everyone knows that produce is seasonal. But what they don't know is packaged foods are seasonal, as well! Each calendar month brings a new batch of sales. Here are the predictable sale cycles for each calendar month:

JANUARY:

- National Oatmeal Month: Quaker
- Diet Foods, including: Healthy Choice, South Beach, Lean Cuisine, Special K, Kashi, Smart Start, 100 Calorie Packs
- Super Bowl Sunday: Pepsi, Coke, chips, dips, cheese, sandwich items, crackers, snacks, wings
- Clearance: Christmas decorations, toys, wrapping papers,
- Winter Health: cold medicines and vitamins

FEBRUARY:

- National Canned Food Month: canned fruit, vegetables; meats: tuna, chicken, salmon; pie fillings

- National Hot Breakfast Month: Malt O Meal, oatmeal, Eggo Waffles, syrup

- Valentines: chocolate, Hershey's, KY Lubricant, etc.

- Chinese New Year: soy sauce, teriyaki sauce, noodles

- Seasonal Produce: artichoke, asparagus, raspberries, potatoes, strawberries, broccoli, carrots, cauliflower, celery, chard, collards, kale, kiwi, avocado, spinach

MARCH:

- Frozen Food Month: frozen meals, TGI Fridays, Contessa, Foster Farms chicken, Eggo, Sara Lee, Healthy Choice, DiGiorno, Freschetta, Breyers, Dreyers, Marie Callendars

APRIL:

- Easter: ham; eggs; some baking supplies: sugar, spices, baking mixes, chocolate chips

- Earth Day: organic foods, energy saver

- Clearance: after Easter sales are the time to stock up on decorating, baskets, etc for the next year

MAY:

- Memorial Day: BBQ sauce, ketchup, condiments, charcoal, salad dressing, potato chips, dips

- Paper Products: plates, utensils

- Outdoor: insect repellant, sunscreen

- Cinco de Mayo: salsa, tortillas

JUNE:

- National Dairy Month: eggs, milk (free milk Catalina, wyb cereal), ice cream, cheese, butter, yogurt, Cool Whip, in-store dairy coupons or booklets

- End of June is Fourth of July Sales: hot dogs, hamburgers, BBQ sauce, ketchup, condiments, charcoal, salad dressing, potato chips, dips

July:

- National Ice Cream Month

- More 4th of July BBQ Sales: hot dogs, hamburgers, BBQ sauce, ketchup, condiments, charcoal, salad dressing, potato chips, dips

- End of July, Back to School Sales begin: crayons, pencils, folders, binders

August:

- Back to School: pudding cups, lunch meat,

- Staples and Office Depot Penny Items

- Disinfectant: Clorox, Purell

- Clearance: insect repellant, sunscreen, charcoal

September:

- Back to School Sales through Labor Day: crayons, pencils, folders, binders

- Diabetes: Bayer glucose meters, Glucerna cereal

October:

- Halloween: candy

- Beginning of the baking sales: canned pumpkin, evap milk, baking chips

- National Seafood Month

- Adopt a Shelter-Dog Month: Pedigree, Purina

NOVEMBER:

- Baking Sales in Full Swing: nuts, chocolate chips, evap milk, sweetened condensed milk, coconut, cake mixes

- Canned foods: soup, broth, condensed milk, vegetables, fruits, spaghetti sauce

- Thanksgiving: turkey, canned pumpkin, Stovetop stuffing, Betty Crocker boxed potatoes, gravy mixes, Rhodes rolls, frozen pies, cranberry sauce, Jello, marshmallows

- Clearance: After Halloween sales are the time to stock up on things for the next year. I like to buy the Halloween candy-alternatives like Halloween crayons, erasers, watches, spinning tops, etc. I mix this in with my next year's candy bowl, and it stretches my loot for all the neighbor kids!

DECEMBER:

- Holiday Dinner: eggnog, deli platters, instant potatoes, gravy mixes, Rhodes rolls, frozen pies, cranberry sauce, Jello, marshmallows

- Baking: flour; sugar; butter; cream; cake, brownie, and muffin mixes; breads, pie crusts, marshmallows, whipped cream

- Canned foods: soup, broth, condensed milk, vegetables, fruits, spaghetti sauce

- Clearance: Buy all your Thanksgiving decorations, extra table settings, and turkey carving products once they're at least 50% off.

By combining your price list, my rock-bottom spreadsheet, a few great tips on buying the must-haves, and this newfound knowledge of monthly trends, you're sure to always stock up when the price is right! No more post-purchase blues. You are now ready to rock the grocery store, stock the garage, and make that money work for you.

FAQs:

Do I have to create my own price list? Won't I eventually figure it out?

Of course, you don't *have* to create your own price list. In fact, many Krazy Coupon Ladies I know have never done this. But many people like to start by creating a price list as a point of reference during their first few months of couponing. So if you're organized and want to take a bit of extra time, this will definitely come in handy at the store. Otherwise, as you become more experienced you'll learn those rock bottom prices and won't even have to look twice.

How do I stock up when stores impose limits?

This can be a little tricky. The thing to remember is that sales cycle around every few months. So if you purchase your limit on a product every time a sale comes around, you'll steadily build your stockpile. It just might take a couple of months instead of a single day!

What do I do when every time I see a great deal on TheKrazyCouponLady.com, my store's shelves are empty?

Frustrating, I know! That's why I love rain checks! Simply approach your checker and ask him for a rain check. He'll write the product, quantity, sale price, and an expiration date all on that special piece of paper. As soon as the shelves are restocked, take your rain check in, and they'll honor the sales price or promotion enabling you to get just what you wanted. I talk more about rain checks in Chapter 10.

SECTION THREE

Taking the Reins

WE CAN LET CIRCUMSTANCES RULE US,
OR WE CAN TAKE CHARGE AND
RULE OUR LIVES FROM WITHIN.

CHAPTER TEN

Timing is Everything:
How and When to Use Your Coupons

You've finally made it. You're now at the point in the book where I reveal all my amazing money saving secrets—the tricks to turning coupons into hundreds of dollars. Remember, a Krazy Coupon Lady doesn't just shop for what she needs *now*. She plans ahead and keeps her savvy eyes peeled for what she *will* need. Krazy Coupon Ladies are picky shoppers and *never* buy products at full price. We match coupons with sales and promos, we stock up, and we save big!

At any given time, I have around ten to sixteen weeks of coupons stored in my binder. Deciding *when* and *how* to use all these coupons is what separates the puppies from the big dogs, the pretenders from the contenders, the duds from the divas...the amateur coupon clippers from the Krazy Coupon Ladies. I only use my coupons when the product is on sale, when the store is running a great promotion, when I can double the coupons, when I can stack a manufacturer coupon with a store coupon or all of the above. Ultimately, I will only purchase a product after I have determined whether or not the final price is acceptable to me.

● ● ● ● ● ● ● ● ● ● ● ● ● ● ● ● ● ● ●

SALES

I know it's not rocket science when I say I wait for a product to go on sale before I use a coupon, but it's key to saving big. Stores run sales on a continuous basis, often cycling every few months. Every single week new items are marked down just waiting for you Krazy Couponers to grab them up. By vigilantly watching the ads, you can easily match up your coupons with the items that go on sale. This results in major savings! Here's a great example of how combining a coupon on top of a sale makes for a super-low price:

> **Buy 1 Advil Ibuprofen, 20 ct. on sale for $2.63**
> Use 1 $2.00/1 Advil or Advil PM from SmartSource insert 5/22
> *Final Price: $0.63*

That's getting Advil for 85% off the regular price of $4.30. Remember, you are allowed to use one manufacturer coupon and one store coupon together on one item. So if a product goes on sale and you have both types of coupons, the final price ends up even lower. Here's an example of how this type of stacking works:

> **Buy 1 Old Spice Body Wash on sale for $3.69**
> Use 1 $2.00/1 Old Spice Body Wash from RedPlum insert 5/15
> And use 1 $1.50/1 Old Spice Body Wash store coupon
> *Final price: $0.19*

Patience is key in the couponing game. Wait for a sale, make sure the price is right, stack your coupon on top of it, and there you have it: krazy low prices!

•   •   •   •   •   •   •   •   •   •   •   •   •   •   •   •   •   •

PROMOTIONS

One of the best times to use a coupon is during a store promotion. Most stores run some kind of promo, usually on a weekly basis. You've probably seen an ad that looks something like this: "Spend $20.00 on these products, Receive $5.00 off your next shopping order" or "Buy this product, get this much cash back instantly" or even the classic "Buy 1 Get 1 Free". These are perfect examples of store promotions. Many national stores use register coupons as their biggest promotional tools. Although these work largely in the same way, each store has a different name for its point-of-sale promotions. When you flip through the pages of your local sales circulars, look for these words to indicate the promotions at each of the following stores:

CVS	Extra Bucks
Grocery Stores	Catalinas (or Your Bucks)
Rite Aid	+Up Rewards
Target	Target Gift Cards
Walgreens	Register Rewards

Every week stores create new promotions involving different products. After you buy that product the store will then give you back a register coupon or a gift card that is good for a certain dollar amount off of your next purchase. Keep in mind, you never receive your register coupon until after you've made your purchase. When you stack a coupon on top of these promotions, the final price drops dramatically.

Here's an example of how stores use promotions.

Walgreens:

Schick Hydro 3 Razor $8.99

Buy 1, Receive $4.00 Register Reward

Use 1 $4.00/1 Schick Hydro from SmartSource insert 6/12

Pay $4.99, Receive $4.00 Register Reward

Final Price: $0.99

Although your initial out of pocket expense is $4.99, after getting your Register Reward it's like you're only paying $0.99. Once you get the hang of it, you can separate your transactions and use the register coupon from your first transaction to pay for items in your next transaction. A Krazy Coupon Lady often can earn so many of these register coupons that soon she never pays anything out of pocket. At the checkout counter she merely hands over the register coupons she's previously earned and walks away without even reaching for her wallet.

An example of a promotion at **CVS**:

Spend $15.00 on any CoverGirl Cosmetics, Receive $5.00 Extra Bucks

Buy 1 CoverGirl Natureluxe Mascara $8.00
Buy 1 CoverGirl Natureluxe Gloss Balm $7.00
Use 1 $5.00/2 CoverGirl Natureluxe Product from Procter & Gamble
insert 6/5
And use $3.00 off any $15.00 purchase of cosmetic CVS store coupon
Pay $7.00, Receive $5.00 Extra Bucks
Final Price: $1.00 each when you buy 2

That's nearly 90% in savings! Notice how I used both a manufacturer coupon and a store coupon in this scenario. This makes for an ideal situation where your savings are even more amazing. Promotions are the perfect time to use your coupons. By paying close attention to your stores' sales circular you will notice how these promotions cycle. Every few months or so they repeat, giving you the opportunity to score these great deals over and over again. You'll soon discover that getting items for nearly nothing is simple. Just wait for the right promotion, and believe me, they always come.

• • • • • • • • • • • • • • • • • •

DOUBLE COUPONS

You've probably heard about stores that "double" coupons, meaning that they accept your coupons at twice the amount of the coupon's face value. Doubling coupons is the store's way of offering a discount to its customers, and, usually, the amount that is doubled is sacrificed by the store, not the manufacturer. If you find a doubling promotion, jump on it. Beware…store policies can vary greatly. Some stores double coupons on a certain day every week. Other stores have a periodic double coupon week, advertised in their weekly ad in the Sunday paper. There are even stores that always double coupons up to a certain value (usually up to $0.50). And lastly, some stores issue a finite number of store coupons that are good for doubling the value of any coupon, up to a specified dollar amount.

If a store doubles coupons up to $1.00 in value, this means that you may present any one coupon valued at $1.00 or less, and its value will be doubled. If you use a coupon worth $1.01 off or more, the coupon cannot be doubled. You will receive no extra savings for any coupon worth over $1.00. You with me? During a double coupon period, a $1.00 off coupon is worth the same as a $2.00 off coupon. The $1.00 coupon doubles to $2.00, but a $2.00 coupon will not be doubled.

Doubling can make your head spin, especially when you're doubling a coupon such as $0.55 off two items. If your store doubles this coupon, it means that you'll save $1.10 off two items, or another way to say it would be $0.55 off one item (must buy two).

Doubling promotions are a huge way to save, but they aren't the only way to succeed at couponing. I shop regularly at a store that never doubles and I still save a tremendous amount of money. Don't get discouraged if your local stores don't double. You can still succeed by just working the sales and promotions. All it takes is a little patience and a vigilant watch on the weekly ads. In no time you'll be saving 70% or more on products you used to pay full price for and your budget will surely plummet.

• • • • • • • • • • • • • • • • • • •

GET THINGS FOR FREE

Now comes the exciting news in our little coupon adventure. FREE! Yes, FREE products! Getting things for free or close to free (often under a quarter!) are common occurrences around TheKrazyCouponLady.com. You can bring home free items every single week. And don't worry, it's not shoplifting.

The only thing to note: you will be responsible for sales tax, even when you get the item for free. Uncle Sam is one smart guy. You pay tax on your total before coupons. If your total is $10.00 before coupons and you have $8.00 in coupon savings, you're usually responsible for any applicable tax on the $10.00 subtotal.

Don't despair about sales tax. When I say I've saved over 90% on some of my shopping trips, that total includes the sales tax I had to pay. I could actually say I've saved more than 95%! When you get an item for free, sales tax will be all you'll have to pay.

With that small disclaimer out of the way, are you ready to learn how to get things for free? Again, it's simply about using your coupons at the right time. Often, all you'll be doing is using a coupon in tandem with a sale price and/or a promo. I'll start with some simple examples:

Kraft BBQ Sauce, sale 10/$10 or $1.00 each
Use $1.00/1 Kraft BBQ Coupon
Final Price: Free

Kraft BBQ Sauce, sale 10/$10 or $1.00 each
Use $2.00/2 Kraft BBQ Coupon
Final Price: Free, when you buy 2

NOT free, but pretty close:

Kraft BBQ Sauce, sale 10/$10 or $1.00 each
Use $1.50/2 Kraft BBQ Coupon
Final Price: $0.50, or $0.25 each when you buy 2

Here's an example of how to get something for free by utilizing both a sale price and an in-store promotion:

Example promotion at Walgreens: Spend $30 on John Frieda products, Receive $12 Register Reward checkout coupon

Sale: John Frieda Shampoo on sale this week 3/$10

Here's how to get shampoo for free:

Buy 9 bottles of John Frieda Shampoo: $30.00

Use 9 $2.00/1 Manufacturer coupons (let's say I have nine coupons because I ordered some extras online)

Pay: $12.00, Receive a $12.00 Register Reward Coupon

Final Price: FREE after factoring in the $12 savings off my next shopping order

Did you follow that? The price of John Frieda shampoo started at $3.33 per bottle.

I then presented my $2.00/1 manufacturer coupon, and the price of nine bottles dropped to $1.33 per bottle, or $12 total. I paid $12 and received a $12 coupon off my next shopping order (of any amount). If I had nine more coupons, I could do another identical transaction and use the $12 register coupon I just earned to pay for the next set of nine. My out-of-pocket cost (which we sometimes call "OOP" for Out Of Pocket) would be nothing, and I would still receive another register coupon for $12 off my next shopping order.

Want another example of getting something for free? This one involves doubling coupons.

> **ACT Mouthwash, on sale 2/$8.00**
> Use $2.00/1 Manufacturer Coupon
> Store is doubling all coupons up to $2.00 this week
> *Final Price: FREE*

The price starts at $4.00 per bottle, and when you double your $2.00 off coupon… free mouthwash!

One more scenario:

> **Huggies travel size wipes, regular price $0.97 in the travel size section**
> Use $1.00/1 Manufacturer Coupon (doesn't specify minimum size)
> *Final Price: FREE*

The manufacturer coupon will usually beep because the $1.00 coupon exceeds the value of the $0.97 product. The cashier should just adjust the price of the coupon down to match the item price (and you can kindly remind the cashier of that if he or she doesn't know). All you have to pay is tax on the original price. As long as the coupon doesn't exclude trial size or minimum size, you can often get free items in the travel section. You may even be tempted to bust out those itty-bitty shampoos and mouthwashes for everyday use!

It's as simple as that. All you have to do is wait for a sale or a promotion or BOTH, match up your coupons with that product and VOILÁ...it's FREE! Can't get better than that, right? WRONG!! How about making a little money?

GET PAID TO SHOP

Make money couponing? I know! You're thinking it's a scam. Kind of like trying to make money by stuffing envelopes in your living room for hours on end? Nope. This is legit. Sometimes you can save so much with coupons that the store actually ends up paying YOU. The best places to make money are drugstores or grocery stores that offer register coupons or Catalinas AND rebates. We will share more about specific drugstore policies in Chapter 19, but for starters, here are some drugstore examples from Rite Aid to help you make sense of this phenomenon.

Rite Aid has a user-friendly rebate program where all you have to do is take your receipt home, enter a few numbers from the receipt into Rite Aid's computer system, and they will send you a check at the end of the month. No clipping proofs of purchase, no envelope or postage to pay, just a few clicks and the check will, literally, be in the mail!

Many drugstores offer products advertised as "free after rebate". Often, you can submit a rebate for the entire product value. I found the following deal just last week at the national drugstore chain, Rite Aid.

> **Crest Pro Health Toothpaste $2.79**
> Submit for $2.79 rebate
> *Final Price: FREE after rebate*

Let's take it one more step to make some money. If you combine a coupon with the rebate promotion, they'll actually pay you. Here's an example:

> **Crest Pro Health Toothpaste $2.79**
> Use the $0.75/1 Crest coupon from 8/2 Procter & Gamble insert
> Submit for $2.79 rebate
> *Final Price: FREE, Plus $0.75 profit after coupon and rebate*

Now, let's take one final step. Let's say there's an additional printable coupon worth $5 off your in-store purchase of $25 or more. This coupon may be used in addition to your manufacturer coupons and rebates. The following example has you purchase six different items to reach a minimum $25 subtotal. This way, you may use the $5.00 off $25.00 coupon to make even more money. Follow along closely:

> Buy 1 Crest Pro Health Toothpaste $2.79 (Submit for $2.79 rebate)
> Buy 1 ReNu MultiPlus Solution $9.99 (Submit for $9.99 rebate)
> Buy 1 Gillette Venus Razor $7.00 (Submit for $5.00 rebate)
> Buy 1 Duck Brand EZ Start Tape 22.2 yards $1.49 (Submit for $1.49 rebate)
> Buy 1 Werther's Original Caramel Chocolate, 5.2oz $2.99 (Submit for $2.99 rebate)
> Buy 1 Soft White Longlife Light Bulbs 60, 75
>   or 100 watt 2 pack - $2.00 (Submit for $2.00 rebate)
> Use 1 $.75/1 Crest coupon from Procter & Gamble insert 8/2
> And Use 1 $2.00/1 – ReNu – (bausch.com)
> And Use 1 $2.00/1 Gillette Venus from Procter & Gamble insert 8/2
> And Use 1 $0.55/1 Werthers from SmartSource insert 4/26
> Subtotal: $26.26
> Use the $5 off $25 any store purchase printable coupon
> Pay $15.96 out of pocket, plus tax
> Receive one rebate in the amount of: $26.26
> *Final Price: Moneymaker of $10.30*

See what I mean? In this deal, I still had to pay the cashier ($15.96 + tax), but at the end of the month, I'll receive a check for $26.26. That's what I call a "moneymaker".

Let's review: If you can find an item advertised "free after rebate" and you have a manufacturer coupon for $2.00 off, it becomes a $2.00 moneymaker. Drugstores often have great coupons like "$4 off a $20 purchase" or "$5 off a $25 purchase." These coupons allow you to make even more money. Rebates may allow you to make money occasionally at grocery stores, but drugstores are the primary place to consistently find these moneymakers.

Oftentimes, a moneymaker comes your way without even having to mess with a rebate. Walgreens, CVS, and Rite Aid all have a Reward Program in which you make a qualifying purchase and receive a coupon to use on your next transaction. You receive this coupon without having to submit receipts or wait for a check! As soon as you pay, the coupon prints either on your receipt or as a Catalina coupon. I recently found this scenario at CVS:

St. Joseph Aspirin $2.00
Buy 1, Receive $2.00 Extra Bucks
Use 1 $1.00/1 St. Joseph Aspirin from SmartSource insert 8/7
Pay $1.00, Receive $2.00 Extra Bucks
Final Price: $1.00 Moneymaker

These simple scenarios happen all the time. I know at first it's hard to wrap your head around. But as you begin to learn the ropes in the coupon world, you'll be astounded at how often you get paid to shop. It's an addicting feeling to leave the store with a bunch of products and an extra jingle in your pocket from all that money you just earned. All it takes is a coupon in the right place at the right time.

The only problem with freebies and moneymakers is that these deals don't stick around for long. Even if a deal lasts all week, the products may sell out quickly if the store hasn't overstocked the items. So what's a Krazy Coupon Lady to do when she finds an empty shelf?

•   •   •   •   •   •   •   •   •   •   •   •   •   •   •   •   •   •   •

RAIN CHECKS

For Krazy Coupon Ladies, rain checks can be like pure gold. Picture this: a flustered Krazy Coupon Lady waits until the last day of the sale to stock up on her much needed Electrasol Dishwasher Tabs. She was out of town all week at her husband's family reunion. While camping with the in-laws in the boonies, she spent the entire time thinking about all the sales she was missing. Fun, right? When she gets home, before she showers or starts a load of laundry, she races to the store to stock up on her dishwasher tabs. She walks straight to the aisle with cleaners and detergent and sees a shelf full of...(begin the ominous music)...empty space. You guessed it. Our dear Krazy Coupon Lady waited too long and is now faced with two choices: start fuming at all the other couponers who "cleared the shelf", or take matters into her own hands by asking for a rain check.

What is a rain check? When a sale item is out of stock, a rain check is a slip of paper that entitles you to come back later and buy that item at the sale price after it is restocked, even once the sale period is over. Ask your store's customer service desk whether or not they write rain checks. Rain check policies vary by store, so make sure you check each store's rules carefully. Some stores have an expiration date on the rain check, while others don't. You will also find that some stores will have a maximum number of items for which they will give you a rain check. Typically, if the sale price involved a limit of, say, four per customer, the rain check will be limited to four, as well.

Rain check tips:

- If you plan to use coupons with your rain check price, make sure that the coupons won't expire before the store gets the items back in stock. No use going through the trouble of getting a rain check just to have expired coupons defeat the purpose.

- Don't bother getting a rain check for something that is also included in a promotion (such as, "Spend $10, save $4 instantly"). Rain checks are only valid for the sale price. The store cannot honor a promo once it's over, even with a rain check.

- You cannot get a rain check on clearance prices.

- When redeeming your rain check, be courteous. Let the checker know that you'll be using one before he or she starts to ring you up. Often, checkers manually need to enter the amount, so they'll love you if they don't have to go back at the end of the transaction to void and re-enter the correct amount.

Remember, if you find a product out of stock, take the opportunity to ask for a rain check. If you want to stockpile the item, ask the person writing the rain check to write it up for the maximum quantity allowed. Then hurry your sweet little self over to the

Internet and buy all the coupons you need, and head back to the store when the item is restocked. Easy as free rain check pie.

FIVE TIPS FOR SHOPPING LIKE A KRAZY COUPON LADY

1. KISS GENERICS GOODBYE

Here's a common concern:

"I've tried using coupons, but after I go to all the trouble of clipping, I find that the store generic brand is still cheaper than the name brand with a coupon!"

Not if you time it right! I used to have the same worry. I'd clip my coupons, take them to the store, hunt down the right product and size, do some math in my head and decide it was still cheaper to buy the generic. So I'd grab the generic and toss the coupon... forgive me! Never again! Now I know the secret!

Here it is. If you visit your local supermarket to use a "$1 off two cans of cream of chicken soup" coupon, it will end up being cheaper just to buy generic.

Campbell's Cream Soup $1.18
Use $1.00/2 coupon
Final Price: $0.68 each, when you buy 2
Generic Cream Soup: $0.55 each

Tossing the coupon and buying generic is just what a casual coupon clipper would do. But not you! You're on your way to getting krazy, and Krazy Coupon Ladies know better. If you wait and use the coupon when the name brand soups are at a rock-bottom price, OR if you match the coupons with a promotion, like I've talked about, *Voilá*! Cheap Soup!

For example, this week Campbell's soup is on sale for $0.68 cents. Let's do that math!

Campbell's Cream Soup $0.68
Use $1.00/2 coupon
Final Price: $0.18 each, when you buy 2

Now that's a stock up price! You're saving over 80% on an average retail price and 67% off even the generic price! When someone asks me whether it's cheaper to buy generics than name brand items with coupons, I ask them whether they pay over fifty cents for a box of cereal or twenty cents for a can of soup. That usually answers their question and is the end of their skepticism.

Coupons can only do so much, and by themselves, those little pieces of paper won't change your life. Only you have the power to use your head, get krazy, and unleash the savings potential!

2. SHIRK BRAND LOYALTY

Keep an open mind. Don't be afraid to try a new product or a different brand.

One reader, Carolyn, shared this story:

[Couponing] has helped me learn to branch out! When I grocery shopped before becoming a Krazy Coupon Lady, I was so stuck in a rut, without even realizing it! I would make my list every two weeks, and it was always the same. Same brands, same size, same meals! Now, I find products that are free and I am given the chance to try them with very little cost out of my pocket.

I love all the new name brand items I've become accustomed to since using coupons. I don't know how I ever ate generic cereal or baked with generic chocolate chips. I grew up on generics, but now that I've crossed over into greener pastures, it would be hard, nay, impossible ever to go back. How much does generic cereal cost at your grocery store? I bet it's not under $1.00, and that's all I pay for my name brand cereal.

My first baby wore generic diapers. I worried that when he got a rash on his little thighs it was because his mother wasn't spending more money on high quality diapers. I think I paid $0.14 per diaper for size 5 generics, and now I pay less than half of that on name brand. But even after you make the switch from generic to name brand through coupons, you'll get to experiment between brands.

Take this example: you need laundry detergent. You've been a loyal Tide user all your life but the All brand detergent just went on sale for $1.00. What do you do? You may want to consider cheating on your previous brand loyalty. Let's take a look:

Tide detergent $7.99 per bottle
No sale price
Use your $0.25/1 coupon
Final Price: $7.74

All Small & Mighty Laundry detergent on SALE for $1.99
Use your $1.00/1 All Detergent coupon
Final Price: $0.99 each

Now is the time to examine your brand loyalty. The decision shouldn't be too hard. But if it is, I'll tell you what to do! Shirk brand loyalty! Go with the best deal!

Although brand loyalty can cripple a budget, there's always room for an exception.

Everyone is allowed one product to which they remain brand loyal. True story: a certain Krazy Coupon husband, Bryan, says he can only tolerate super soft, triple-ply Charmin toilet paper. His Krazy Coupon wife brings home cases of cheap, name-brand toilet paper that she gets for free...the only problem? It's not Charmin. Their family's solution?

Bryan has his own roll of toilet paper in the cupboard and the rest of the family uses the free stuff. This compromise has saved them $5 to $10 per month! Bryan and his wife do their best to buy his brand of toilet paper by stacking a coupon with a sale. And, if the toilet paper and coupon constellations ever align, and the high-end Charmin falls to a rock bottom price, you'd better believe they will be buying every roll they can find.

If you have a brand-loyal family member who, like Bryan, just can't budge, it's okay to have brand loyalty for one product. Just make sure it's not more than one. I was never a very brand loyal person to begin with, so this was never a hard adjustment to make. In fact, it's been just the opposite. Because of coupons I've been able to purchase more name brands than ever before! I can't tell you the number of great new products I have brought home since couponing. Products that I never would have looked at twice are now staples in my home. You just might like spicing up your pantry a little!

Another bonus to couponing is that coupons allow you to get the newest products at the store. When a product is about to be launched for the very first time, a manufacturer will often release a coupon right along with it. This is great for the manufacturer because it helps motivate buyers to try out that new product. But it's even better news for a Krazy Coupon Lady; I get to try all sorts of brand new items all because of my beloved coupons. So the next time your child sees a commercial and shouts, "Mom! I want those robot-shaped crackers!" or some other newfangled treat on TV, you will very likely say, "Sure! We have coupons for those!" Couponing allows you to try many different new products, so make sure you keep an open mind when finding the best deals. Search by price, not by brand. And above all, stay loyal to your coupons, not your brands! *Keep to the coupons!*

3. WAIT FOR IT!

Don't look desperate!

One Krazy Coupon Lady's mother-in-law eagerly reported that, upon learning her local store doubled all coupons up to $0.50 in value, she spent every single $0.50 coupon she had and "saved a lot." I wanted to yell, "Come on! Don't spend a coupon just because you've got it." That's one of the biggest coupon mistakes you can make. Don't spend it because it's about to expire or because it took you ten minutes to successfully find the coordinating product in the store. A Krazy Coupon Lady isn't afraid to play the waiting game. Save your coupons for when they'll maximize your savings.

If you end up using your coupons just for the sake of redeeming them, the manufacturer will be the only one happy. A week or two later, you'll regret your purchases when you realize you could have found better deals elsewhere. Watch the prices at your grocery store, in the weekly ads, and on various couponing websites, including **TheKrazyCouponLady.com**, of course! Only use your coupons when you are comfortable with the final price. Couponing is all about timing. Just like finding the right time to talk to your husband about his "honey-do" list, or the right time to buy and sell on the stock market, your timing can make or break your couponing success. Be patient. No one wears desperation well. Stay sharp, and wait for the right time to buy, then stock up!

Don't use a coupon just because you have it. For example:

Cascade Dishwasher Detergent tabs, 32 ct. $6.49
Use your $0.50/1 coupon
Your store automatically doubles coupons $0.50 and under
Final Price: $5.49 ($0.17 per tab)

Now is NOT the time to buy! Wait for the Cascade to go on sale, or wait for a better coupon. Next week, the smaller 16 count dishwasher tabs may be on sale for $2.49. That's more like it!

Cascade Dishwasher Detergent tabs, 16 ct. $2.49
Use your $0.50/1 coupon
Your store automatically doubles coupons $0.50 and under
Final Price: $1.49 ($0.10-$0.11 per tab)

4. Play Hard to Get

Don't buy a jar of peanut butter just because the store advertises that it's on sale.

Krazy Coupon Ladies know these tricks, and we don't succumb. Jumping on a not-so-hot sale or using a coupon just for the sake of using it is exactly what the manufacturer wants you to do, and it will prevent you from saving some krazy cash. Wait for the stars to align. When a manufacturer coupon matches an item on sale, plus you have a store coupon and a promo going on at the same time, I like to call it the perfect storm. Well, except that instead of George Clooney sinking his boat, you'll float home happy, basking in savings.

The Perfect Storm
Sale Price + Promo + Coupon

The following is a real life scenario:

Buy 2 Gillette Venus Razors on SALE $6.99
Promo: Buy 2, Receive $5 off your next order
Use 2 of these coupons: $4.00/1 Venus Razor
Pay: $5.98 out of pocket, receive $5.00 off your next order
Final Price: $0.98 or $0.49 each when you buy 2 (after factoring your $5 savings on your next order)

Remember, holding out for a great sale and waiting for the perfect storm only applies to building your stockpile. If you're a new coupon virgin, out of peanut butter, and itching for a sammich, find a decent price and go ahead and buy it. When you're shopping for the future, my general rule is to wait until you find a product 75% off after all coupons and discounts. That's the magic number and that's the time to stockpile!

5. WEED OUT THE GIMMICKS

Remember, grocery prices like to play games.

They'll swing up and down by $0.50. Sometimes the store will even turn the tag green as if to signify a screaming deal, when you know it's the same price as the week before. Just ignore these games and pay them no mind. Stay in the zone and you'll be just fine. Grocers and manufacturers are salespeople. Sure, they're not selling you rusty cars, but they're trying to push products by enticing you with big colorful ads that are largely worthless gimmicks. Don't fall prey to their tantalizing, overpriced gourmet foods and their sleek shopping aisles. Don't be fooled by their finely dressed end caps or the sweet snacks at the register.

Bogus Gimmick

Buy 5 Kraft Mac & Cheese, save $1.00!
Kraft Mac & Cheese: $1.29 each
Final Price: $5.45, or $1.09 each

Don't fall victim to gimmicks that aren't any good or a green price tag with a not-so-red-hot price. Remember your bottom line and let the prices and pressures dance around you.

There you have it! All the tricks to shopping like a Krazy Coupon Lady. Cheap, free, moneymaking phenomena! Now you know exactly when and how to use those beloved coupons. Never forget: in order to maximize savings, patience is KEY! Wait for the right time, whether it's an amazing sale price, an incredible promotion, or a stacking scenario. You CHOOSE! Hopefully, the stars align often and you get the opportunity to relive the perfect storm time and time again. You'll be amazed at all the items you can get for free and how exciting it feels to come home with more money in your pocket than you left with. That's the way to shop like a Krazy Coupon Lady. We're not only eagerly grabbing up deals; we know how to play the waiting game better than the best! By doing so we save the big bucks!

FAQs:

If my store doubles coupons up to $2 and I use a $2.50 off coupon will the store take an additional $2 off for a total of $4.50?

No! When the store states it will double coupons up to $2.00 in value, any coupons $2.01 or higher will receive no special treatment of any kind.

Are online rebates worth the time?

Absolutely! Most rebates take less than three minutes. The first thing I do when I walk in the door from shopping with rebate items is head straight to the computer with my receipt, enter in a few short numbers and the rebate is calculated for me. I receive my rebate in the mail once a month. Basically I get a paycheck in the mail for shopping.

Do I have to submit UPC barcode with all my rebates?

No. Most rebates only require you to enter a few key facts from your receipt. Nor bar code clipping, no stamps, no hassle. Although there are a few old-school rebates that require you to clip a UPC and mail it in, we general say it's still worth the time for rebates of at least $2-5.00.

Do you ever really get paid to shop?

Some grocery stores will pay overage, meaning if you have a $1 coupon to use on a $0.80 item, they will physically pay you $0.20 to buy the product. But most stores' policies adjust the price of the coupon down to match that of the item, meaning they won't pay you money. Most Krazy Coupon Ladies will tell you that it still feels like you're getting paid when you walk out of the store with register coupons or rebates worth more than the cash you brought in.

If chocolate chips are on sale for $0.98 per bag and the store is out of stock may I get a rain check for 20 bags and go ahead and pay now? My coupons expire tomorrow so I can't wait for the re-stock but I can pay now and then pick up the chocolate chips when they arrive, right?

Unfortunately, you cannot prepay for items with coupons. It technically constitutes…horrified gasp…coupon fraud. You may get a rain check for as many items as the store allows, but you may not buy the items with a coupon until they are physically in your cart.

Can I really save more than 50-75% without double coupons in my area? I'm never going to be a Krazy Coupon Lady without doubling!

This is so far from the truth, it actually causes me chest pain. Doubling coupons is just gravy. You can absolutely save 75% without doubling a single coupon. Just by matching coupons with a sale price, and maybe a register promotion, you will be saving more than you ever dreamed!

CHAPTER ELEVEN

Befriending the Bigwigs:

LEARNING THE STORE POLICIES AND TALKING TO STORE MANAGERS

Now that you know how to clip, file, shop, talk the talk, and walk the walk, you're almost there, but you're not done yet! All your confident coupon skills are useless without a solid understanding of store policies. *Pick Another Checkout Lane, Honey* is the only book where you will find actual store policies for real U.S. stores! Each store sets its own coupon policy, and policies vary even within stores of the same chain. Find your stores and view those policies in Chapter 19.

Chances are you'll want to shop at stores besides the ones I have listed for you. For this reason, and because store policies are constantly changing, you need to know how to get a hard copy of your own store's policy. In this chapter, you'll learn how to find a store's policy, but even after you get a copy, you'll want to speak to local store management. Take the policy into your local store manager to verify that the policy is accurate and will be enforced as it is written. Does that sound like a pain? Well, short-term, yes, long-term, no. As frustrating as it sounds, the truth is that many stores have a great policy that is unlearned and unenforced at the local level. Cover your bases by making sure you and your local stores are on the same page.

● ● ● ● ● ● ● ● ● ● ● ● ● ● ● ● ● ● ●

GET A COPY OF THE POLICY

To search on your own for a store's policy, first try the store's official website. Use the search bar and keyword search for "coupon policy". The policies can be difficult to find, so the surest way to get a copy of the policy is to email customer service under the store's "contact info" or "contact us" links. Take twenty minutes or less one afternoon, and do this for all the stores in your area where you wish to use coupons. It will be time well spent. Here's a short sample email you can send to request a copy of the policy and to make sure you're asking all the right questions.

You can find a copy of this draft email at my website. Just copy, paste it, and send it to any stores you wish!

To whom it may concern at _____,

My name is _____.

I'm learning how to become a Krazy Coupon Lady, and I'm looking forward to shopping in your store with coupons. Before I begin, I would like to request a copy of your coupon policy. Can you please clarify your policy and answer these questions?

- What kinds of coupons do you accept? manufacturer coupons, printable coupons, eCoupons on my loyalty card?

- Do you offer store coupons? Where may I find them?

- May I use a store coupon and a manufacturer coupon on one item?

- Do you exclude any coupons? E.g. above $5 off, BOGO offers, coupons for free products?

- Do you accept printable coupons? May I print them in black and white?

- Do you match competitor prices or take competitor coupons?

- What is your policy on overage (when the value of the coupon exceeds the value of the product)?

- If the coupon exceeds the item's value, do you adjust the price of the coupon down? E.g. $1.00 off coupon on $0.97 cent product.

- Do you limit the number of coupons I may use per transaction?

- Do your employees understand "one coupon per purchase=one coupon per item," not "one coupon per transaction"?

- Does your store ever double or triple coupons?

- Concerning buy one get one offers: if your store runs a BOGO FREE promo, may I use a manufacturer coupon with that sale?

- Are individual stores allowed to impose their own rules or vary from this policy?

Thank you for taking the time to educate me on your store policies. Please mail your response to: [provide your name and address]

Sincerely,

I suggest requesting the response be mailed to you (rather than emailed) because a hard copy is much more powerful to have on hand. The policy will come on company letterhead, and it will have YOUR name on it. If you have a miscommunication with a local store manager, you can show your personalized, official letter from the manager's boss. This will be a powerful tool to use, and it will come in handy more times than you may know! Trust me, it's a wonderful feeling.

Even though you might feel bulletproof now, you've got one more step to take in this process.

● ● ● ● ● ● ● ● ● ● ● ● ● ● ● ● ●

MEET WITH STORE MANAGEMENT

"But do I have to? May I please skip this step?" Sure, you can skip it if you'd like, but you may end up regretting it. One way or another, you are going to meet your store managers, I can promise you that. They'll be coming around your checkout lanes to answer checkers' questions and do overrides all the time. So, why not ensure that it happens in a peaceful, controlled environment instead of during a heated discussion with your cashier? You have two options. One, take the initiative to make an appointment or two, wait for them to come talk to you. It is much easier (and wiser) to go ahead with a meeting when it's on your own terms, NOT when you're standing at checkout with a screaming toddler. After you set a meeting with the managers, they will love you! You want these managers on your side. Having a good relationship with store managers takes any stress right out of couponing.

Depending on how serious you want to get with this, there are two options.

First, if you want to go big, then call your store and ask for the general manager. When you get her or him on the phone, say, "Is there a time I can come into the store and meet with you briefly to discuss your coupon policy?" I have yet to have a manager turn me down on this request.

You might be a Krazy Coupon Lady if...
you go a bit "Nancy Drew"
when you meet with store managers.

The second option is to go into the store, preferably during off-peak hours, and ask to speak with the manager on duty, sometimes called the "front-end manager". Whichever manager you meet with, you'll want to show up on time and take your copy of the store's coupon policy with you. Allow the manager time to look over the policy and ask whether he or she is aware of all of these regulations. If you live in an area that has not yet seen the rise in Krazy Coupon Ladies, you will very likely be providing an education to the store manager, blazing a trail for all the coupon ladies and gentlemen to follow. Keep your meeting to around five minutes—ten minutes, at most. The manager is certainly busy, and you want to stay on his or her good side. Make sure you cover all of these questions:

- Would you like to photocopy this policy to post or share with employees?

- Will your store enforce the policy as outlined from corporate customer service?

- What should I do in the event that a store employee or manager refuses to uphold this policy?

- Is there a number where you may be reached for such an occasion?

- Will you please write or sign your name (and possibly a cell phone number) at the bottom of this policy so I can remember that we have spoken?

Thank them profusely for their time. It is imperative that you leave a good impression with management. Make sure they know you are a valuable customer and that they want your business. Assure them by your actions that you are a confident and responsible shopper. You're making every effort to learn and play by all the rules. (And now that you know the rules, GAME ON! Those in your path had better step back and watch with their jaws gaping open as you work those store sales to your advantage.) Maybe if they're nice enough to you, someday you'll tell them how to save all that money!!

CARRY YOUR STORE POLICIES IN YOUR BINDER

Can you see how good it will feel and how powerful you will become when you have your accurate store policy and you've discussed it with the store manager? You are just about ready to begin this journey. The last thing I want to address regarding store policies is what to do with all those policies now that you've collected them and discussed them with local management.

Those Boy Scouts have it right: be prepared. Print each store policy and tuck it safely away in your binder where it's out of the way but easily accessible. You will find that when a checker hasn't been educated about store policy, and the coupon beeps, requiring a response from the checker, she'll just say, "Sorry! We can't take this!" The checker will just assume the coupon is rejected. But if you have your coupon policy on hand, it's easy to nicely and firmly explain how the store's policy works.

Here's an example. You go to Target to buy one trial sized bar of soap priced at $0.97. You have your $1 off coupon (which states $1 off any sized soap). You hand the checker your item, then the coupon, and when she scans the coupon, it beeps, requiring the checker to respond. She hands the coupon back to you and says, "The system won't allow me to take this coupon." You pull out your Target Policy and say: "Your corporate policy states that you are able to adjust the coupon down to equal the amount of the item. Would you like to see a copy of your policy?" This will generally clear up any confusion, and you and your free soap can head home to organize your shiny, towering stockpile.

• • • • • • • • • • • • • • • • • • •

PROVIDE FEEDBACK

How can stores improve their written policies as well as their implementation? Through all of our feedback, of course. *Always give feedback.* If you have a poor experience with a policy or store employee, don't be too afraid or lazy to take it up with the corporate store offices. We can't expect stores to improve if we don't report the problems.

On the other side, make sure you provide just as much positive feedback as you do negative. If you have a favorite store location, one that is particularly coupon-friendly or especially helpful, please send positive feedback to corporate headquarters. If you have a favorite, knowledgeable checker, make sure you tell his or her manager how impressed you are.

I used to have a favorite grocery store not half a mile from my home. It had the best stock, the nicest checkers, and the most knowledgeable management. This store even clipped coupons and handed them out to customers for free! One of the store managers' names was Bill. His store was so well known as the hot coupon spot that when I ran into policy problems at other locations, I'd say, "At my location, I was able to use both a manufacturer and a store coupon on one item." The response would always be something like, "Oh, they're too liberal with their coupon policy over at your location." Instead of complaining about the bad store, I decided to praise the one that was doing so well. I wrote a short article on **TheKrazyCouponLady.com** titled "Marry me, Bill." In it I told how awesome his store was and how much I appreciated him. It made him feel good, and rumor has it that he printed out the article and put it up at his store for all the employees to see.

Once as I was checking out at my favorite Albertsons location, my checker helped me with a huge order of merchandise which made him miss part of his lunch break. As I was profusely thanking him, he said, "If you really want to thank me, let my manager know that I helped you; this way he may give me more hours next week". Before I left, I filled out one of their Customer Service Feedback Cards and talked about James and his above-board commitment to customer service. The next time I was shopping, James ran over to me and thanked me for taking the time to offer my feedback to management. He happily reported to me that he had received more hours for the next week, in large part because of my comment. I like to look at couponing as a team effort with our checkers and managers. In some ways, they hold the power to our success. Remember to treat them with kindness and respect and they will usually do likewise.

●　●　●　●　●　●　●　●　●　●　●　●　●　●　●　●　●

LEARN THE RULES
SO YOU CAN PLAY BY THE RULES

Learning the ins and outs of your store policy allows you to do two things. First, it allows you to play by the rules because you know the rules. What do I mean? Well, you won't have to be nervous that you're accidentally or unknowingly being unethical about something because you've taken the time to educate yourself and learn the facts. In the olden days, when I began couponing, I made many errors out of ignorance. Sure, I made these mistakes without meaning to, but I accepted responsibility for my lack of education.

When I moved to California a couple of years ago, a co-worker mentioned to my husband, "Make sure you don't talk on your cell phone while driving. It is now illegal in California." Then later that week, while driving (and wishing I could pick up my phone and make some calls!), I wondered, "Between my out of state plates and my pasty white complexion, I clearly appear to be an out-of-stater. Do I have to abide by the same law as California residents?" If it hadn't been for my husband's co-worker, I wouldn't have even known that there was this "new cell phone law". For a minute, I began to justify my actions. I said to myself, "If I were pulled over, the cop couldn't expect that I know this new law. I'm an out-of-towner!" But then I realized: if I want to drive on California roads, it is my responsibility to learn California laws and abide by them—or pay the price. The same holds true for learning store policies. Don't get by on ignorance. We all have a responsibility to learn and follow the rules.

The second thing learning the rules allows you to do is to save big. Learn the rules, because that knowledge will allow you to take advantage of things you may have once considered loopholes, but, after further inspection, found were perfectly honest and legitimate ways to save big bucks!

Learn that when a store says 10/$10, it almost never means you have to buy ten to get that price. You can simply buy one for only $1. Learn that if milk, regularly priced at $3.29, is on sale for $2.99 when you buy 2, it usually means two or more: if you want to buy 3 gallons, you'll only pay $2.99 each. Learn that during a "Buy one, get one free" promotion, you can often use one manufacturer coupon on the item that is not free, to bring your price down even lower! Learn that during a "Save instantly" promo, such as "Buy 5 cereals, Save $5", you can nearly always purchase 10 boxes and instantly save $5 twice, or 15 and save $5 three times. As long as the sales ad doesn't have a stated limit, and your store policy doesn't exclude it, you can buy more to save more!

Every Krazy Coupon Lady knows that knowledge is power. Ignorance will lead you to mistakes, either in the form of embarrassment or less-than-spectacular savings. Neither alternative is acceptable, and neither is conducive to achieving The Krazy Coupon Lady's mantra. So seize the day, take the reins, and get out and learn your policies! The confidence that comes from a sound understanding of store policy is vital. Preparation plus knowledge equals coupon confidence!

FAQs:

Do store policies change frequently?

Most stores update their coupon policy one time per year, but they can change at any time. For the latest policy information stay up-to-date at TheKrazyCouponLady.com.

TheKrazyCouponLady.com doesn't cover all the stores in my area. How can I find coupon match-ups for one of my local stores?

If I don't cover your store, I am sure there's someone who does! There are many great and free coupon sites scattered across the county. Search the web to find one that covers the store where you shop.

What if I find my store is inconsistent in enforcing its coupon policy? Sometimes I can get certain deals and others times I cannot. What do I do?

Inconsistent policy enforcement is both common and frustrating. One particular supercenter is the worst offender. The best way to combat inconsistency is to find the opportunity to talk to the head manager at your store. After your meeting you should have the 411, and you can throw the head manager's name around the next time you have a run-in with an on-duty assistant manager.

CHAPTER TWELVE

Fight the Krazy:
HOW NOT TO GO NUTS
AT CHECKOUT

With all of your newly acquired coupon knowledge, you're ready to take it to the store. During your first few shopping trips, as you use your new krazy coupon skills, you may feel a bit like you're stepping out on the high dive for the first time. When you get in line to pay, you may feel an air of uncertainty, the looming fear of something going wrong, and the impending confrontation that might ensue. But just like the high dive, standing at the top and over-analyzing is the worst part (well, that and the whole wearing a bathing suit in public thing). So take a deep breath, and get in line; it'll be over soon, and it's never as bad as you think it might be. As you push your cart out the door after your first successful trip, you'll experience the couponer's "buzz", and you'll be hooked for good! So go ahead, and don't be afraid to jump in head first and make a splash.

This chapter will offer you a few more tips that are going to make certain you're totally prepared. Let's ensure that you can, in fact, swim before I tell you to jump.

• •

SEVEN STEPS FOR CONTROLLING THE KRAZE

There are seven things you can do to really help cut down on that urge to panic at the checkout counter. By being aware of those simple tools you can approach the cashier with confidence and ease. No more jitters! No more apprehension! Here's exactly how to keep your sanity:

1. Get organized.

Do you know what can make or break your couponing experience? Organization…or the lack thereof! How organized you are when it's time to check out is what will ultimately make the difference. So before you even leave the house, first make a list of what you want to buy. You might choose to write yours by hand, or just print the store's coupon match-ups from TheKrazyCouponLady.com. If you plan to purchase items that are part of a Catalina promo where you will be doing multiple transactions, do yourself a favor and write out your list, separating each transaction. Write the item, price, and quantity you plan to buy. Have a calculator handy, and make sure to take it in your purse to the grocery store. If you're not organizing your pre-clipped coupons by category, find your coupons, and clip them now, before you leave the house. Place them in an envelope or in the front of your binder where they'll be easy to find.

2. Choose wisely the time of day that you shop.

I have found that in the morning, early afternoon, or late at night is best for me. You and your checker will be less stressed if there is not a line behind you. In fact, your checker may enjoy having something to do to kill the time during a slow shift. Don't try to do five separate transactions with eighty coupons during the 5:00 p.m. rush and then act surprised when you get a grouchy checker or a bunch of grumbling customers behind you.

3. Just for moms:

If you're like me and you have young children, the key is to do your shopping early in the morning or right after naps. It's hard enough for kids to behave at the grocery store, so I try my best not to take them out when they're already cranky and exhausted. Checking out as a Krazy Coupon Lady is going to be a much longer and more intensive process than you're used to. It's worth it, but remember that your kids will need something to do while you get your coupons rung through. You won't regret packing some toys or snacks to entertain your kids at checkout. You might even check your grocer's bakery to see if they have free cookies or snacks for children, and, if so, make that your last stop before checkout. The ideal first shopping experience would be to shop without kids, if possible, so you can totally focus on what you're doing. The first trip or two, consider shopping late at night when your spouse is home or even getting a babysitter for your daytime shopping trip. Couponing will soon be second nature, but if you have the luxury of a babysitter close by, take her up on any offer she's made to watch your kids for an hour or two while you go shopping, just until you get the hang of it.

4. Consider shopping with a friend.

Friends make everything more fun. This is especially true for beginning Krazy Coupon Ladies. On a big, multi-transaction trip, having one person to watch the items ring through and hand the cashier the coupons while the other person sets items onto the conveyor belt and separates them into transactions is an absolute lifesaver. Even on smaller trips, it's still great to shop with a buddy. You can share coupons, take turns watching each other's kids, or help each other check out one at a time.

5. Talk to your cashier before your transaction begins.

Greet her and let her know you're going to be using coupons with your purchase. If you're participating in a Catalina promotion, make sure to ask whether the Catalina machine is on and working! (You would not believe how often they're turned off or non-functional. Most customers don't care a bit, so the store doesn't have much reason to upkeep the machines.) If you're planning to do several separate transactions, let your cashier know. Sometimes if I say, "I'm doing five different transactions with coupons today. Is this lane okay?" they'll either open a new lane for me, or they'll pull across behind me the coiled black wire that holds the "this lane closed" sign. They don't do that very often, but I love it when they do. It's nice not to have to say, "Pick another checkout lane, honey" eighteen times. If I am shopping during a time of day that is busy, I only put one transaction on the conveyor belt at a time. This way, if a line starts to form behind me, I can finish my purchase and get back in line.

Ask your cashier how she would like to take your coupons. Would she like to scan an item and then take the coupon? Or would she prefer to scan everything through and then take all my coupons? I find cashiers usually prefer the latter, but I still talk them through the stack of coupons. I'll let them know the quantity and value of each coupon as they scan them in. And I'm ready to answer any questions they might have. The easier I can make their jobs, the happier they are—and that's always a good thing! If you are particularly Type A, or if you are nervous about cashiers not ringing in some of your coupons, insist that they ring up one item, and then the coupon. This will help you keep track of your savings and will make sure each coupon gets scanned.

6. Do not be afraid to ask for a member of management to come clarify something for you.

Often, you know more about the store coupon policy than the checkers, so don't be afraid to ask nicely for a manager to explain something to you. Many times, I have had them call over a manager, and it ends with the checker saying, "Huh. I never knew that!"

7. Keep a copy of the store's coupon policy in your binder.

This is slightly repetitive but it's that important. Keep the store policy with you, and don't be afraid to show it off. The reason you went through the trouble of getting a copy of the policy is twofold: first, to educate yourself, and second, to let it do your talking at the register. One reader writes:

> *Thank you for insisting that we keep the store policies with us while shopping. I just returned from a shopping trip that would have been a waste of time had I not been carrying the policy. My checker was uninformed of the store's policy, and I may have been too nervous to stand up for myself had I not had a written copy to use as reference. I was able to pull out the store's policy and have the checker read it. He immediately accepted the coupon and apologized for the trouble!!*

These seven steps will be sure to help you avoid the frazzles. Checkout will be a breeze and you'll leave without a hitch...hopefully! And yet, sometimes, after all that you do, the preparation, the organization, the careful calculating, there's still one thing that can either make or break your shopping experience: the cashier. So what we recommend next is a little good-old-fashion profiling.

● ● ● ● ● ● ● ● ● ● ● ● ● ● ● ● ● ●

CASHIER PROFILING

Imagine...

With my basket full and my shopping complete I slowly approach the checkout counter eyeing each cashier as I go. Studying them carefully, my mind begins to reel. Who's the friendliest? Who is most proficient? Who's going to give me the biggest attitude? Who won't mind a Krazy Coupon Lady with dozens of coupons? Question after question floods my thoughts as I quickly try to evaluate each one. I notice gender, age, attitude, and appearance. I feel like a hawk slowly circling above, planning my strike carefully.

Lane 1. The middle-aged management type, carrying a sense of authority on his shoulders. Probably pleasant, possibly stern, most likely proficient. And yet there's always that chance he'll be annoyed with the amount of coupons I'm using.

Lane 2. The extra-cautious, snail-paced, elderly woman. Sweet and accommodating or clueless and crabby? From experience, I've learned that either is an equal possibility. I'd hate to add an extra hour just because she might be technologically out-of-date.

Lane 3. The young girl in her early twenties. Will she have the necessary patience for my multiple transactions and dozens of coupons?

Lane 4. The young clean cut male with obvious efficiency. I notice how effortlessly he scans the groceries and watch as he punches the buttons at an incredible pace. Speed of checkout seems to be his top priority.

Finally, after a few short strolls past the checkout lanes and a bit of inner debating my decision is complete. I choose Lane 4. Yes! It's called cashier profiling, and I do it!

From a recent poll conducted on **TheKrazyCouponLady.com** 76% of couponers have a cashier preference. Of those, 53% base that preference on outward appearance, gender, and age, with young males coming in first. Only 8% of couponers pick the shortest, fastest moving lines. Judge us couponers if you must, but picking the right cashier is crucial.

Prior to coupons I would have simply picked the shortest line in hopes of leaving the store as quickly as possible—or maybe the lane closest to the exit in an attempt to shorten the jaunt back to my car. Not now. Speed and proximity no longer play a role in this equation. It's all about who will treat me and my coupons the best.

What I've learned through my years of couponing is that so much of my shopping experience lies in the hands of the cashier. I either leave full of exhilaration from successfully saving my family hundreds of dollars, or I leave irritated, flustered and deflated, unable to forget the feeling of being treated like a coupon criminal. I need a cashier who will treat me with respect and exhibit some patience with all the extra scanning.

You might be a Krazy Coupon Lady if...
your favorite cashier knows your family
by name and your preferred card by heart.

As you begin couponing, pay attention to the available cashiers. In no time you will uncover the friendly ones with all the necessary coupon proficiency and patience. One will soon emerge as your favorite, and each time you return to that store you'll pray the whole way there that he or she will be standing right behind the register waiting for you. It's true that if I don't know any of the cashiers I tend to lean towards the young males. But in my case, there is the friendliest elderly woman at Rite Aid who always makes me feel amazing for saving so much money. At CVS I look for the girl with the crazy hair who enjoys watching the total plummet as much as I do. So remember, although profiling is helpful and necessary at times, it's important to stick with what works for you.

• • • • • • • • • • • • • • • • • •

WHEN THINGS GO WRONG

Armed with this knowledge, you're ready for success. You can go shopping with confidence and expect only the best. Well...expect the best, but prepare for the worst. Brace yourself, as I'm about to share with you my worst shopping experience to date. I hope that for you, it won't get any worse than this. I was shopping at that oh-so-friendly supercenter where we've all likely shopped. I had about twenty items to purchase, each with its own coupon. Most of the items were to be totally free, and I would just be paying sales tax. The cashier was friendly enough, as most cashiers usually are. The checker scanned all my items through, bagged them, and we were almost done... or so I thought. She started scanning the coupons, and the coupons began beeping and misbehaving. I had expected this, since I was using coupons that exceeded the value of the items (e.g., the soaps were $0.99 and my coupons were for $1.00 off). I explained to the cashier how to adjust the price down, but she went ahead and called a manager over. Although it can be frustrating when checkers call managers about every little thing, remember that checkers get in trouble if they do something wrong or against the rules. They are just being careful, so Krazy Coupon Ladies should be patient with them.

The manager stormed over like a very-past-middle-aged-woman-who'd-been-working-way-too-long-at-this-supercenter-and-was-mad-at-the-world. She took one look at my coupons and told me I couldn't use them because they all said, "One coupon per purchase". She glared at me. "You may only use one of these coupons." I explained to her that one coupon per purchase means one coupon per item, and when she didn't understand, I asked to speak to another manager. When the second manager joined her, neither one would listen to my explanation of their store's policy. I asked whether there was anyone else I could speak with so they called out the "front end manager". (How many levels of managers are there? None of which is the actual store manager. Apparently, they keep finding new ways to promote mediocrity at this establishment.) He started off upset, angry that he had to bother with a customer. He agreed with the other managers, but he took it a step further and began questioning the validity of my coupons. He sneered, "How do I know these aren't fake?" These weren't even printable coupons. These were clearly from inserts, on shiny paper, the whole bit.

It gets worse. He then told me he was going to refuse me service. That's right; he told me I couldn't buy anything. He told me the store has a right to refuse service to anyone. I was upset but refused to back down. I told him he'd have hell to pay if he refused to serve me just because I was trying to shop with coupons. I then proposed, "If you think purchase means transaction (which it doesn't) then let me do twenty-plus transactions." He laughed out loud, threw up his hands and said, "Fine, do them all separately!" and walked away. Whew! I spent the next twenty minutes paying separately, and my only regret is that I should have swiped my credit card (so the store could pay a fee each time) instead of paying in cash.

Of course, I set up an appointment with the head manager at the supercenter. When I met with him, I showed him the perfectly and obviously legitimate coupons I was trying to use and asked what he was going to do to rectify this situation. Although this man was polite, he was totally clueless about coupons and about policy. He wanted to look at my binder and grill me on where customers get coupons. I had my notepad with a bunch of questions for him, and he wasn't able to answer many of them. The supercenter where I shopped is one of the worst places to coupon. Corporate has a policy, but it is officially up to each individual store to enforce its own version of the policy, and the store where I shop has an official policy to leave it up to the managers on duty. When I asked for an apology from the managers who had mistreated me, I was denied. I asked to receive an apology in writing, and this is what I received a few weeks later:

> *I wanted to take this opportunity to apologize for the confusion in policy and let you know that we would love the chance to have you back in our stores.*
>
> > *Signed, Curly, Mo & Larry (names have been changed to protect the three customer service-challenged employees)*

I'm not telling this story to scare you. Chances are you won't run into anything nearly as bad as that experience. The lesson is just that no matter how prepared you are, you'll sometimes still get the runaround. You'll then have the choice as the consumer whether you wish to take your business elsewhere, or go back for more deals on the chance that you might get a manager who knows the policy. Looking back, I can laugh at that ridiculous day. I have since learned to keep my cool and walk away before the situation escalates. When a polite manager is simply unaware of the store policy, it's easy to explain and help him or her out. But when someone starts attacking you and treating you like a criminal, your resolve to stay polite will truly be tested.

One Krazy Coupon Lady, Kinsey, wrote about the battles she has faced as a coupon-user. Sometimes it helps just to know that you're not alone when you run into these all-too-familiar hiccups!

> *As I approach the doors of the store, I quickly make a mental checklist.*
>
> - *Specific products and prices written down, CHECK.*
>
> - *Coupons clipped and neatly arranged in a crisp white envelope, CHECK.*
>
> - *Money in my pocket ready to be spent, CHECK!*
>
> *I feel completely prepared and yet there always exists a slight tremor in my hand. My nerves are just barley on edge, and I can't help but unconsciously bite the inside of my lip. Maybe because I'm a little new at this whole couponing thing, and I'm never quite certain how a scenario is going to work out. Or*

maybe because for every time a coupon trip goes perfectly smoothly there's another time that something goes wrong and I have to stand up and ROAR!

- *Like the time my $2.00 Ovaltine coupon was scanned at the register but never applied to the total. I had to stand in the customer service line and explain to the sweet lady there that for some reason my coupon didn't show up on my receipt. She then went on a hunt to locate that coupon, found the register where I had checked out, searched through the drawer for that coupon and then compared it to my receipt. Fifteen minutes all to get my $2.00 back.*

- *Or the time my $10 Extra Bucks didn't print out and the annoyed cashier brushed me aside hoping her lame excuse would be enough for me to leave. But really it made me stand my ground and patiently demand to speak to the manager.*

- *Or the time my $5.00 Catalina didn't print out. Another trip to the customer service counter. Another chat with the representative there. Except for this time she didn't believe me, wouldn't take my word for it, and without coming out and saying it, pretty much called me a liar.*

Whatever the circumstance may be, with each new coupon trip I do feel more comfortable, more knowledgeable, and actually, more empowered. I'm learning to stand up and be heard. I'm learning to speak up and be strong. And I'm learning to let that inner lioness out and sometimes let her ROAR, politely... that is, even if it is over just $2.00. Because sometimes that's what it takes!!!

Sometimes you'll hit those little bumps in the road and it will be important to stand your ground. But generally speaking, you're going to be just fine. In fact, you'll make some great friends out of the cashiers and employees at your local grocery stores. Just remember to *play nice*. Be courteous to your cashier, the managers, and fellow shoppers. It's okay to question what a cashier is telling you and to ask for clarification from a manager, but be polite. If you need to clear the shelf of an item, consider asking to special order. If you are going to be doing multiple transactions, shop during the slow hours and let other customers go in front of you in line. Follow the store policies and the individual coupon rules. Don't expect stores to bend their rules or make an exception for you. Respect the expiration dates, quantity limits, and manufacturer's rules. Most of the time, stores will treat you with respect when you treat their store policies with respect. Your couponing experience will go so much more smoothly if you prepare for your trip by making a list and grouping your coupons together. It's amazing how much nicer I am if I am not stressed about getting all my coupons together come checkout time.

One last thought: conduct yourself so that you wouldn't be embarrassed if you ran into an old friend or neighbor at the store. I've heard horror stories about women racing for diapers or even grabbing them out of other shoppers' baskets or hands. Don't be that shopper. They give everyone a bad name.

Shopping like a Krazy Coupon Lady with a basketful of groceries and a binder full of coupons is definitely worth it even though it can be daunting. In order for it to be a pleasant experience you must be prepared. Plan and organize before you ever leave the house, choose your cashier wisely, and cultivate that strength within to sweetly stand your ground. By following these simple rules you'll discover that couponing really *is* all it's cracked up to be, even when the register starts to beep.

FAQs:

Do you ever get really angry in the store?

Yes. Oh, yes! And I must admit I got worked up a time or two when I was just starting out in this whole coupon-world. Now I've learned that the best way to get what you want is to bulk up on knowledge and leave your ego at the door. Stay calm, pull out a copy of the store policy and try to reason with and teach the cashiers and managers how their own coupon policy operates. It's baffling, but at this point in the book you already know so much more than the average cashier.

Why do you like young male cashiers? Isn't that sexist?

Well, maybe it is sexist. But I find that young male cashiers are generally more easygoing. When I share a point of coupon policy with them, they are more likely to accept it than other cashiers. They are generally impressed by my coupon savings and want to know how I do it. Sometimes other cashiers have been immediately skeptical thinking this is too good to be true and that I must be a scammer. Feel free to conduct your own case study and get back to me with the results. Generally, if the cashier smiles at the beep of a coupon, it doesn't take Pavlov to tell me that this is the kind of cashier I'll be going back to again and again.

How long do you take at checkout?

Using coupons doubles your checkout time. After the cashier rings through all your groceries, you have reached the halfway point. Now the cashier will ring through each of your coupons. If you have complications or need a manager's approval, additional time is required. Don't freak out when you read this, but the longest I've spent in a checkout line is almost an hour. One of my first coupon trips, I did about ten transaction in one morning. It was a slow process but well worth it!

This is too overwhelming!
How am I going to do this?

Relax! You can do it, and at this point in the book you already have most of the knowledge you need to be successful. There are two easy tips for success. First, choose wisely the time of day you go to the store. *Don't go at rush hour.* Your trip will be much more relaxed if you shop during a slow time. Second, start small. Plan on only doing one transaction on your first few trips. Make a shopping list and calculate all your coupon savings before you leave the house. Keep your transactions small, under twelve items on your very first trip, and you'll soon be able to do more and more until you're a pro.

I don't want to argue with my checker!
Is there any way I can avoid it?

Your best shot to avoid an altercation is to carry your store policy. Let the policy do the talking if you can.

My checker is unwilling to take my coupons. Should I still go ahead and buy the items in my cart?

No! Do not buy the items if your coupons are refused. Politely let your checker know that you will not be purchasing the items at this time. Follow up with your manager or corporate office on the phone. When the matter is resolved go back to the store and use your coupons.

CHAPTER THIRTEEN

Leading Your Family:

LIFE AS THE CFO

Now that you've learned all the tricks to using coupons the *krazy way*, you have the chance to transform your family finances. *Now's your opportunity to change your family's future.* It's time to step up and grab the title of CFO, Chief Financial Officer, of your household. The job requires confidence, serious discipline and some street smarts (or rather, shopping-aisle smarts), many of the same qualities that every Krazy Coupon Lady already has in spades. Shopping like a Krazy Coupon Lady isn't always an easy thing, as we've just discovered. It takes a little gumption, self-assurance, and a spring in your step that says, "Watch out, world. I won't settle for less." To see how easily you fit the mold, take the following quiz. You'll either discover you're totally compatible, or you'll see that a little newfound bravado is just what the doc ordered!

• •

KRAZY COUPON LADY QUIZ:

WHAT KIND OF SHOPPER ARE YOU?

1. You're shopping with your young and wiggly child in the cart. As you watch your items ring through on the screen, you notice that a sale item, marked down to $1.99 rings up at regular price $2.69. What do you do?

A. Nothing. $0.69 cents is not worth the time and headache to wait for the cashier to correct the problem.

B. What screen? You've got way too much going on even to think about checking the computer screen!

C. You mention that you think the item was on sale. The checker asks, "Well, do you want me to call someone to go do a price check?" You say, "No, it's fine."

D. You tell the cashier that the item did not ring up correctly. When the cashier offers to go get a price check, you accept and thank him or her for fixing the error.

2. At the checkout, your cashier takes one look at your stack of coupons and informs you that the coupons state "one per purchase" and declines your request to use more than one, unless you're wanting to do twenty-plus separate transactions.

A. You remain calm and start explaining nicely that "one coupon per purchase" means "one per item". All it's really saying is that you can't use two $1.00 off coupons for one $2.00 product. The cashier gets mad and calls over a manager, but you politely stick to your guns. You invite them to call their own 800 guest services number to clarify, and you wait for fifteen minutes while they sort out the debacle.

B. You throw up your hands and cuss like a sailor, shouting, "I can't believe you don't know your own policies! Re-shelve these items or stick them [bleeeeeeep]."

C. You tell them you'll do separate transactions and proceed to swipe your credit card over twenty times.

D. You buy all your twenty-plus items at full price and only use one of your coupons.

3. Which of these statements best describes your attitude regarding the way stores treat those who shop with coupons.

A. "Thanks anyway!" Even if the store refuses some of my valid coupons, I'm still grateful for the ones they do accept.

B. The store should go out of its way to help me. They should open up a new checkout lane for me, and take ALL my coupons even if they don't scan, look questionable, or exceed any store limits. After all, look how much stuff I'm buying! I'm talking so much about my new obsession that it's free advertising for the store.

C. My valid coupons are my currency. They are just as good as cash, and the store will treat me with respect.

D. It's okay for the cashiers and managers to huff and puff and treat me like a subclass shopper. After all, I'm slow at checkout, and I'm sure coupons are a pain.

4. You're buying an item with one store coupon and one manufacturer coupon. The item is $2.00. You're using a $1.00 off manufacturer coupon and a $0.50 store coupon. The cashier tells you, "One coupon per item, lady. You can't use both of these. Pick one." What do you do?

A. You say, "Well, I know your policy says I can use both coupons, and I'm not leaving until you ring these both through." Ask for her name and how long she's been working here. Write down all this info as if you're turning her in to the authorities.

B. You politely whip out the store's coupon policy from your binder, and show her where it states you are allowed to use one store and one manufacturer coupon together. Then apologize to the line of people behind you. Let them know they might want to...."Pick another checkout lane, honey."

C. You take one look at that long line behind you and tell the cashier you'll just use the $1.00 off coupon and save the $0.50 for later.

D. You don't explain anything. Just turn on your pouty face and ask whether she'll please make an exception, just this once.

5. You're buying some trial-sized items with coupons. The items are $0.97 and your coupons are for $1.00 off, so you're gonna get them free. But guess what? Trouble at checkout! The cashier says he cannot accept a coupon that exceeds the item's value, AND coupons can't be used on trial-sized. What do you do?

A. You ask him to read the coupon and tell you where it says "excludes trial sized" (it doesn't, you already checked), but he maintains his stance, and you storm out with no purchases.

B. You tell him his store policy states that he should simply adjust the price down to match the value of the item, so instead of taking off a full dollar, just take off $0.97 cents.

C. You insist that he must take off a full dollar because, after all, the store is going to be reimbursed for the full $1.00. Why are they stealing your $0.03??

D. You buy the trial sized items anyway, without the coupons.

Now, find below the answers you chose, and give yourself the corresponding points.

For example, in question 1, if your answer was "c", give yourself 3 points. Then total your score.

1) a.2 b.1 c.3 d.4

2) a.4 b.2 c.3 d.1

3) a.1 b.1 c.4 d.1

4) a.3 b.4 c.1 d.2

5) a.3 b.4 c.2 d.1

16 points +

You are well on your way to being a savvy and successful couponer! You're not afraid to stand up for fairness and policy, even if it inconveniences you to do so. You stay calm and collected and are always a picture of politeness, but you are unwavering in your dedication to getting what is rightfully yours.

7-15 points

You are still a coupon rookie! You're learning as you go, and by the end of this book, you'll be ready to assert yourself. You might be intimidated by the idea of having to go toe to toe with some overconfident store manager who thinks he's the king of the world. You might think you're too busy, and you don't have time to deal with shenanigans at the store. I've still got some convincing to do with you, but you'll get the hang of this soon.

Under 7 points

Stand up for yourself, girl! You deserve better than what you are accepting. Don't let others walk all over you. It doesn't make you ungrateful or rude when you calmly and assertively make sure you're treated with respect. Go look in the mirror and tell yourself that you deserve respect…and while you're there, remind yourself that you're beautiful.

Now that you know what kind of shopper you are, let's talk about the kind of shopper you can become! It's really quite simple. Treat yourself with the same honesty and respect you give others every day. Stop selling yourself short, eating the heels of your bread, and letting others walk all over you! Here's one more quiz question for you:

Imagine you just got home from one of the aforementioned coupon trips. Exhausted, you drop your grocery bags to the floor and toss your purse on the counter only to see a shiny wrapper peeking out of the top. You walk over and find a bag of candy in your purse—a contraband candy bag thrown into your purse by your four-year-old while you were neck deep in your coupon debacle for what seemed like an eternity. Your child walks up behind you and says, "My candy! Can I have it, Mom?" What do you do?

I don't have to give you options because I already know what you're going to do. I know what kind of stand-up individual you are and that you're going to take advantage of this teaching moment. Whether you're loading that four-year-old back in the car right this instant (or maybe some of us less-than-perfect folks would wait until the next day), you're going to drive him back to the store with that candy bag. I know you're going to march straight up to customer service with his trembling, sweaty little fist in your hand. I know you're going to ask him to give that candy back to the store because, "We didn't pay for it." Why are you going to all this trouble? Is it because the store might go bankrupt if it loses that $0.33 you owe it for some candy? Of course, not. It's for the principle. You're teaching your child to treat others with the utmost honesty. This will likely be the last time you find surprise candy in your purse as you've just effectively taught an important parenting lesson.

It's an equally important lesson to teach this same child that, just as you should treat the grocery store with honesty and respect, the grocery store should treat you the same way. When my child watches me politely interject as my item rings up at the wrong price, when my child sees me calmly and confidently speak to a store manager, he is being taught, and I am proud of what I'm teaching. I'm glad to be raising children who know how to speak up for themselves, politely.

● ● ● ● ● ● ● ● ● ● ● ● ● ● ● ● ●

TEACH THE VALUE OF MONEY

As CFO, you need to recognize that managing your money is not your only job description. It's also your responsibility to pass that knowledge on to the other members of your family. Teaching your children about money is vital if you want them to grow into responsible adults. Parents wonder, *How do I raise a financially responsible child? When do I begin teaching my child about money? Where is the balance between starved and spoiled? How young is too young for a child to begin earning money of their own? How do I teach my child to manage money?*

One reader, Richelle, wrote in to tell us why she coupons with her children. She said:

"I want my kids to learn to save and be frugal! If you want something, it's okay to wait until it's on sale so you don't have to spend all your money on it."

Remember, teaching your child about money is a process, not an event.

As soon as your child is old enough to beg for a toy or treat at the grocery store (and throw a tantrum when you don't buy it), you know it's time to start teaching about money. Here are a few great ways to involve your children, even from a young age, in the process of saving!

- **Let them play with scissors:** If they can use a pair of scissors then they can cut coupons. Teach your children how to look for the coupons and explain that coupons hold value just like coins.

- **Miniature wallet and coupon holder:** Take your lessons to the store by purchasing a small wallet or miniature accordion file at the dollar store for carrying coins and coupons.

- **Make coupons a game:** Turn couponing at the grocery store into a scavenger hunt; ask your child to match each coupon to the products on the shelf.

- **Hand over the money/coupons:** At checkout, let your child hand over the coupons with the money, to reinforce that these are both valid forms of payment.

- **First taste of entrepreneurship:** Give your kids their first experience with earning money by helping them create a lemonade stand or, even better, sell cookies, which they helped to make, at your neighborhood garage sale. Make sure the price points are all single-coins, such as $0.25/ea.

If your children are a bit older, you can implement even more strategies in addition to those listed above! Try a few of these, age-appropriate tips:

- **Math:** Put math skills to the test by asking your child to determine if buying a product with a coupon is a better deal than purchasing another brand. Older children can calculate price per unit and percentage saved.

- **Allowance:** An allowance can be an effective teaching tool, especially when children have to earn it. Giving your kids money for no reason is like teaching them to live off the system. If you choose to give an allowance, make sure you require something from the child before you hand over the cash. Then encourage her to save and budget that money for a future purchase or goal. Here's an example: Explain in June that your child will be responsible for purchasing her own back-to-school outfit or that special birthday present for her friend's party. Let her know that all summer long you'll be giving her a list of weekly chores and $5 per week upon completion of those chores. Tell her it will be her responsibility to save enough of that money to afford her first-day-of-school look.

- **Menu Planning:** Show your child a weekly sale circular. Teach him how to read it and allow him to help plan one dinner, based on the foods he sees are on sale that week.

- **Prioritize spending:** Help children learn the differences between wants, needs and even wishes. As adults, my husband and I still sometimes disagree on wants verses needs, so why not start teaching the principle at a young age?

- **Teach them to work:** Summer jobs such as dog-walking, yard work, window washing and weed pulling build character! Don't wait until your kids reach the legal age of employment! Children can start earning money as soon as they show an interest. If your child is too young for the above ideas, offer extra chores around the house. Get kids excited about the rewards of work!

- **Match Savings:** For every dollar your child saves, offer a matching contribution. Teach kids to save, but help them, too. This is a great system to begin early and carry on to college tuition and beyond! Help them visualize their savings by posting a simple drawing of a thermometer that they can color in as their savings grows. Your children will have more respect for the things they own when they earn part of the cost themselves!

As a teenager, I didn't have things handed to me: no car, no clothing budget. I had a job and I paid for my own expenses. I'd be lying if I said I wasn't envious of the friends who got cars on their 16th birthday, or even were handed a $5 bill for lunch every day. But I now see the value in how my parents chose to raise me. When things weren't handed to me, it taught me to figure out a way to earn them for myself.

By the time you've got teenagers in the house, you'd better be working with them to learn about work and money.

- **Savings account:** Teach your children that adults use the bank to save money. Take them to the bank so they can watch the process of opening an account. Studies show that children with savings accounts have less stress and more hope for the future.

- **Checking account:** By opening up their own checking account, teens learn to write checks, balance a checkbook and use a debit card. Make sure to have two separate accounts; don't give a checkbook or debit card on the savings account!

- **Learn about credit:** Seniors in high school may be ready for their first credit card. Prepaid credit cards are a good alternative to regular credit cards for teens and can serve as their "training wheels" to ease them into using credit wisely. Low-limit credit cards are another alternative. Parents co-sign with their teen on these cards and set a low credit limit of $200 to $300.

- **Teens can take work-from-home to a new level.** Encourage them to start their own lawn mowing or babysitting service. Help them organize a family yard sale and let them keep the earnings.

- **College savings:** As I mentioned before, I love the idea of matching contributions. If you are financially able, continue to match your teen's earnings in their college savings account.

As you teach your children about money, you'll find it becomes so much easier to manage your family finances. You won't be the only one frugally shopping and consciously saving. The entire family will be in on the fun, working towards similar goals. It not only makes your job as CFO easier, it also prepares your children for the time when they become their very own CFO.

● ● ● ● ● ● ● ● ● ● ● ● ● ● ● ● ● ● ● ●

REPLACE SPENDING WITH SAVING

So now that you're completely aware of your newly acquired job title of CFO and the multiple job descriptions it includes, you've got to stop giving your power and your money away as a mindless consumer. Recognizing that saving money can be equally as exciting as spending money will be the key to how extensive your budget transformation becomes. The great news is that all this saving still involves shopping. I love to shop. There's something about acquiring things that gives my spirit a boost. Do you feel that way? One of the best things about couponing is that grocery shopping is no longer a mindless chore. It's a shopping trip. Now, instead of stalking the clearance aisles at Macy's, I satisfy my shopping urges by trolling the grocery aisles for freebies!

A reader, Fernelius, wrote in:

> It's better to surf the Internet looking for ways to save more money than to spend the money. I once was addicted to [online shopping], but now I'm addicted to couponing and free items. I average about $45.00 a week in savings that I normally just threw away when I would go shopping. We put that money in a jar, and it goes in the family trip fund. I like that I am teaching my kids to be frugal and really weigh the options in buying things rather than buying just to do it.

Couponing is not a housewife's chore. It truly will become your hobby, your obsession, and your new responsibility as the CFO. What better pastime can you have than saving money?

● ● ● ● ● ● ● ● ● ● ● ● ● ● ● ● ● ● ● ●

TRADE TIME FOR MONEY

Saving $500 per month or walking out of the store with a cartload of groceries for under twenty bucks doesn't come free. You know you'll have to reallocate your time in order to make that extra hour or two per week to become a coupon shopper. But as the CFO you are already perfectly capable of rearranging your schedule to maximize your benefits. Is it worth it? Of course. If you're not convinced yet, just ask yourself: who would you rather pay—the store or yourself? As the chief financial officer of my household, I know the answer. I'll pay myself every time! Last year, the Wall Street Journal wrote an article suggesting that clipping coupons would do more to help your financial situation than getting a part time job! They calculated that a coupon clipper earns, on average, $86.40 per hour! A few hours of my time for hundreds in my pocket: it's hard evidence to refute.

Now, you must rise to this occasion and take on the responsibilities of the CFO, whether you're a stay-at-home-mom, full-time working mom, savvy shopping dad, college student, bachelor, retired grandma or grandpa—you name it! (Although bachelors, beware. Walking around a grocery store with a cartload of groceries and your coupon binder might make you the hottest chick-magnet ever!)

You might be a Krazy Coupon Lady if...
while your neighbors lower their garage doors
you leave yours open to showcase your stockpile.

Each of us must become more conscious of our spending, more aware of what we're teaching our families, and more vigilant in balancing the dollars that come in and out of our households. Evaluate your budget and your daily life. Commit to setting aside the time, and get excited as you watch the return on that investment roll in!

FAQs:

What if I don't feel comfortable standing up for myself at checkout?

You'll get there. Remember that standing up for yourself doesn't mean being rude or causing a scene. You can stand up for yourself firmly and kindly and then everybody wins. Anyone can stand up for him or herself! I have a friend who is extremely shy and soft-spoken. When she told me she wanted to learn to become a Krazy Coupon Lady, I was concerned. I thought there was no way she would ever be able to talk back to a store manager. She has totally surprised me. She has grown in confidence like krazy. She uses the store policies to do a lot of the talking for her, but she asserts herself as well. Even if you're painfully shy or afraid to ruffle any feathers, isn't that something you'd like to overcome? I think anyone can grow into the role of becoming a sassy coupon lady.

What if the store manager is insistent and you can't agree?

Walk away. Sometimes store managers are pretty bull-headed. Even after you show them the policy, don't be surprised if you hear lines like, "We just had a meeting addressing this..." or "Well, the new policy states....". I think we often intimidate managers, and they scramble for a reason to be right. In their store, they win. So after we've done our best, sometimes we have to walk away. Do so politely. Let them know, "I'm sorry. I won't be able to complete my purchase today." Then get in the car, and after you pull out of the parking lot, commence screaming. When you get home, call the corporate office. They will invariably apologize and take care of you. Sometimes they'll even call and speak to the store manager while you're still on the line.

Shouldn't we be more understanding of a store that doesn't like coupons? Don't they lose money?

No! Stores are reimbursed for every penny. You aren't costing them anything, and they benefit by selling more stuff. My coupons are my currency! They are just as valid as a dollar bill. All the store has to do is mail them off to a clearinghouse that does all the sorting for them. In addition to reimbursement for the coupon's value, the store also receives up to $0.08 in handling fees per coupon, which covers the cost of this process.

The store pays a fee every time I swipe my credit card. It earns money when I pay with coupons and change. Never feel like a sub-class shopper, and never allow yourself to be treated like one.

CHAPTER FOURTEEN

TheKrazyCouponLady.com:

USER GUIDE

At this point you might be thinking "Great! Now that I know all the tricks to couponing, how do I find all the deals? Do I have to spend hours each week searching through every different store ad? Should I be visiting each manufacturer's website on a daily basis for those printable coupons? How in the world am I going to accurately match up all the coupons in my binder with sales?" Well I'm here to bring you the best news you've heard in years. All the work is done, and it's yours for absolutely......FREE. That's right. Zilch, nada, nothing, zip. At TheKrazyCouponLady.com I've created the most comprehensive, up-to-the-minute website for all your coupon needs. You're gonna love it! Only problem is, you may find it difficult to stop hitting the refresh button! Seriously, sometimes I think the website is so addictive it should come with a surgeon general's warning.

TheKrazyCouponLady.com reports deals at most of the major grocery and drug store chains around the nation, as well as retail stores, restaurants, and online sites. You'll find coupon tips for beginners, a database full of thousands of printable coupons, and even ideas on how to increase your income, all in a user-friendly, simple to navigate format. There is so much available at TheKrazyCouponLady.com that this chapter is dedicated just to helping you understand it.

Think of this as your Navigation Manual. I'll start by explaining some of the ways to sort through all the information available on the site.

EXTREME COUPONING

Click "Extreme Couponing" if your binder's itching for a trip to the store. Here you'll find the most recent deals from every grocery store, drugstore, and supercenter all in one place, sorted by most recent.

Wouldn't it be nice if each week all the coupon deals could be purchased at just one store? It would certainly make shopping a whole lot easier. But the previous 13 chapters have just taught you that some weeks you may need to shop at multiple stores in order to take advantage of the most deals. Can you imagine the time it would take to match each coupon with each sale price at the 10 different grocery chains in your area plus the time it takes to shop? I know you love your coupons almost as much as you love your own mother, but I think even you might waver in your allegiance to deal-finding if you had to do all that work yourself! That's why **TheKrazyCouponLady.com** is so vital to your coupon survival. I've got everything you need right here in one place. Under the section titled "Extreme Couponing" you'll find strictly grocery, drugstore and supercenter deals, uninterrupted by any other info on my site.

FIND MY STORE

Click "'Find my Store" to select any one store and see all of its current deals.

Each store has an individual page, so if you're interested in only one store, no need to mess with the rest. Bypass all the others, and go directly to your store's page by clicking on the tab at the top titled, "Find my Store", then highlight the one you want. You'll be taken straight to that store's page where you'll find all their current deals, their coupon policy, as well as a basic tutorial on how to shop there.

With each store's new sales circular, a "weekly deals" post is added to the site, highlighting all the sales and promotions that correlate with that particular ad. In this post I take each store and type up the weekly ad, search my coupon database for coupons that match the products on sale, and then calculate the final price you will pay on that product. All you have to do is get on the site and start reading!

I currently publish deals for the following stores:

(Bear in mind, if you don't see your favorite store below, I am continually expanding the stores covered on my site.)

Grocery Stores

- Albertsons
- Carrs
- Dominick's
- Genuardi's
- HEB
- Kroger
- Pavilions
- Publix
- Randalls
- Safeway
- ShopRite
- Tom Thumb
- Vons
- Whole Foods

Supercenters

- Kmart
- Target
- Walmart

Drugstores

- CVS
- Rite Aid
- Walgreens

As a first time visitor to one of these store pages, you might think the coupon deals look a bit confusing. But once you understand how everything is listed and what everything means, it'll be a breeze. Each product "match-up" (because I'm matching coupons with sale products) looks something like this:

L'Oreal Voluminous Mascara $5.00
Use $2.00/1 L'Oreal Paris Eye Product from RP /17
or $1.00/1 L'Oreal Paris Eye Cosmetic from RP 3/20
or $1.00/1 L'Oreal Paris Cosmetic from SS 5/1
or $1.00/1 – L'Oreal Paris Eye product – (lorealparisusa.com)
Final Price: as low as $3.00

The product is typed in bold with the sale price next to it. All the available coupons for that product are then listed underneath. These include both manufacturer and printable coupons. Next to the manufacturer coupons is the name and date of the newspaper insert where they can be found. The Procter & Gamble insert will be abbreviated as *PG*, the RedPlum insert as *RP*, and the SmartSource insert as *SS*. The printable coupons are underlined and linked to the appropriate website. Remember, you are only allowed to use one manufacturer coupon and one store coupon per item. So although I list multiple coupons underneath the product, you can't use them all. You choose the one you have access to that will result in the best deal. The final price is then calculated and entered on the last line below each product. It's as easy as that. All the products are listed this way. Once you understand what everything means, it's a cinch to read.

Along with the weekly match ups I highlight any great new deals I can find. New additions are being added to the website constantly. Often I post several per hour. Sometimes I'll find a new coupon that makes a current deal even sweeter and I'll post it. Or I'll discover an item on clearance that wasn't even listed in the ad and will post that too! You'll be amazed at the sheer volume of great deals out there.

In addition to the posts of all currents deals, on each store's page you'll find a summary of its coupon policy as well as a basic tutorial and maybe even a video on how to shop there. This information is helpful when trying to navigate a new store. It's not always easy to keep store policies straight, so if there is ever a question concerning policy or rewards systems, these pages have all the answers.

. . . .

STYLE

Click "Style" to see the latest deals on fashion and beauty products!

What good is saving all that money on groceries, if you're going to turn around and blow it all on full-price clothes and cosmetics? Okay, okay, maybe blowing your hard earned (hard *saved*) money on a new wardrobe is a little more fun than spending it on groceries, but why pay retail when you don't have to?

Why spend up to $500 a visit at a salon when you can get the same results for less. Ever considered getting your spa treatments at a beauty school? You could save 60%! What if I told you I can teach you how to make beauty products in your own kitchen that work just like the real thing? I've got all that and more! Saving money and looking your best? Now that's a beautiful thing!

This section is full of tips on how to help you look and feel your very best, including: *How to get makeup samples for free, How to get salon style results at home* and even *How to wear that red lipstick you got for free last week at Walgreens!* Find designer accessories and their budget look-a-likes, and learn to dress like a celebrity from head-to-toe with *The Look for Less!* Trust me, *Saving Never Looked so Good!*

. . . .

TRAVEL

Click "Travel" to find discounted vacations and tips on how to save at destinations across the globe.

Never thought you'd ever be able to afford that dream getaway? Check out this section of my website where you'll find new articles and deals all about traveling on a dime. Whether it's a budget escape like a $15/night hotel deal in Vegas, or a splurge $499 Mediterranean cruise, I won't post the deal unless the savings are, well, krazy!

Affordable travel isn't just about getting there! The travel section will also help you find free attractions from museums to national parks all across the country. There's no need to spend a fortune on activities while traveling. You work hard for your money; I'm here to help you keep some of it while *Turning Travel Dreams into Reality!*

●　●　●　●　●　●　●　●　●　●　●　●　●　●　●　●　●　●　●

FAMILY

Click "Family" for a refreshing take on parenting topics to help you save money and sanity! This is also the home for bargain children's toys, clothes, baby and maternity items.

Kids are never too young to learn the concepts of saving money. With advice for every member of your family, from toddlers to teens, there's something in the family section for everyone. Learn about topics such as: *How to talk to young children about money* or *How to give a child's haircut* (and how to find a deal at a salon in case it goes terribly wrong). With a strong following of teenage Krazy Coupon Ladies, I'll also keep this section stocked with tips such as: How to save on the SAT, *How to rent your college textbooks* and more!

Whether you're shopping for a birthday, a baby shower or a bar mitzvah, this is the place to find gift ideas for everyone! This section will also include fun, free ideas about "repurposing" household items into new toys for kids! Think of the family section like therapy for your household budget. I like to call it *Family Time on a Dime.*

●　●　●　●　●　●　●　●　●　●　●　●　●　●　●　●　●　●　●

HOME

Click on "At Home" if you dream of Pottery Barn style on a Target budget.

When it comes to my biggest money pit, my budget's strongest vacuum and my pocket's most mysterious black hole, I've got one phrase for you: "There's no place like home". I could spend a small fortune on decorating if my husband would let me. Since he doesn't (and thank goodness for that), I've developed some pretty great strategies for getting the Pottery Barn look for less, which I share in the home section.

I want to help you create the atmosphere in your home that you've always wanted. In this section you'll find articles and deals on all things home, from the inside out: redecorating, refinishing, and gardening. And, of course, there's my personal favorite *Knockout Knock-offs*, where I show you how to get almost exact copycats of the most requested high-ticket items: rugs, furniture, housewares and home decor, often at less than half the cost! Don't worry—I'll keep it secret that you're *Saving in the Suburbs*! We think of ourselves as *House-wise Housewives*.

• • • • • • • • • • • • • • • • • • • •

FINANCE

Click "Finance" to read ingenious tips on how to make money from home and better manage your finances.

Coupons can help you lower your monthly expenses, but what if that isn't enough? I know the stress of living paycheck to paycheck, and I hope this section will help! The finance page is filled with articles about how you can increase your income while decreasing your spending. Many of the articles are directed toward stay-at-home moms who have a unique set of obligations that often make it impossible to work full-time. Some of the topics you'll find include: *How to become a mystery shopper, How to earn money by taking surveys online, How to start your own online business, How to flip furniture on Craigslist* and countless others. It's the place to help you *Earn More, Save Better*.

• • • • • • • • • • • • • • • • • • • •

BLOG

Click "Blog" to see the latest and the greatest posts from every category.

If you're one of those ten-times-a-day visitors, I have a feeling this is where you'll want to visit first! When you click "blog", you can read every post in its entirety no matter the category. This is the place to view it all, unbiased and uncensored. This is a constantly revolving section where you can read anything and everything I add to the site. Fashion deals, new coupons, grocery deals, a travel article—it's all here, mixed together, for your betterment, newest deals at the top of the page! Click refresh every 10 minutes and it's the game that never ends!

• • • • • • • • • • • • • • • • • •

PRINT COUPONS

Click "Print Coupons" to reach all of my comprehensive coupon databases, filled with thousands of coupons you can print, clip or load electronically!

With thousands of available coupons from many hundreds of online sources changing, refreshing, and expiring daily, it would be nearly impossible for you to keep track of them all on your own. *Trust me on this, it's all I can do to keep all of them updated myself!* Since it's way too big a job for any busy Krazy Coupon Lady, I (with a little help from my friends!) keep a comprehensive list of all current printable coupons as well as coupons from the Sunday newspaper inserts and eCoupons.

- **Printable Coupons.** To select a printable coupon from the more than 2000 alphabetized links, just click the coupon you'd like to print. The hyperlinked URL will open in a new window and you can take the steps to print your desired coupon. This is *The Legal Way to Print Money!*

- **Newspaper Coupons.** Wondering if there has been a Colgate toothpaste coupon in the last 3 months to pair with a sale next week? Click the Newspaper Coupons tab to be taken to an alphabetical listing of all unexpired coupons as well as the name of the coupon insert and the Sunday when it was released.

- **eCoupons.** Similar to the printable coupons, simply select the eCoupon you wish to load electronically to your store card and you'll be taken to the page where you can log in and proceed.

My database is updated constantly: thousands of coupons listed alphabetically and separated into their own database according to the type of coupon. Who needs sugar when you've got alphabetization?

BEGINNERS

Click "Beginners" to review the basic principles of couponing.

It's not always easy being the new girl in school, what with all those eyes on you. It can be a little nerve-racking and a bit intimidating. But it's like that whenever you start something new. There's always a learning curve, even with couponing. Don't get frustrated, and above all don't give up. Because I know how hard it can be, I've dedicated an entire section of my site to beginners, or as I affectionately like to call you, "coupon virgins'", in hopes of lessening the sheer grade on that learning curve. I want to be there for you in as many ways as possible. On this page of my site you'll find a fun ten-step program to becoming a Krazy Coupon Lady that covers all the basics in a very straightforward manner. You'll find the *How to Become a Krazy Coupon Lady in Ten Days* series reiterates a lot of what you've already learned in this book and reminds you of the most important tools.

BRAG LOUNGE

Click "Brag Lounge" to upload a photo of your shopping trip and share how much you saved!

Couponing will soon become so much more than saving money. With each new shopping trip you'll try to outdo the last savings total, all in an attempt to increase that savings. It's a challenge that can quickly turn into a game! The "buzz" that comes from it is so amazing that sometimes you just can't keep it in. Because of this I've created an entire section of my site called *The Brag Lounge* dedicated just to that: bragging! It's one of the only places left on earth where bragging is not only socially acceptable, but welcomed! In fact, you can brag as much as you want without annoying anyone. It's the perfect place to share all your coupon successes. I love to go on and read all about what other people are able to do with coupons. It's motivating and inspiring!

FREE DAILY EMAILS

No matter how many times you check the website, chances are you probably missed something! Since I loathe the thought of you unnecessarily paying retail price, make sure to sign up for my newsletter by adding your email to my mailing list. You'll receive a once-daily email with every post from the last 24 hours. And don't worry, this timely, daily, afternoon delivery won't wake up your napping children with a loud ring of your doorbell. More than I can say for those other delivery guys!

FACEBOOK & TWITTER

http://www.facebook.com/thekrazycouponlady/

http://twitter.com/krazycouponlady

Not only do my facebook and twitter fans get the most recent deals through my feeds, they're also privy to sneak previews, giveaways and exclusive discussions. It's just another way to keep you in the know.

 This chapter isn't meant to try and sell you on the website. I'm just proud of all that is available to you. I know how hard it can be to try and save money or pay off debt. I know how strapped for time and how overextended life can get. That's why I'm letting you know that I'm here to help—just a click away.

FAQs:

Why am I not getting all the coupons listed on TheKrazyCouponLady.com?

Coupons, as well as price and promotion, vary by region. So sometimes a deal I list on the website won't be available to everyone. Or it might just not be as great in your area. On any given Sunday, someone in California may get a $0.50 off raisins coupon, while someone in New Jersey gets a $0.75 off 2 raisins coupon and someone in Texas gets a $1.00 off 2 raisins and someone in Florida doesn't get a raisin coupon at all. This is why I list all of the available coupons for every deal on my website. Don't let these variances get you too frustrated—it's just the way it is.

Why do my out of pocket expenses always end up being way more than I'm expecting?

It's important to remember that you pay taxes on the pre-coupon price of the product. For example, you buy Huggies at a price of $8.00 and use both a $3.00 manufacturer coupon and a $3.00 store coupon dropping the final price to $2.00. You'll be paying taxes on the $8.00. So sometimes the actual out of pocket (OOP) expense is a little more than expected. And at **TheKrazyCouponLady.com** I can't calculate taxes on the final price because taxes vary state to state.

You might be a Krazy Coupon Lady if...
your husband clips coupons
to get you in the mood.

SECTION FOUR

Banking the Cash

WHEN A WOMAN HAS DONE HER BEST, HAS GIVEN
HER ALL, AND IN THE PROCESS SUPPLIED THE NEEDS
OF HER FAMILY AND HER SOCIETY, THAT WOMAN
HAS MADE A HABIT OF SUCCEEDING.

Couponing for Life

Now that you have all the tools to save massive amounts at the grocery store, let's talk about what you're going to do with all the money you are saving. Some of you will coupon to survive. For you, there is no money left in your account at the end of the month. Your finances are fixed and you're feeling the pinch. You've learned how to save on groceries, but what else can you do to help pull yourself out of this confining financial predicament? How about extending the principles of couponing into other areas of spending? You'll start to see that your checking account has more and more wiggle room the longer you practice couponing. You'll then need to start deciding exactly what to do with that money. Invest? Save? Donate?

Either way, let's talk. Don't get me wrong; I'm no Dave Ramsey or Suze Orman, although I have read books from both of them. I'm no accountant or economist or other expert VIP. I am just a stay-at-home mom who has learned to live on less and can now afford the things that are important to me.

The best part about learning how to budget like a Krazy Coupon Lady? I'm not depriving you of any one thing. I'm teaching you how to get what you want at a price you can pay—not a price you can "charge".

Jean Chatzky, financial analyst for *The Today Show*, writes in her book *The Difference*:

There are only four things standing in the way of any one individual and financial security.

- You have to make a decent living.

- You have to spend less than you make.

- You have to invest the money you're not spending so that it can work just as hard for you as you are working for yourself.

- You have to protect yourself and this financial life you're building so that a disaster—large or small—can't come along and take it all away from you.

These points aren't rocket science. Just like the principles in this book, they don't exactly make your eyes glaze over with their complexity. It's common sense. But it never hurts to live your financial life on tried and true common sense practices! Remember, couponing isn't about saving nickels and dimes. It is about saving enough money to make a big difference in your budget and build a stockpile to protect you in an emergency. Soon your family and your finances will be thriving with the sound implementation of these principles. That light at the end of the tunnel might seem far away for some, which is why the following section is geared toward the many of you who are already in debt, struggling to pay your bills, and becoming desperate. Don't give up; hope is not lost. Congratulations! You're about to become a coupon survivor.

CHAPTER FIFTEEN

Couponing to Survive

Let's start with those of you who are couponing because there is no money in your budget for groceries. Maybe your spouse is out of work. Perhaps your family is growing faster than your income, or maybe you're up to your eyeballs in credit card debt. Whatever the reason, there is hope.

• • • • • • • • • • • • • • • • • • •

HEATHER'S STORY:

About 4 years ago, just after I had my second son, my husband and I looked at our income and our expenses and realized we were in some financial trouble. I had been working as a hair stylist from my home. But with the birth of our second child, it became too hard on our family for me to continue working. We crunched the numbers and projected that in a few months we wouldn't comfortably be able to make all of our payments. So we decided to take action and get drastic. We put our house up for sale and made an offer on another house 25 miles away. The new house was smaller, older, and half an hour away from our friends and family. We sold our house and moved our family to a little city where we knew no one. As drastic as this was, we weren't done yet. This move allowed us to lower our monthly expenses, but we also wanted to increase our monthly income. My husband found a second job, and within a few months we were able to lower our expenses by about 30% and raise our income by 30%. Over the next four years, with the help of my Krazy Coupon Lady habits, we were able to pay off credit cards, medical debt, and student loans to the tune of nearly $60,000. Our family is now debt free (with the exception of our house, which I plan to pay off in the next four years!) and my husband was able to quit his second job! The years that it took to pay off our debt weren't easy. We went without family vacations, eating out, nice cars, new clothes; and we worked long hours. But what we have gained in return has been life changing! We are now enjoying financial freedom; we have a growing savings account; we are teaching our small children about being financially responsible; and we have enjoyed taking our "giving" to a new level by helping those in need. And, not to be forgotten, we're planning a long-overdue family vacation!

If you are living paycheck to paycheck (or even worse, with the help of a plastic card), it's time to stop. Evaluate your situation and develop a radical strategy to get out of your financial mess!

The two basic ways to become more financially secure are (1) spend less and (2) make more. Not exactly advanced calculus, right? But like all too many things in life, these principles are a little tougher to implement than they sound.

●　●　●　●　●　●　●　●　●　●　●　●　●　●　●　●　●　●

SPEND LESS

If you're anything like me, you need more specific guidance than someone just saying, "Hey, spend less!" Here are a few tips to help you scale down your expenses and take control of your funds.

WRITE OUT A BUDGET

Make, use, and stick to a budget. For me, that means no debit card in my wallet...seriously! I give myself envelopes with cash in them for each of my categories. This strategy might not be necessary for every family, but if you have a history of trouble when it comes to managing your spending habits (be honest), give this idea a serious look. When my cash is gone, I am done spending for the month. My categories include:

- **Groceries:** I use a weekly budget for this category, rather than monthly.

- **Household/Miscellaneous:** this includes little trips to Target, McDonald's, the dry cleaner, etc.

- **House Maintenance:** this gets mostly used at Home Depot and usually gets spent on paint, weed killer, etc.

- **Kids:** this is the envelope I bring to Chuck E. Cheese, miniature golfing, or the water park.

- **Date Night:** I try to be religious about date nights. Some weeks, it's what keeps me sane. We don't do anything extravagant—usually just dinner with a coupon and a dollar movie—but having it budgeted gets us out, and I need that. Even if your budget is really tight, set aside $10 per month. Find ways to do things for less. Take a walk, get ice cream, or put the kids down and rent a movie. You can even check out my website for free RedBox and Blockbuster Express codes.

PURGE YOUR POCKETBOOK

Cut back on extras. It may sounds heartless, but as they say, a sharp knife is better than a dull spoon. Break up with whatever is holding you back. Ditch the cable TV, ditch the gym memberships, and stop eating out. You can watch all the good TV shows free online anyway, the park is a nice (free!) place for a jog, and with your couponing, you'll have plenty of groceries to cook with at home. Get rid of anything you can live without.

Have a garage sale, or sell big items that you haven't used for a few years on Craigslist. Sure, if it's a grandfather clock that's been in your family for three generations, you can keep it. But look around and get rid of your outgrown clothes, unused toys, and over-indulgent things you really shouldn't have bought in the first place. Be ruthless about what you get rid of. Ask yourself, honestly, "Have I used this in the last year or two?" If the answer is no, it's gotta go. I recently (and sadly) parted with some pretty hot designer jeans that I'm just not fitting back into and finally decided to sell online. While it was sad to say goodbye to that small of a bottom, it was pretty nice to have an extra fifty bucks.

ELIMINATE CREDIT CARD DEBT

Before you can pay down your debt, you must get real about the debt you have. Find your credit statements or call your credit companies. Write down on paper the numbers and balances of all your credit cards. When I know I'm overeating, I avoid the bathroom scale like the plague. I go months without making eye contact with it. Within these months, I can easily gain five to ten pounds. Then, one morning I get brave and in my moment of resolve, run into the bathroom, step on the scale, and look at the number. It usually ruins the rest of my day and I feel a bit depressed. But this day is always the beginning of the next phase where I buckle down and re-lose that five to ten pounds. I run through this cycle over and over. But I have never once been able to lose any weight without first stepping on the scale to weigh the damage. I can't lose weight until I have the hard numbers. Paying off debt is the same as losing weight. Without the actual numbers in front of you, you won't succeed. I know it sounds scary, but don't be afraid of totaling your credit card balances. Right now! Put this book down and go get your statements. One proven method you may use when paying off your credit card debt is to begin paying extra on the card with the lowest balance. Another method is to begin by paying on the card with the highest interest rate. Once you completely pay off the first card, take the money you were paying on the first card and put it toward the next smallest card, and so on. Do what it takes to become debt-free.

ELIMINATE CAR PAYMENTS

If you have a car payment, sell your car and buy something reliable enough to get you from point A to point B (or, in couponing, from Safeway to Walgreens). There is no use driving a Lexus while you are living paycheck to paycheck. That's like putting on your prom gown for dinner at McDonald's. Sell your car. Don't trade it in. Don't lease. Sell, and pay cash for a car you can afford. With the money you'll be saving by couponing, if it's that important to you, you'll get your Lexus back soon enough, and this time you'll be able to afford it!

MAKE MORE

Maybe your household has one income, or maybe you have two. You may already be working full-time, or perhaps you're a stay-at-home mom. Either way, figure out a way to bring in some more cash. The rest of this chapter addresses people who are currently staying home with their children or would like to begin staying home. Whatever your situation may be, adjust these principles so they work for you.

COMMIT

I love to start projects and I love the exhilaration of beginning something new. It's the finishing that always bogs me down! About halfway through a project, the glamour is gone, the work becomes a reality, and my attention span is mostly spent. This is where the real test of my spirit begins…and reveals character I'm still working to improve. If you're serious about making money, you have to be serious about seeing this vision all the way through. Don't expect to give it a try, and then, if it doesn't smell like roses in three months, dream and scheme up a new idea. Commit, stick to it and finish.

Newsflash: all those spam emails in your inbox offering $1,000 per week by working from home are big whopping lies. If it sounds too good to be true, it is. There are no get-rich-quick schemes, and there are no magic diet pills (and if there were, Oprah would have already told you about them). There are two things to which I attribute my corner of success: one is God's blessings in my life and the other is LOTS of hard work. I think Jillian Michaels, trainer from *The Biggest Loser*, said it best: "I believe in blood, sweat and tears." Though she may have been referring to a workout, it really all boils down to discipline. So, do like Jillian says, "Unless you puke, faint, or die, keep going!"

FIND YOUR PASSION

What do you enjoy? If you had to spend four hours a day doing something, what would it be? Is there any way that your hobby or some related field could earn you an income? If you scrapbook, could you sell your services or pre-packaged materials? Could you buy products wholesale and resell them online? If you love working out, could you teach classes from your home or at a local park? Maybe a "Mommy and Me" class? Think about something that is really worthwhile in your life that you'd love to share with others. Teach a class; teach voice lessons, music lessons; do tutoring of any kind. Offer babysitting or even clean houses.

A dear friend of mine, Arlynne, mother of six children, needed to supplement her family's income during the time of her husband's unemployment. But how can a mother of six have time to work, especially with the youngest two boys too young for school? Arlynne got creative and decided to clean bathrooms or houses a few days a week with her two littlest boys in tow. Although her job is neither glamorous nor easy, she makes it work in order to supplement her family's income. She's a wife, a mother, and she's not afraid to roll up her sleeves and work hard. And whether she's scrubbing a floor or strutting across it, she looks good doing it! She's got confidence, she's got sass, and she wears it well, no matter which of her many hats she's wearing. That is what being a Krazy Coupon Lady is all about.

Whatever your business vision, can you come up with a way to have zero overhead cost? If you have business expenses, get creative with financing. When I needed to print business cards for the first time, I didn't pay a printer. I found a stationery company and offered them advertising space on my website in exchange for business cards. Many of my business expenses have been financed in the same manner. I remember being a little nervous to go out and ask for swaps or get ad accounts on my website. But I didn't let that stop me, and it shouldn't stop you either. Find your niche and then find others who are trying to appeal to the same demographic. You can swap products or advertising and build positive networking relationships at the same time.

Evaluate Time

Where and when will you have time for this new endeavor? What can you cut from your life to make room for this? Don't add one more giant chore to your platter. You'll have to reorganize and prioritize your schedule to make time to earn an extra income. The wise Stephen R. Covey says, "The key is not to prioritize what's on your schedule, but to schedule your priorities."

Get Support

Make sure that your spouse and children are on board. If they aren't supportive, you'll have a hard time making your business successful. Often business opportunities present themselves as hobbies at first. Then slowly they turn into a way to make money. At this point, you will need to re-evaluate with your spouse the expectations both of you have.

Is this something that you can start and run on your own? One of the most crucial pieces of advice I can offer you is to choose wisely when deciding on a potential business partner. The water can become very rough when you mix a friendship and a business. We [Heather and Joanie] function like clockwork. One of our strengths compensates for the other's weakness, and we're still best friends. But it's fair to say that we're the exception, not the rule. Someone you would choose to be your best friend may not be the same person with whom you would do business. If you can run this business by yourself, try it out. If it becomes too hard, then bring someone else in. If you start a business with a friend, make the terms very clear. Get everything in writing and specifically include what you expect from each person.

Don't give up. Release your inner Mom-preneur, and email me if you need a pep talk. You can do it!

For more advice on becoming debt-free and financially independent, I recommend:

- *The Total Money Makeover: A Proven Plan for Financial Fitness, 3rd edition* by Dave Ramsey (December, 2009)

- *Suze Orman's The Money Class: Learn to Create Your New American Dream* (March, 2011)

- *The Difference: How Anyone Can Prosper in Even the Toughest Times* by Jean Chatzky (March, 2010)

Whichever of these methods you apply in your life, just remember, in order to change your financial situation you have to spend less and make more. As simple as it sounds, this is how you make a difference; this is how alter your current course; this is how you change your stars. Have hope. It can happen!

FAQs:

Am I allowed to use using coupons on top of food stamps?

YES! You can! While you absolutely can use coupons to make your food stamps go further, you may want to bring some spare change with you. Since a 3rd party (the manufacturer) will be reimbursing the value of the coupons you use, the store must charge sales tax on the value of the coupons. Remember, coupons are a form of payment NOT A DISCOUNT—so essentially, the manufacturer is paying that portion of your bill, and you are responsible for the tax.

How do I know if I'm setting a realistic grocery budget for my family of 5?

According to the USDA, if you are being thrifty, a grocery budget for 3 young children and 2 adults should sit around $650 per month. Obviously, with the use of coupons you can cut that budget tremendously. The most helpful thing you can do is calculate your pre-coupon grocery budget. As you begin couponing, pay attention to how this number drops. Soon you'll get into a groove and you'll learn exactly what your family needs. Then you'll be able to readjust your budget to account for coupons.

How do I get my spouse on board with these spending cuts?

It may take a few months, but as your grocery budget plummets, the numbers will speak for you. As you begin to see more wiggle room in your wallet, your spouse just might catch on. Remember to be patient and set the example, and hopefully he'll eventually see the light!

CHAPTER SIXTEEN

Couponing to Thrive

Once you pay off your debt, the real fun begins. Now what do you do with all that extra cash? To save or to spend; that is the question. There are endless possibilities. No matter what you choose, just make sure that money improves your life today AND in the future. There's nothing worse than mindless, uncontrolled spending bringing a bit of joy now but ultimately resulting in financial hardship in the future. Long term financial independence is your ultimate goal. So use your brain, your time, and your savvy skills to keep improving your situation.

When I first started couponing, I had a very impatient husband. He wanted quick results, and he wasn't seeing them. I was having so much fun building my stockpile that I was spending almost the same amount each month on groceries as my pre-couponing days. My very skeptical sweetie saw me spending hours more a month on the computer, at the grocery store, organizing my binder, bragging to my friends, but he wasn't seeing me spend less money. He was worried. Suddenly, when our stockpile was established, we saw an enormous drop in our spending. After about three months, we were spending half of what we'd spent before. I can't even express how great it felt to realize how much room we'd just made in our budget.

At my house, our average savings runs between $600 and $800...PER MONTH. Here are a few examples from our monthly budget for a family of four. In April, I spent $286.15 on all my grocery shopping, including household shopping, cleaning supplies and toiletries. Without coupons, my total would have been $1,133.60. That's a savings of 76%. In May I spent $267.62 on all my shopping, and my total before coupons was $942.72, a savings of 72%. I did thirty-one transactions in May—yikes! That's like going to the store every day. (Don't worry, I didn't *actually* go to the store every day. I just did multiple transactions in one shopping trip.) And those were big stockpiling months where I spent more than I usually do! June was more typical. I spent $117.01 on all my groceries, toiletries, produce, meat—everything! My totals before coupons were $540.58, a savings of 78%.

I never kept a strict grocery budget before couponing, but between my weekly shopping trips, my late afternoon grocery runs, and my wholesale club massacres, my monthly grocery budget was around $500.00. I did my best to shop generics, sales, and cook cost-effective meals, but my grocery budget still sat around $500 per month.

Now that I coupon, during a big spending month, I'm still spending only about half of my old grocery budget. The most beneficial result of couponing is my stockpile of food and toiletries worth many thousands of dollars. But my family also has an extra $250-$400 dollars in our pockets each month.

Once you have your stockpile and some extra money on hand every month, you're left with a decision. What do I do with all that extra money? It's tempting to take biannual trips to Tahiti or douse your home in Pottery Barn, but hang on a second. I do love vacations, Pottery Barn (and don't forget my beloved Banana Republic), as much as anybody, but let's start thinking long term.

●　●　●　●　●　●　●　●　●　●　●　●　●　●　●　●　●

SAVE

Now that you're sold on the idea of paying off debt, what's the next step? With no more credit card debt, vanished car payments, and student loans a thing of the past, you've definitely got some wiggle room. The most important thing to do is stay the course. Once you become debt-free, the trick is to stay debt free. This means it's time to stockpile money. That's right. Build up your cash reserves! This way, if your car breaks, your dryer blows up, you need a new roof, or whatever surprise comes next, you won't need to borrow from your in-laws or even worse, a credit card company. You'll be able to meet unexpected expenses with ease just by going to your own bank account.

Paying yourself is one of the most important things you can do with your money, especially now that you have extra! Saving is KEY to financial security. Whether it's for that glam vacation, college tuition, or a retirement that will inevitably come sooner than you think, putting away money is essential. The principles here mimic those of stockpiling, and the rewards are the same: peace, security, and self-reliance. So one of the smartest things you can do with your newfound financial freedom is to put a predetermined amount of money into some sort of account every single month.

● ● ● ● ● ● ● ● ● ● ● ● ● ● ● ● ● ● ●

Where is the Best Place to Put Your Savings?

A few options include:

Money Market Accounts

These accounts are great for money that needs to be accessible like your cash stockpile. Money Market accounts allow your investment to earn a little interest while still remaining completely available to you, if need be. An average money market interest rate sits between 1.0-1.5% APY, slightly higher than a simple savings account. It's frequently suggested that you let your cash reserves build in a money market account until it's enough money to sustain your family completely for 4-6 months, including make your mortgage payment.

401K

This is a retirement plan for employees of participating companies. Check with your employer to see if he offers this type of investment vehicle. Contributions to a 401K may be made with pre-tax dollars, and often employers will match a maximum monthly contribution. 401K money will be taxed when you begin to take money out, so it is not the ideal investment for money you may need prior to retirement age.

IRAs

Individual Retirement Accounts are another great way to save and grow your money long-term. You may contribute up to $5,000 per year (unless you're over fifty, then you may contribute $6,000). IRAs are another great way to avoid paying taxes as you're trying to save. In a traditional IRA you make pre-tax contributions, and much like a 401K, your money will only be taxed when you take it out. A Roth IRA is my family's personal savings preference. A Roth IRA allows you to contribute after-tax money, but then when you want to retire in twenty, thirty, or forty years, you can withdraw the money tax-free! I love not giving the government more of my money almost as much as I love giving less of it to the grocery stores!

Education Savings Accounts (ESAs)

Think about your kids' college. Whether they are fifteen, five, or five months, you should be building some sort of college fund for them. The best option is an Educational Savings Account. This sort of account earns interest, and it is tax-FREE as long as it is used for Education.

MAKE IT FUN

Many people don't realize it, but saving can be just as fun and rewarding as spending. Think about it beyond the traditional bank account options. Maybe make it a family event. Put the money in a jar earmarked for a family activity, trip, or big purchase. See how supportive your little grocery helpers and coupon clippers become when they're working toward that one thing they've always wanted. Have your heart set on something just for you (how about a nice duvet cover from Pottery Barn, a favorite hardcover book, or some new MAC makeup)? Cut the picture out of the magazine and tape it to a jar just for you! In a few months, you'll be knocking on the glass doors at the mall, waiting for them to open so you can go get what you've so painstakingly earned. What about all the extra change in your pockets? If you're anything like me it gets lost somewhere between the couch cushions, the dryer, or the bottomless pit of my bulging purse. Ever thought about putting it in one place, like a large jar and letting it accumulate? A friend of mine does this with his change, and in no time he returns from cashing it in at the bank with a couple hundred dollars in his pocket. Who would've thought all those nickels and dimes could turn into that? Every penny makes a difference!

However you choose to save, make it a priority. Use as many options as you can and feel the security that comes from knowing you've got extra to take care of the unexpected. When you pay yourself first, it's much easier to know how much is left over for you to spend!

●　●　●　●　●　●　●　●　●　●　●　●　●　●　●　●　●

SPEND

I love pretty things: furniture, picture frames, fireplaces, jetted tubs, jewelry, shoes, dessert, diamonds, Hawaiian vacations...you get the idea. Sure, living large *sounds* nice: strawberry daiquiris at the beach by day, pampering and ice cream by night, with handsome foreign men rubbing my perfectly manicured feet while I read ridiculous novels. But at the end of the day, all the treats would rot my teeth, and I'd be spoiled and unhappy. What makes us truly happy are the people around us and our relationships with others. Money problems corrupt relationships and bring stress into the family home. My husband would spend himself into techno-oblivion if I didn't bring him back to reality, and my daughter would be dressed like Suri Cruise if he didn't do the same for me.

But, I'm not one to advocate all work and no play. So sure, go ahead and treat yourself to something nice every now and then. If you save $400 a month by couponing, why not spend $100 on a new pair of jeans and invest the other portion? Or put half of it in your family vacation fund and the other have in college savings? The Krazy Coupon Lady is not about deprivation. I'm not suggesting you move to a trailer and sell all your belongings just so you can be debt-free. Just make sure to be moderate in your spending. Become content living on less. Make that attitude shift that allows you to be happy with just what you have.

Often it takes more than just a few good ideas floating around upstairs to avoid overspending. It takes a real, tangible plan. Write down those few things you'd love to purchase. Figure out how it fits into your budget, and always make sure to pay yourself first. This ensures that you won't end up like a washed-up reality TV star.

SPEND TO EARN

Once you've figured out what you're going to do with your extra cash and IF you're good with credit cards, why not consider using one of the better cards to earn cash back on your expenditures? Since spending is inevitable, this is a great way to spend and earn at the same time. Some cards will give you up to 6% back on your balance. Some help you earn flying miles that you can put towards that awesome destination you have your eye on. Look for a card that pays the highest cash back in the areas where your spending is greatest: things like gas stations, department stores, and grocery stores! No matter which you choose, always make sure to pay the balance off every month. No amount of cash back will make up for the interest and finance charges you'll incur if you forget to pay your bill!

PAY OFF YOUR HOUSE

You don't always have to think of spending in terms of frivolous, unnecessary items. Why not spend your extra zeroes on something that will allow even more financial freedom in the future? I dream of the day when I've completely paid for my home. I get a little giddy imagining writing the last check to my mortgage company. Once you have paid off all your credit cards, student loans, and car loans, make it a priority to pay extra toward your mortgage. Simply by making two extra mortgage payments per year on a fixed, 30-year mortgage, you'll pay off your loan 10 years early—saving you thousands!

Spending is fun and exhilarating. It brings moments of joy and excitement. And it certainly can be rewarding, especially when done in the right way. You deserve some fun after all the hard work you've done transforming your budget and couponing your way to financial freedom. The key is moderation combined with a very clear plan! Save a little here, spend a bit there. Whatever you choose, create a plan and stick with it. Make your future as bright as your today! Remember, you don't want to end up on *Lifestyles of the Rich and the Stupid.*

FAQs:

What's the best savings account to start for young children?

Any of type of savings account is great. The key is to save! Look for a bank with a higher interest rate and no fees. Consider putting money in an Education Account where you can earn interest over a long period of time, tax free!

How much of your income should be put into savings?

It's safe to say that putting nothing less than 10% of your income into some type of savings program is a good place to start. Of course, contributing more than that will only set you up for a more stable future. But 10% is a good number to live by.

CHAPTER SEVENTEEN

Couponing to Live

Have you ever found yourself wondering how that friend of yours can afford her designer jeans? Or how your neighbor pays for all those family getaways? What about that flat screen TV your husband's been drooling over for the last 12 months? In this chapter I'll walk you through all the ways to save on restaurants, clothes, hotels, and furniture, while teaching you the tricks to get what you want at a price you can afford! Really, nothing is off limits. See how far that extra bit of money you've dedicated to spending goes when you put these tips into practice.

•   •   •   •   •   •   •   •   •   •   •   •   •   •   •   •   •   •

ALL THINGS RETAIL

Why would anyone ever be content paying full price for a product? There's no need. It's ridiculous, unnecessary, and completely avoidable. When it comes to retail stores, you can almost always get what you want at a fraction of the cost. But you've got to know the tricks. Sometimes all it takes is a big dose of that thing called patience. Other times you've just got to know where to look.

LEARN THE SCHEDULE

Stores run on a schedule just like the rest of us. Uncovering this coveted information can be the secret to savings. Usually, a store does mark-downs on a regular basis, often on the same day each week. By knowing when this occurs, you can be sure to have first dibs on those newly reduced prices. Oftentimes you come by this information simply by being a frequent customer. Other times you may need to ask when things go on sale and when new promotions begin. At my mall, Wednesday is the day when prices are marked down and new promotions begin at The Children's Place. So you'll never find me shopping there on a Tuesday. Instead, on Tuesdays, I'm shopping the fresh sale racks at the Gap. Knowing the schedule can help you buy at the right time and ensure you never go home with a product that ends up half the price the following day!

But don't worry if you forget the sale schedule at your favorite department store. I've still got you covered. Most retailers offer a one-time price adjustment. If a post-purchase clearance price has you feeling buyer's remorse, simply take your receipt back into the store within the specified time period (usually 7-14 days) and the retailer will refund you the difference between what you paid and the newly reduced price.

SHOP CLEARANCE AND THINK AHEAD

I'm the kind of customer that walks into a store and heads straight to the back. I seldom let those full priced products entice me, no matter how appealing they may be. Why shop any other way when I've had so much success with the clearance section? Recently, I went into a rather high-end clothing store. I found an amazing dress and the perfect cardigan for nearly 70% off the retail price. I rarely shopped at this store simply because I thought I couldn't afford it. Oh, how wrong I was! The clearance section really has become one of my best allies in my quest to save money.

One way to really make the clearance racks work for you is to think ahead. If I buy a child's winter coat in September or October when the stores are just breaking them out, I could pay the full retail price of $49.50. But I wait and buy the exact coat in March for $9.97 in a size up for next year. Now when the next winter comes around, my daughter will have a brand new $50 coat that I got for almost nothing. It's sort of like stockpiling—but for clothes instead of canned tomatoes! Take kids' clothes, again, for example. If you find your favorite brand of jeans on clearance for $6.97, why not buy them in a couple of different washes in a few bigger sizes. Next year, when the old pants are worn out or too small, you won't even need to leave your house. All you do is go to your little clothing stockpile and grab from your stash. If I didn't spend a penny on clothes for the next twelve months, my kids would be so well-dressed no one would know the difference. Believe it or not, I have an entire year's worth of clothes boxed up in my garage. I've taken the idea of stockpiling clearance finds and applied it, not only to my kid's clothes, but also to gifts, office supplies, and school supplies.

This same principle of waiting for clearance and planning ahead applies to holiday and seasonal items, as well. Why buy that brand new patio set at the beginning of the summer when you know in just a few short months it will be a fraction of the cost? As a newlywed, I had almost no Christmas decorations. But instead of heading to the store at the beginning of December and breaking the bank, I decided to wait and purchase all my decorations right after Christmas. When I walked in the door following this after-Christmas shopping trip, my husband almost fell over. I dropped several large, bulging bags to the floor and proudly announced that my total of almost $350 dollars dropped to barely $70. Shop clearance, think ahead, and buy in multiples. These three simple principles can save your budget and help you afford things you never thought possible.

Shop for Coupons

Oftentimes, before I even leave the house I do a quick Internet search for any online discounts. I type in the store name, and almost always some type of coupon will pop up. These discounts usually come in 2 forms. They're either the traditional coupon format that can be printed off and physically taken into the store or a coupon code that you type in at checkout when shopping online. These discounts come in many varieties: free shipping, $ off a certain purchase amount, or a percentage off your total. Whatever the coupon or code may be, it's definitely worth your time.

Participate

I love when my checker hands me my receipt and there on the bottom of it is the option to participate in a survey. You better believe I go home, get online or call the number and spend my 5 minutes completing the survey. I'm always rewarded with an amazing coupon for my next trip to that store. One of my favorites is 15% off my next purchase. It may not sound like a lot, but since I'm always buying clearance, this 15% makes my final total even more unbeatable.

When you hear those dreaded words, "May I have your email?" maybe rethink your reflex response of "no" and consider adding your name to a store's email list. Most retailers, if not all of them, have great emailing programs. If you're on the list, you're guaranteed first notice of all the newest mark-downs, upcoming promotions, and even special discounts that apply just to you. You only know if you let them in. So go ahead and hand over that .com of yours. Don't want an inbox full of junk mail? Set up a separate email account for all of your bargain hunting. You'll give this email strictly to retailers at the mall and at home on websites that require you to sign up in order to print coupons.

Many stores have some type of program you can join. Most of them are absolutely free with little or no hassle. All you do is sign up and enjoy. These come in many varieties: reward programs, birthday clubs, memberships. By simply joining a reward program, for example, you earn points with every purchase. These points accumulate, eventually turning into money towards future purchases. Some stores' birthday clubs send out free gifts on your birthday or free % off coupons. Why not join? It's just another way that retailers try to keep their customers happy and loyal.

• • • • • • • • • • • • • • • • • • •

STORE TO STORE

Now take these simple rules and see how they work in individual stores. Here's a quick look at some of my favorite places to shop:

Amazon.com

- Sign up for *Amazon Mom* to receive free shipping, discounted diapers and wipes, and exclusive offers via email.

- Join *Amazon Student* to receive free two-day shipping and more deals exclusively for students.

- Consider *Amazon Prime*, a membership program that gives you and your family unlimited fast shipping, such as FREE Two-Day shipping and One-day shipping for $3.99 per item for an annual membership fee of $79.

- Consider buying slightly used items. Look for the products that say "Like New" and "Very Good" with high ratings.

- Receive *Free Super Saver Shipping* on qualifying orders over $25.

- Look into the *Subscribe & Save* program that offers an extra 15% off and free shipping when you purchase products you routinely use, and choose to have them delivered at specified intervals.

Ann Taylor

- Shop during the *additional 50% off sale* for shockingly low prices.

- Search for coupons. Several times a year Ann Taylor releases high percent-off printable coupons. It's easy to uncover coupon codes online, like *30% off your total purchase* and *free shipping*.

- Pay attention to price adjustments. Ann Taylor offers a one-time price adjustment within 7 days of your store purchase. If the price of the item you bought drops within that time frame, take your receipt back to the store, and they will credit your original form of payment with the difference.

- Sign up for Ann Taylor's mailing program. Every quarter or so you will get really exciting coupons in the mail, like *$25 off your purchase (no exclusions)* or *$10 off your $25 purchase*!

Banana Republic

- Consider shopping online rather than in-store. You'll often find discount codes, like *25% off any purchase over $100*, or *40% off any women's style*.

- Shipping is free for any purchase of $50 or more, and you can make free returns in store, if needed.

- Be aware of price adjustments. Banana Republic offers a one-time adjustment on in-store and online purchases within 14 days of purchase.

Barnes & Noble

- Search for discount codes and coupons before shopping.

- Check out their *Bargain Books* section in stores.

- Check out their *Deal of the Day* online. You can often get their featured deals for over 50% off the retail price.

- Shipping is always free on purchases of $25 or more.

Bath & Body Works

- Look for those coupons hanging out in the bottom of your bag after your purchase. Many of them offer up to *20% off your next purchase* or *Buy One Get One Free* on a certain product.

- Do a quick online search for printable coupons before heading to the store. You'll typically find coupons such as: *Free Item, with minimum $10 purchase* or *$10 off $30 purchase.*

- Remember, some of the best times to shop at Bath & Body are after the holidays or when a scent/product is being phased out.

Bed, Bath & Beyond

- Get on the mailing list (snail mail, that is) and receive frequent coupons worth *20% off any item* or *$5 off a $15 purchase.* If your coupon expires, don't toss it yet. Many BB&B stores still accept mailer coupons, even after expiration date.

- While in store, always check the clearance racks, usually located on the end caps or center aisle.

- Create a gift registry and receive a 10% discount on items you don't receive.

- Get a friend to create her registry and get a $25 gift card for yourself.

Best Buy

- Price match in Best Buy stores and online! You can request a price match at the time of purchase or any time during the return period (14-60 days)!

- Check out their online outlet where you can access their *Deal of the Day*, last chance items, refurbished items, and any other item that has been recently discounted.

- *Ship to Store* for free shipping!

- Sign up for *Best Buy Reward Zone*, especially if you're making a large purchase. Get 1 point for every dollar spent. Earn 250 points and receive a $5 gift card.

- Take advantage of *Best Buy's Buy Back Program*, which allows you to trade in your old electronics within 2 years of the purchase date and receive a gift card to use on your next purchase.

- Don't forget to shop on Black Friday. Arrive early and stick to your shopping list for best results.

Gap

- Shop the clearance rack, especially during *extra 25% off* sales, when you'll get additional savings on top of the clearance price. Season ending clearance sales are often the most competitively priced.

- Sign up for emails from Gap.com and immediately receive a *$15 off $75 purchase* coupon just for signing up.

- During Gap's semi-annual *Give & Get* sale, customers save 30% for about a week, both online and in stores.

- Never shop online without a discount code; just do a quick Internet search to find a valid code.

- Don't forget that Gap offers a one time price adjustment up to 14 days after your purchase.

Hobby Lobby

- Sign up to receive weekly emails. You'll be privy to special discounts and new promotions.

- Look for their coupon for *40% off any regular priced item* in their weekly ad, and make sure to sign up to receive this ad via email, as well.

- Shop after-holiday clearance to save on decorations and seasonal merchandise.

Home Depot

- While shopping in-store, look for items that have a slight flaw or irregularity. If you don't mind fixing it or living with it, pick it up and ask an associate for a discount.

- Don't pass up Home Depot's online rebate center to see all current rebate offers. This allows you to earn money back on your purchase.

- Price Guarantee: If you find a current, lower price on an identical, in-stock item from another local retailer, Home depot will match the price and then beat it by 10%.

- Select *Pick Up In Store* when shopping online to avoid shipping charges.

J.Crew

- Students and teachers with valid ID receive 15% off every day. Cannot be combined with other offers.

- Find coupon codes online, such as free shipping or percent off savings.

- Shop clearance racks in stores.

- While in store, search for the red phone if the full priced item you want is out of stock. Or ask an associate, and order the item with free shipping to your home.

- Don't forget the price adjustments up to 7 days after your purchase.

JC Penney

- Sign up for mailers (snail mail). At least twice a month they send out $ off coupons like *Save $20 on a $100 purchase, $15 on $75*, or *$10 on $50*.

- Shop during the *Lowest Price of the Season* sales, *Back to School*, or *Black Friday* where prices are super-low.

- Shop the *Red Zone Clearance* section at JCPenney.com where merchandise is marked down by up to 80% off.

- Take the customer satisfaction survey on the back of your receipt for a 15% off code good on your next purchase.

Jo-Ann Fabric & Crafts

- Sign up for Jo-Ann's mailer (snail mail). Every month their new circular includes an array of coupons. There's almost always a *40-50% off one regular priced item*.

- Teacher Reward program offers eligible educators savings of 15% off.

- Shop the clearance after major holidays and at the end of a season.

Lowe's

- Look for coupons at your local post office in the *Change of Address Packet*, namely 10% off entire purchase.

- Check with *Lowe's Rebate Center*, where you can earn money back on qualified purchases.

- When shopping online, choose the *Ship to Store* option to avoid any shipping fees.

- Price Guarantee: Lowe's will beat competitor prices by 10%. If a competitor is offering a percent off discount, Lowe's will reduce their current price by the same percentage discount that the competitor is offering.

Michaels

- Utilize the *50% off one regular price item* coupons from the weekly circular.

- Bring in coupons from stores like Jo-Anns and Hobby Lobby. Michaels will honor competitor coupons.

- In many Michael stores, AARP members get an additional 10% savings on Tuesdays.

Office Depot

- Join the free *WorkLife Rewards* program and receive money back on qualifying purchase.

- WorkLife members are eligible to receive a $2 reward for every used ink or toner cartridge they bring in (up to 10 per month).

- Shop Office Depot's Penny Sales during back to school season.

Old Navy

- Shop clearance racks in stores, where you can find items as low as $1.00!

- Search for coupon codes and check out their facebook page for exclusive coupons.

- Price adjustments available one-time within 14 days of purchases made online or in-store.

Overstock.com

- Flat Rate shipping is $2.95 on your entire order.

- If you're a frequent overstock.com shopper, consider joining *Club O*. For an annual fee of $19.95, you will receive 5% back on every purchase and free shipping every day.

Payless Shoes

- Shop during *Buy One, Get one 50% off* sales, which occur several times per year.

- Select *Ship to Store* to avoid shipping fees when shopping online.

- Shop end-of-season clearance deals: buy sandals in the fall and boots in the spring for the best prices!

Pottery Barn

- New movers receive 10% off total purchase coupons. Not moving? Look for sellers online who may be offering their coupons!

- Shop the end of season clearance, which makes Pottery Barn affordable: Holiday decorations will be 75% off in January. Outdoor furniture is deeply discounted by October.

- Shop during semi-annual clearance sales, where merchandise is marked down up to 75% off.

Sephora

- Enjoy free shipping on online purchases over $50, free returns, and free samples with every order.

- Sign up for the free *Beauty Insider* program and earn points when you make purchases and then redeem them for great samples or gift collections.

- Relax with an unbeatable return policy. If you are not completely satisfied with a Sephora or Sephora.com purchase or gift for any reason, return it for a full refund. If, after opening and using your beauty purchase, you decide you don't like the item, Sephora will refund your purchase, no questions asked.

Snapfish

- Don't make a purchase without a discount code! Coupons, such as free shipping, percent-off savings and free products, are nearly always available.

- Create an account and get special discounts and offers on greeting cards, photos, canvases, mugs, calendars, photo books, and much more. You can even pick up your prints at over 10,000 locations.

Staples

- Check out their *Dollar Deals*, especially during back-to-school season.

- Staples offers the price match guarantee at time of purchase or during the 14 days after purchase.

- Sign up for Staples' *Easy Rebate* program. The program is entirely online— no clipping or mailing receipts. Look for Easy Rebate products every time you shop, then go to StaplesEasyRebates.com and enter the required information right online. You'll automatically receive your rebate within 4–6 weeks.

- Sign up for their reward card to earn 10% back on all ink & toner, case & ream paper, and copy & print purchases.

- Teachers are also eligible for a 10% discount on all teaching and art supplies.

- Recycle any ink or toner cartridge and get $2 in Staples' Rewards. Keep a lookout for double or triple recycling reward promotions in your emails and weekly ads.

- Most Staples stores will accept competitor coupons, so if you can't find a valid Staples coupon before shopping, try doing an Internet search for one of their competitors.

The Children's Place

- Join their *Birthday Club* to receive special coupons on your birthday.

- Participate in their store surveys to receive a code for *15% off your next purchase*.

- Shop their clearance section both in stores and online.

Toys R Us

- Sign up for *Rewards "R" Us* program to receive a $5 reward certificate for every $150 you spend, along with discounts, exclusive member-only-shopping events, free baby formula, free diapers, free greeting cards, and much more.

- Use your manufacturer coupons on diapers, baby food, and more at Toys R Us and Babies R Us. Take advantage of stacking coupons with promotions such as *Buy 2 Huggies Diapers boxes and receive $20 Babies R Us gift card.*

Victoria's Secret

- Sign up for Victoria's Secret mailers and receive regular coupons including a *Free Panty (no purchase required)* and *$10 off any purchase (no minimum).*

- Shop clearance bins to find deep discounts on overstocked items.

- Join *Pink Nation* and print coupons such as a free product with any Pink purchase.

DAILY DEALS

Daily Deal sites offer buyers deals on everything ranging from salon services to oil changes. When purchasing from a Daily Deal site, you are actually buying a voucher, which can later be redeemed for the good or service. 99% of the time, purchasing a daily deal will not get you that product. You must later order it or redeem it in person in a separate transaction. Here are some of my favorite Daily Deal sites where I recommend you sign up:

- BuyWithMe.com
  Sign up with BuyWithMe to receive deals in your inbox. You can purchase discounted vouchers to redeem at a variety of retailers. If you refer 3 friends to any one BuyWithMe offer, you'll get the deal for free!

- **Citydeals.com**

  If you're looking for a great night out on the town, this is the place to go. This widely popular site is the perfect avenue to score amazing deals on restaurants, spas, salons, theater and movie tickets and so much more. Search for restaurants in the city of your choice and uncover gift cards selling for half of the face value. You'll easily be able to get a $50 dinner for only $25. Interested in the theater, karate lessons, a night of bowling? All of this and so much more are featured at a fraction of the cost.

- **Eversave.com**

  Another great daily deal site offering online deals that most anyone can use and redeem. There are a few local deals for some regions, but for the most part, this site offers national deals only, usually for products, not services.

- **Goupon.com**

  The largest daily deal site in the nation, Groupon offers both local and national deals on most anything. They negotiate prices with local business and then send the deal alerts to your email. You simply sign up, tell them a bit about yourself, and then sit back and receive offers in your inbox. You can also search for deals by city to find hotels, spa experiences, and even health services like a visit to the dentist! Make your purchase and print out a voucher that can be redeemed at the applicable merchant. Every once in a while there is a smokin' hot national deal like 50% off gift cards at Gap, The Body Shop or a photo deal from SnapFish! And if you refer a friend, a $10 Groupon voucher is all yours!

- **KGBDeals.com**

  Similar to its competitors, KGBDeals offers discounts by city, specializing in entertainment. So go to KGBDeals to search for anything to entertain yourself: movies, dinner, spas and more.

- **LivingSocial.com**

  Recently acquired by Amazon, this site offers just one deal a day in your city. Like Groupon, LivingSocial works with local businesses to bring you deals of up to 90% off. Water parks, massages, paragliding, restaurants, and theater tickets are a few of the kinds of things they feature. This site, unlike others, tends to focus more on dining and service vouchers, and it's all unique to where you live. Living Social also offers Escapes, which are discounted vouchers (usually around 50% off) for getaways to places like Cancun, Lake Tahoe and other luxury destinations. The destinations typically have to be booked within a set period, so be sure to read all the fine print before making your purchase.

- Mamasource.com
  Formerly known as Mamapedia, this site offers multiple national deals everyday, as well as local deals for select markets. Mamasource focuses on baby and kid clothing and toys, as well as pregnancy, nursing and mothering gear.

- PlumDistrict.com
  A daily deal website that's specifically designed for moms, the busiest people alive. They offer up to 80% off on restaurants, baby, beauty, health, fashion, fitness, garden, spa, tickets, travel, pets, kids, home and events.

• • • • • • • • • • • • • • • • • •

FLASH SALES/GROUP BUYING SITES

Flash Sales/Group Buying sites offer discounts on overstocked retail goods from manufacturers. Because these sites promise to deliver large sales volume, companies will allow their items to be sold at a significant discount. Most of these sites do not keep the items that they sell in stock; rather, they forward customers' orders on to the manufacturer who then fulfills the order. Beware, this can often result in slow shipping times (2-6 weeks) but also some really great deals. Here are some of my favorites:

- BeyondtheRack.com
  This site is a private shopping club for women and men who are on the lookout for designer brand apparel and accessories up to 70% off retail. All merchandise is available for a limited amount of time, usually only 48 hours. Members are notified by email in advance of the upcoming deals and encouraged to shop

early in order to score what they want most. Membership is by invitation only; you may be invited by a friend, or by **TheKrazyCouponLady.com**!

- **Gilt.com**
  Gilt Groupe provides instant insider access to today's top designer labels. It's specific to high-end fashion and luxury brands. As a members-only site, they offer these high-end products for up to 60% off the retail price.

- **HauteLook.com**
  This site sells some of the best names in women's and men's fashion and accessories, beauty, kids' apparel and toys, home décor, and travel getaways at up to 75% off. Sales start at 8 AM Pacific time. Be the first on their site so you don't miss out.

- **Modnique.com**
  This is a boutique sales event website for all members of your family. Modnique offers access to brand name sale events on hand-picked designer merchandise. Members save 50-85% or more. Modnique sells designer apparel, jewelry, watches, sunglasses, handbags, home goods, and other premium quality brand name products at discounted prices. Sales usually start at 7 AM or 7 PM Pacific time.

- **Nomorerack.com**
  A unique alternative to the traditional way of shopping. Every day at exactly 12 Noon EST, eight items go on sale at a huge discount, often up to 90% off the retail price. The popular items sell out within minutes, so in order to score those great items you've got to be on the site immediately at 12 Noon (or before). This site features a wide range of name brand products including shoes, clothing, electronics, toys and handbags.

- **RueLaLa.com**
  An exclusive, invitation-only website offering premier brands from private bou-

tiques. Membership is free. Deals are available for a limited amount of time. Shop here for unique and high-end items.

- Totsy.com

  The best items here tend to sell out quickly, so be sure to check out this web-site as soon as the sales begin. They cater to mothers and children, and products include baby gear, travel accessories, bedding and bath, clothing, prenatal care, toys and even educational materials. Totsy offers free shipping on your first order.

- Whiskeymilitia.com

  Another great deal site. They feature one discounted item at a time until it sells out, at which point another item becomes available. This site features snowboarding, skating, and surfing brands, including T-shirts for $5, shoes for $15, even surfboards for $300, (which might sound like a lot until you consider regular retail was over $700).

- Zulily.com

  This website offers daily deals of up to 90% off for mom, babies and kids. Simply sign up; membership is free. Discounted items include toys, shoes, maternity clothes, baby gear and much more. Shipping is a flat rate of $7.95 to most parts of the country.

● ● ● ● ● ● ● ● ● ● ● ● ● ● ● ● ●

TRAVEL

You know where you want to go on vacation. You know when you want to travel. You even have your expense budget saved up and set aside for the trip. Now, how do you go about making your reservations? How do you ensure that you're getting the best deal? With the myriad of travel sites competing for your attention, it's difficult to know where to turn for the best values and best service. To help make planning your next vacation a little easier, here are thumbnail reviews of eight of the top travel booking sites.

- Expedia.com

  Originally founded by Microsoft, this Washington-based travel giant is the world's largest travel agency and has many travel arms, including Hotwire and Hotels.com (listed below). Particularly noteworthy is Expedia's deal page, which offers a variety of deeply discounted offers that change daily. Expedia has recently formed a partnership with Groupon to offer weekly travel discounts. On **TheKrazyCouponLady.com** I featured a Groupon deal for a hotel and spa in Sedona that represented a savings of more than 50 percent. Expedia also offers a price guarantee. If you find a better price online within 24 hours of booking your vacation with Expedia, they will refund the difference to you and give you a $50 gift certificate towards your next vacation with Expedia.

- Hotels.com

  This hotel booking site, a division of Expedia.com, offers more than 135,000 hotels worldwide. In the past they would not reveal the name of the hotel until after you completed the deal, but they have since changed that policy. I've found some great prices with this site. Last year I booked a room in Chicago that normally goes for $199 per night for just $69 per night. Hotels.com is also a good resource if you're traveling to a city during a major convention or sporting event. They frequently have rooms available when other booking sites do not.

- Hotwire.com

  Another division of Expedia.com, Hotwire sells deeply discounted hotel rooms, flights and other travel components, usually very near to the travel date. You can find some good prices here if you are flexible about your travel dates and destination AND if you can accept not knowing the airline or exact hotel until after you've paid for the trip. For hotels, they DO tell you if the property is a three, four or five-star hotel and give you a basic location (such as airport, downtown, east side, etc.) The site advertises up to 50 percent discounts on hotels and up to 40 percent discount on flights (although this is likely off of the full price and not off of any discounted price offered by the airline or hotel company).

- **Kayak.com**

  The best part about Kayak.com is that it's an impartial site. Unlike some other travel sites, Kayak is a search engine and grabs information from a variety of sources, including Orbitz, major hotel chains and online travel agencies. Founded in 2004, Kayak.com is a good place to research a variety of hotels and/or flights all in one place. I like this site, but some of the information pages, such as the hotel description pages, can be somewhat outdated. Kayak recently formed a partnership with the search engine, Bing, to offer an even broader range of information, such as airport gate locations and driving directions.

- **Orbitz.com**

  There has been a lot of controversy involving Orbitz over its ten-year history. The most recent incident involved American Airlines pulling its flights from their booking site's database in 2010. These flights are back, but Orbitz' reputation hasn't quite rebounded. Today the travel booking site facilitates more than 2.5 million travel searches each day. Like Expedia and Travelocity, Orbitz offers hotels, flights, cruises and car rentals. They also offer a price guarantee where they will send you a refund check if the price of your flight, hotel or other travel package decreases before you depart on your vacation. Personally, I find that Expedia and Travelocity offer better information and are easier to use.

- **Priceline.com**

  Priceline was the original travel bidding site and is best known for its "Name Your Own Price" offers. Today, the site offers discounted pre-priced flights, hotels, car rentals and cruises as well as the bidding offers. If you can be flexible in your travel and can abide not knowing your exact flights and times, exact hotel or exact car rental company until after you've paid for your vacation, you can save big money here. Personally, I'm not that flexible, and I wouldn't recommend it for families with small children (since you could be stuck flying all day). However, if you don't mind giving up a little control over your travel plans, there are deals to be had here.

- SmarterTravel.com

  I just recently learned about SmarterTravel.com and haven't had an opportunity to use it to book a vacation, but I like what I see. According to their website, they are the "largest online travel resource for unbiased travel news, deals, and timely expert advice". They personally comb hundreds of travel sites and hand-pick the best ones to feature on the site, with real people, not bots. I like, too, that they offer general travel information on things to see and do from area Convention and Visitors Bureaus in addition to selling flights, hotels and such.

- Travelocity.com

  Unlike some of the other travel booking sites, Travelocity is a full-service travel agency, the sixth largest in the United States. This company is owned by Sabre Holdings, who used to own American Airlines. Although Travelocity claims to have no bias, it's good to keep in mind that their system probably favors, at least somewhat, American Airlines flights and tours. Travelocity's complete travel offerings include flights and hotels as well as cruises, tour packages, rail tickets and passes, car rentals, and even tickets to attractions at your destination, like Sea World.

  I particularly like Travelocity's hotel program. The company negotiates special rates at a wide range of hotels that can only be booked via Travelocity. These offerings change frequently, but recent deals included $97 for the Super 8 near Union Square in San Francisco, the Hyatt Regency in Denver for $76, and $135 for the Omni Hotel at CNN Center in Atlanta. Travelocity also has a "secret hotel" program that promises up to 55 percent off of your hotel rate. With this program, you don't get the exact name of your hotel until after you pay for the hotel.

  Travelocity also offers a price match program where they will refund the difference to you if you find a better price after you've booked your reservation with them. They also add a gift certificate for $50 towards your next vacation with Travelocity. Unlike the price guarantee with Orbitz, which is automatic, you have to find the better price for Travelocity and bring it to their attention.

USING TRAVEL SITES WISELY

To get the most from travel websites, just like shopping for groceries or back-to-school supplies, you want to know the "regular", everyday price of the flight, hotel, cruise or travel package before you make your reservations. Just like grocers put large, eye-catching displays at the end of the aisle, so travel sites entice readers with spectacular prose even when the "deal" isn't all that great. To research, visit the individual airline, hotel and cruise line sites first before you shop on the travel sites. Often these sites charge a booking fee that airlines don't. There have been plenty of times when I've been able to get a lower fare by purchasing my ticket straight through the airline. If you're really looking to save, airlines recommend calling Monday–Friday between the hours of 12 Midnight–1AM in the time zone of the airline's "home base". Sounds kind of crazy, but if you're on a budget even the most drastic measures can make a difference!

By now you know, a Krazy Coupon Lady isn't afraid to do something a little extreme in order to afford the lifestyle she's dreaming of for her family. Creating a separate email account so you can sign up for reward programs at your favorite retailers or staying up past midnight to call the airline aren't too great a sacrifice for me. I like to think of it, not as extreme sacrifice in order to find a deal, but extreme ingenuity—knowing the secret to finding the deal! With all these different insiders' tips, you should now be equipped to find what you want at a price you can afford. Put some of these tips into practice and you'll be amazed at how much further your dollar goes.

FAQs:

I recently heard about people regretting purchases made on daily deal sites. Why is this?

For whatever reason, people are making purchases on these sites and then not redeeming their vouchers. This is where the buyer's remorse comes in. It might be that their plans change and they aren't able to spend the weekend at that spa or that they put their voucher somewhere and let it expire. If you are going to purchase a voucher on a daily deal site, it's your responsibility to remember to redeem it. Put it in your wallet or someplace visible as a constant reminder.

I used Groupon once to purchase a spa treatment but was never able to get through to the Spa to make my appointment and they would never return my calls. Is it a scam?

No! It's absolutely not a scam and Groupon stands behind every single voucher. If for a reason outside of your control you are not able to redeem your voucher, give them a call and they will refund your purchase! Most daily deal sites have a 100% Guarantee, which makes purchasing from them totally risk free!

Is it honest to buy discounted vouchers or gift cards?

Yes. It's the same principle as marking down products. It's another way for the store to increase sales. Instead of a shirt going on sale, they're marking down a gift card. The principle is the same. The store would rather earn $25 than nothing!

CHAPTER EIGHTEEN

Couponing to Give

Believe it or not, I'm not a salesperson. I don't even like salespeople, generally speaking. I cringe at multi-level marketing and would rather shred my coupon inserts (and that's really saying something) than pressure others into buying something for my personal gain—even though many great, legitimate businesses operate successfully with that strategy. If I had collected all the invitations I've received to sales parties (Tupperware, jewelry, books, candles, cooking supplies, you name it), many from people I hardly knew, I'd have a mountain. I've never had a knack for sales. In college I signed up to sell makeup and failed miserably. No pink Cadillac for me! I'm just not comfy as a saleswoman.

So how did I end up here, writing and selling this book? A couple of things make me, the world's worst salesperson, want to get others involved in couponing. First, I'm so proud of the fact that, other than the cost of the book, all the information you need is free. No monthly subscription fees, no donations, no nothing. The Krazy Coupon Lady might be krazy not to charge, but I'm sincerely excited about helping families like yours save money. Don't crown me with sainthood yet. TheKrazyCouponLady.com earns revenue through affiliates and advertisers, which allows the site to remain totally free for all readers. Your patronage is all the business I need.

Call me corny; call me idealistic. This information will enrich your life. Overly optimistic? Maybe. But these skills, and especially the mental shift that comes along with them, are life changing. Something this valuable is not meant to be kept to yourself but to be shared, to be shouted! So don't quickly hide this piece of the golden pie you've stumbled upon, so as not to share or compete for products. The information is meant to help as many homes as are willing to listen.

Once you get krazy, the subject of couponing will come up naturally all the time. Almost every time I shop, I'm approached and asked about my binder or my cartload of twenty-four laundry detergents. I explain to these people how I do it and how they can save money too. I then tell them about my website and ask whether they'd like to know more. I feel like a Christian missionary spreading Bible messages and inviting folks to church. Sometimes the shoppers I speak with are thrilled, and other times they think I'm nuts. One of my Kraziest Coupon Guy readers, Rick, described his experience trying to convince other people to use coupons in this way:

> You would have thought I had asked them to go to a chiropractor instead of a doctor or believe in the wave theory vs. particle theory of light or hope that Jen and Brad will ever reunite.

The skeptics will always think something about your claims is too good to be true. Don't let the skeptics bother you. Just remember that once you figure this stuff out, you can help other people achieve their financial goals, too.

Here is a story from a reader who is sharing the coupon love:

> I just started this coupon thing two weeks ago…I have a brother-in-law who has struggled with stage 4 melanoma for the last four years. He is unable to work, and his outcome is very uncertain. My sister has to be the sole breadwinner in her family. They were a young couple and had no life insurance when he was diagnosed. Oftentimes we wanted to do more for them besides watch the kids and clean their house.

> Couponing allows me not only to let her know about these easy deals that she can take part in but also to send food her way to ease some of those burdens.

> So thank you, Krazy Coupon Ladies!!!! There are many ways you make a difference. You've given me an opportunity to help them. — Sara

. . . .

DONATE

Think of all the ways you can give back or help someone else by couponing. Here are just a few ideas:

- Donate to your local food bank. When you've got mac and cheese or breakfast cereal coming out your eyeballs, and it goes on sale for $0.25 again, why not spend ten bucks and donate twenty-five boxes of cereal to the food bank? Your groceries are way more valuable than a cash donation when you can shop like that. You might even talk to your local food bank and see whether they'd like any help with their shopping.

- Donate toiletries or food to a women and children's shelter. How about all those $0.17 bottles of shampoo? How much can your family go through in a year, really? And you know that sales cycle through regularly. Wouldn't it be great if the shelter had so many toiletries they could send some full bags home when the women get back on their feet? Shelters often accept diapers, toys, games, school supplies, and many of the other items we know exactly how to get for super cheap.

- Donate to nursing homes. Some of the items I frequently donate are Bayer Blood-Glucose monitors. Often Bayer releases high value coupons that make these products free. Monitors are usually about $40-50, so if I can buy ten of them to donate, it's quite the contribution. Take your kids with you to make your donation. You'll teach them how important it is to give, and the residents will enjoy seeing them.

- Donate your expired coupons! Did you know that overseas military families can use coupons up to six months after expiration? Join with The Krazy Coupon Lady in sponsoring my military bases. Come on over to the website for the latest details.

There are countless ways to give back with the items you receive with coupons. Call your local hospital, Boys and Girls Club, Ronald McDonald House, or church to see what items they need. Maybe they'll name something you have stockpiled. If you don't already have the items they need, you can easily put them on your radar and watch for deals over the next month. The only thing more satisfying than stockpiling your own garage is giving away food and supplies to someone in need. Recently, I was able to donate 300 lbs of food to my local food bank, all from my stockpile. It's an amazing feeling to be able to share the love, and coupons have given me this opportunity.

•   •   •   •   •   •   •   •   •   •   •   •   •   •   •   •   •   •

HELPING OTHERS HELP THEMSELVES

As amazing as it is to give, one of my favorite ways to pay it forward comes from a Chinese Proverb: "Give a man a fish and you feed him for a day. Teach a man to fish and you feed him for a lifetime." I like to say, "Give a woman a basket of food and feed her family for a day. Give a woman a lesson on coupons and feed her family for a lifetime!" It's been incredible to watch people transform their own lives by implementing the simple principles of couponing. Story after story floods my inbox with tales of positive change and life-altering hope brought into lives just because of coupons. What a gift it is to be able to teach others how to save money, how to feed their families on pennies, and how to take control in their lives. Change is powerful, and it's happening all over the nation because of coupons! As you become comfortable with couponing, go ahead and pass on the knowledge. Teach your family and friends how to save 70% on their grocery bills. Even after just a month of couponing, you'll be ready to dole out points of wisdom and help someone else make this journey to become another one of the Krazy Coupon Ladies. Jump on an opportunity to teach a volunteer class in your community. Instead of just dropping off the toiletries at the women's shelter, ask whether you'd be welcome to teach a class on money management and share with them a few of your strategies. Teach a class to the adults or even to the teenagers at your church.

Even though my garage is fully stockpiled with all that my family needs, I haven't backed down on my couponing. The newspapers keep coming; my binder is still full; and my eyes are forever on the lookout for those irresistible deals. When I see free toothpaste and deodorant, or $0.50 cereal and crackers, I never pass them up. I purchase them with another plan in mind. They won't end up on the shelves in my garage but in the hands of someone in need. Couponing has given me the gift of giving. Whether with a basketful of food or class full of tips, I've been blessed to be able to share the love, lighten loads, and help people survive.

• •

READY. . .SET. . .GO!

In a very real way, couponing has the power to transform your life too. Yes, it takes a little work, a bit of extra time, and some obvious effort, but the results are amazing. So why wait? You can do this. Taking the reins is just what The Krazy Coupon Lady is all about.

I remember participating in a high ropes course as a teenager. Was it fun? Yes. Was it terrifying? Absolutely. One of the obstacles was a tiny wire ladder that took me to the top of a telephone pole. Then the task was to walk across another wire with only another couple of lines to hold onto. My emotions were a frantic mix of fear and excitement. I had the desire to climb up that ladder and walk out on the wire, but it was hard to take the first step. On the other end of that wire, standing on another telephone pole, stood my coach. He encouraged me and believed in me (and reminded me of my harness that would prevent me from falling to my death). As I stood with one foot on the wire, I knew I had committed, and it was now my job to go for it. I looked down to the ground where all my girlfriends stood to encourage me. I then realized I was being overdramatic and I walked out onto the wire. It was a rush and tons of fun, especially the zip line ride down.

Couponing is your high wire. You want to do it, and you know it's going to be fun, but it's still scary to take those first steps. **TheKrazyCouponLady.com** is going to be your coach. Ask your questions and soak in all the information the site has to offer. You'll be coached through until you reach the other side. I'm on the site every day (if not every hour) answering questions and guiding you through the process. Come to The Krazy Coupon Lady to meet your team of girlfriends who will encourage you from down below. You won't find any judging or name-calling on The Krazy Coupon Lady. No question is too stupid, and if you make an error, we'll help you know what to do next time without jumping down your throat or calling the coupon police. We're women helping women, and we love our sprinkling of coupon guys too! If you're comfortable in a highly frugal, highly estrogenized environment, come on over.

Are you envisioning your surplus monthly budget? Can you see yourself confidently speaking to a store manager at checkout? Are you ready to re-allocate your time and make this a priority for your family? Then let's go! Make sure to keep track of all your savings and send The Krazy Coupon Lady a letter in a year when you reach $10,000. We'll start a club. And think of the bragging rights!

NEED A RECAP?

Now that you understand how much fun (and money) couponing will add to your life, let's review.

To get started, you need to:

- *Be willing to set aside an hour or two each week.*
- *Collect multiple copies of coupons.*
  - ❖ With newspaper coupons, find a way (through extra subscriptions, neighbors or co-workers, or befriending the newspaper boy) to get at least four to six copies of your local Sunday paper.
  - ❖ Watch for coupons in the weekly store ads, often available in-store.
  - ❖ Online you can buy newspaper coupons from coupon clipping websites, print coupons from the Internet (visit **TheKrazyCouponLady.com** for a comprehensive list of current printable coupons), and find store coupons on the store's website.
  - ❖ Watch for peelies, tearpads, and blinkies in the store.
  - ❖ Keep your eyes and ears open for Catalina deals, both advertised and unadvertised.

Don't be afraid to special order items or ask for rain checks if they sell out before you can make your purchase.

- *Organize your coupons.* Choose whichever binder method you find most appealing (organizing by date or organizing by category). Find the list of supplies you need to get started in Chapter 7. Put your contact information in your binder in case it gets lost, and bring it with you every time you go to the store.

- *Learn how to spot rock-bottom prices.* Never buy if the price isn't incredible. When you find a great deal, stock up! With perishable goods, purchase as many as you can reasonably use before they expire. With nonperishable goods like cleaners, buy as many as you'd like.

- *Learn store policies.* For stores you frequent, obtain your own copy of their policies and keep them in your binder. Sit down and talk with local store management to make sure you're on the same page.

- *Get ready for checkout.* Choose wisely the time of day you head to the store. Try to go when it's slow so your cashier will be in a good mood, and there won't be a huge line behind you. Get organized before you leave the house, with separate lists for different transactions, if necessary. If you have kids, take them to the store early in the morning or right after naptime. Feel free to "profile" and choose a cashier who looks coupon-friendly. Talk to your cashier before he or she begins ringing you up to see if he or she has a preference (coupons now or coupons later?) and don't be afraid to ask management to clarify, if necessary.

Whew! Are you ready or what?? You can do it! Don't worry; if you're new to this, you'll be a pro in no time. With *Pick Another Checkout Lane, Honey*, there's nothing you can't have. Krazy Coupon Ladies can have our cake (at $0.25 a box of mix!) and eat it too, washed down with an ice-cold, dirt-cheap soda, and cleaned up with free paper towels if we spill. We sleep well at night with minty fresh breath (thanks to free toothpaste), knowing that we're in control of our financial futures, and awake to gourmet breakfast cereals we bought for next to nothing.

I know you'll love the rush you get from loading the car top to bottom with groceries you snagged at rock-bottom prices. If you still have questions or need a pep talk along the way, I'm ready to guide and cheer you on to couponing success at **TheKrazyCouponLady.com**. Let me know what you decide to do with the $600-$800 per month you save, and send me a postcard on your next ritzy vacation made possible by careful coupon clipping. I can't wait to hear your success stories! Just don't tell me if your stockpile begins to gleam brighter than mine...I don't know if I could take it.

Happy couponing!

You will be a Krazy Coupon Lady,
when you pay off your debts, command your
finances & coupon your way to prosperity.

FAQs:

What if I don't feel like I have the means to donate?

Do not feel obligated to donate. Your first and most important mission is to help yourself. Build your stockpile, get out of debt, be financially independent, and take your power back. Once you have a surplus of a few items, you can consider donating. If you feel like it's too much, don't worry about donating right from the start. Take care of yourself first, and then you'll be able to help others.

What if I don't want to share my couponing secrets for feat that my stores will become overrun with couponers?

Others are gong to try to figure out how to coupon. When they hear your deals or those of someone else, they will try to cash in on those same deals with or without your help. Without you they are bound to make mistakes and break some rules unintentionally. Everyone will be better off if you help him or her learn how to do it right the first time.

CHAPTER NINETEEN

Insider Tips:
SECRETS TO SAVING BIG AT TWENTY STORES ACROSS THE NATION

Now that you've got the tools and you're ready to shop, how about a bit more guidance on where the best places may be to shop in your area? Below you will find insider secrets on how to maximize your savings at twenty of the best places in the nation to shop with coupons!

I'm sure there are plenty of great stores in your area that are not on my list. I couldn't cover them all here. Follow the steps in Chapter 11 to acquire store policies for all your local stores! Flip back to Chapter 3 to review the different types of grocery stores and what to look for when choosing where to do your shopping!

Please note that while The Krazy Coupon Lady has used the most updated versions of the store policies as of the printing of this book, I am not responsible for any changes that stores implement. So it is recommended you still double check the store policies online or contact the stores to make sure you have the most recent versions. For the latest information visit **TheKrazyCouponLady.com**.

ALBERTSONS

Before you shop at Albertsons with coupons, here's what you should know about its policy:

- Albertsons accepts newspaper, printable, and other manufacturer coupons. Internet coupons for free items or coupons with a value of $5.00 or more will not be accepted.
- Albertsons accepts one manufacturer and one store coupon per item.
- Albertsons does not accept competitors' coupons.
- Albertsons runs promotions each week. You may use coupons on the items in these promotions to save even more!
- Albertsons sales typically run Wednesday to Tuesday.
- Select regions distribute store coupons in the weekly ad, which you may use with a manufacturer coupon.
- Select regions distribute "twice the value" coupons. This store coupon matches the value of a manufacturer coupon up to $1.00 off. A $1.00 off coupon will become $2.00 off, a $0.50 off coupon will become $1.00 off, a $1.50 off coupon will receive no special treatment.
- Select regions use a store loyalty card, or "preferred card". Ask at your store and sign up!

*THE SECRET *
Stack coupons with Albertsons sales and promotions!

Albertsons runs two kinds of promotions, the "Save Instantly" promo and the "On Your Next Order" promo.

1. The "Save Instantly" Promo:

Example: Spend $20, Save $5 Instantly.

After you scan your preferred card, the register instantly deducts $5 once you spend $20 (total before coupons) on participating products. You can usually take advantage of this type of promo multiple times in one transaction. Example: If you spend $40 on participating products, the register will deduct $10 (twice in $5 increments).

Example: Spend $10 on Nabisco products, Save $3 Instantly

Buy 4 Nabisco Wheat Thins $2.50
Use 4 $1.00/1 Wheat Thins manufacturer coupons
Save $3 Instantly
Final Price: $3.00 or $0.75 each

2. The "On Your Next Order" Promo

Example: Spend $20, Save $5 on your next order.

Your total before coupons and tax is $20. Present any coupons and pay. With your receipt your cashier will hand you a Catalina coupon worth $5.00 off your next order. These Catalinas can typically be rolled. This means you can do one transaction, receive the Catalina, do another identical transaction, pay with the first Catalina, and a new Catalina will still print. Often, OYNO promos can potentially be "moneymakers".

Lunchables $2.79
Use $1.00/1 Lunchables manufacturer coupon
Pay: $1.79, Receive a $1 Catalina to use on your next order
Final Price: $0.79 (after factoring in the Catalina)

You could roll this Catalina and buy another Lunchables. Then you would only pay $0.79 out of pocket, and still receive a new $1 Catalina.

BJ's Wholesale Club

Before you shop BJ's with coupons, here's what you should know about its policy:

- BJ's is the only wholesale club that accepts all manufacturer coupons. When paired with items that are marked down or deeply discounted, you can save big.
- BJ's is a members-only wholesale club. Membership currently costs $50 annually.
- BJ's accepts newspaper, printable, and other manufacturer coupons.
- BJ's distributes store coupons via BJs.com, Instant Coupons via email, BJ's member magazine, BJ's mailers, and BJ's in-club coupon fliers.
- BJ's will accept one store coupon and one manufacturer coupon per item.

The Secret

Shop BJ's low prices and stack a store and manufacturer coupon together to maximize savings!

At BJ's, if you buy a multipack, you can use multiple manufacturer coupons. For example, if you buy a twelve-pack of mandarin oranges and each can has its own barcode, you can use twelve manufacturer coupons on that purchase.

Example:

Filippo Berio Olive Oil, Extra Virgin 2 liter, 2 pk. $17.89
Use two $2.00/1 Filippo Berio manufacturer coupons
Final Price: $13.89, or $6.95/2 liter

CVS

Before you shop CVS with coupons, here's what you need to know:

- CVS accepts both newspaper, printable, and other manufacturer coupons.

- CVS accepts one manufacturer and one store coupon per item.

- CVS does not accept competitors' coupons.

- CVS only allows one manufacturer coupon on a BOGO scenario.

- CVS weekly sales run Sunday to Saturday.

- CVS tracks your purchases and Extra Bucks rewards through your CVS Extra Care card. Make sure you apply for a card!

- CVS offers weekly "Extra Bucks" promotions. Extra Bucks are coupons worth a $ amount off your next purchase, similar to Catalinas. Extra Bucks print at the bottom of your receipt after your transaction is complete. There is no limit on the amount of Extra Bucks you can use in one transaction. Example of an Extra Bucks promo: Spend $15 on participating candy products, receive $5 Extra Bucks. You must reach the required $15 subtotal before coupons!

- Extra Buck offers have limits per card. If the stated limit is 1 you will only be able to get the Extra Bucks one time, regardless of visits or transactions.

- CVS also has purchase-based coupons: common values include $2 off $10 purchase, $3 off $15, $4 off $20, $5 off $30, etc. These purchase-based coupons expire the most quickly, around two weeks after printing.

- CVS offers coupons online through their website. All you have to do is sign up, and you can download these coupons straight onto your Extra Care card.

- CVS offers store coupons through their "Coupon Machines" located inside most stores. Simply scan your Extra Care card and coupons will print out. Sometimes you can get multiple coupons in one trip, so keep scanning until coupons no longer print. An example store coupon could be $1.00 off any deodorant. Each of these coupons has a different expiration date, so beware.

THE SECRET

Stack manufacturer coupons with store coupons on an "Extra Bucks" promo item!
Then, get a few deals like the one below. Do them in one transaction and add a
purchase-based coupon such as $3 off $15 and save even more!

Example Promotion: Buy 1 Old Spice, Receive $1.49 Extra Buck

Buy 1 Old Spice Deodorant on sale $3.49
Use $1.00/1 any deodorant CVS store coupon
Use $1.00/1 Old Spice deodorant manufacturer coupon
Pay $1.49, Receive $1.49 Extra Buck
Final Price: Free! (after factoring in the Extra Bucks)

This deal could be even sweeter if you had previously earned Extra Bucks to pay with, offsetting your out-of-pocket expense. If you'd had a $1.00 Extra Buck, you could have used it and paid only $0.49. You would still receive the $1.49 Extra Buck after the completion of your transaction!

FOOD LION

Before you shop Food Lion with coupons, here's what you should know about its policy:

- Food Lion will only accept coupons that are in date and the product or purchase requirements have been met.
- Competitor coupons will not be accepted.
- Food Lion accepts manufacturer, store, Internet and Catalina checkout coupons.
- Coupons with limits specified on them must be followed.
- No "cash back" will be given for coupons of any kind.
- Customers may not use more than (1) one coupon per item with a maximum of (10) ten coupons for the same item per customer.
- Food Lion will only accept Internet coupons that appear to be originals.
- Food Lion will not accept Internet coupons from other retailers.
- Food Lion will not accept Internet coupons for free items.
- Food Lion will accept manufacturer and store coupons for FREE items.
- The value of the FREE item cannot exceed the purchase price of that item.
- Food Lion reserves the right to limit the quantity of coupons that may be redeemed in one shopping visit. They also reserve the right to refuse any coupon that may appear to be fraudulent.

THE SECRET

You can no longer stack a store coupon and a manufacturer coupon (coupon policy: "one coupon per item"). Food Lion has printable store coupons on their website, or they have "mobile coupons"— basically eCoupon updates sent to your phone, and you can add them to their store loyalty ("MVP") card. Food Lion often has 3-day sales that are usually loss leaders, meaning they are deeply discounted. Take advantage of these sales, along with other sale priced items and stack with a manufacturer or store coupon.

Example:

Huggies Jumbo Pack Diapers, $6.99 (3 Days Only, Friday-Sunday)
Use $3.00/1 Huggies printable manufacturer coupon
Final Price: $3.99

GIANT EAGLE

Before you shop Giant Eagle with coupons, here's what you should know about its policy:

- Giant Eagle accepts newspaper, printable, and other manufacturer coupons. Internet printables will not be accepted if they are over $3 in value, for a "Free" product, or are BOGO coupons.
- Store sales run Thursday to Wednesday.
- You must use the store loyalty card to get sale prices.
- Select Giant Eagle stores double manufacturer coupons up to $0.99. eCoupons, Catalinas, and store coupons cannot be doubled.
- Giant Eagle stores have Catalina Promotions (both advertised and unadvertised).
- Giant Eagle offers store coupons.
- Coupon Policy states limit 1 coupon per item purchased, so either a store coupon OR a manufacturer coupon. You can, however, use a Giant Eagle eCoupon + a manufacturer coupon on one item. Maximum of 12 coupons per same 12 items purchased.
- Accu-Scan policy: If the charge price of a product appears on your register tape at an amount higher than the displayed, posted or advertised price, you will receive the first improperly scanned item free.
- Coupon value cannot exceed the price of the item(s) purchased.
- If you forget to use your coupons at the time of purchase, Giant Eagle will accept them with your receipt and Advantage Card® up to 7 days beyond the date on the receipt.

THE SECRET

Giant Eagle has so many ways to save, but the greatest savings comes when you stack a promotion or sale price, a manufacturer coupon (that can be doubled up to $0.99) and an eCoupon! Giant Eagle runs two kinds of promotions, the "Save Instantly" promo and the "On Your Next Order' promo.

1. The "Save Instantly" Promo

Example: Spend $10, Save $2 Instantly.

The register instantly deducts $2 after you spend $10 (total before coupons) on participating products. You may usually take advantage of this promo multiple times in one transaction. Meaning, if you spend $20 on participating products, the register will deduct $4 (twice in $2 increments).

2. The "On Your Next Order" Promo

Example: Spend $20, Save $5 on your next order (OYNO)

Your total before coupons is $20, then redeem any coupons and pay. With your receipt your cashier will hand you a long, receipt-like Catalina coupon worth $5.00 off your next order. These Catalinas can be rolled. This means you can do one transaction, receive the Catalina, do another identical transaction, pay with the first Catalina, and a new Catalina will still print.

Example Promotion: Buy 5 Post Cereals, save $5 on your next order

Buy 5 Post Cereals $2.00 each
Use 5 $0.75/1 Post manufacturer coupons (each coupon will double to $1.50)
Pay $0.50 each, Receive a $5 Catalina to use on your next order
Final Price: $2.50 Moneymaker! (after factoring in the $5 Catalina)

HARRIS TEETER

Before you shop Harris Teeter with coupons, here's what you should know about its policy:

- Harris Teeter accepts newspaper, printable, and other manufacturer coupons. Internet coupons for free products are not accepted.
- With the purchase of two like manufacturer products, Harris Teeter accepts two Internet coupons, per store, per day.
- Harris Teeter uses a store loyalty card, called VIC for Very Important Customer. Apply in store so you can get the lowest sale prices and double your coupons.
- Harris Teeter sales run Wednesday to Tuesday.
- Harris Teeter accepts competitor coupons (not subject to doubling or tripling).
- Harris Teeter doubles coupons up to $0.99 in value, and up to twenty per day. Additionally, you can only double three coupons for the same item.
- Scan guarantee: "If an item scans higher than the shelf tag or sign, you will receive one like item free. We will honor five 'scan guarantees' per customer."
- Select Harris Teeter locations have Triple Coupon Events. (These are the times where you pull out a map and consider a road trip just to get to the deals!)

THE SECRET

Shop promotions and double your coupons for maximum savings! Harris Teeter runs two kinds of promotions, the "Save Instantly" promo and the "On Your Next Order' promo:

1. The "Save Instantly" Promo

Example: Spend $20, Save $5 Instantly

The register instantly deducts $5 after you spend $20 (total before coupons) on participating products and scan your VIC card. You may take advantage of this promo multiple times in one transaction. Meaning, if you spend $40 on participating products, the register will deduct $10 (twice in $5 increments).

Spend $15 on GM products, Save $5 instantly
Buy 5 Green Giant Frozen Vegetables $1.00
Buy 4 Betty Crocker Frosting $1.25
Buy 3 Betty Crocker Warm Delights $1.67
Use 5 $0.25/1 Green Giant manufacturer coupons (3 coupons will double to $0.50)
Use 4 $0.50/1 Betty Crocker Frosting manufacturer coupons (3 coupons will double to $1.00)
Use 3 $0.50/1 Betty Crocker Warm Delights manufacturer coupons (3 coupons will double to $1.00)
Save $5 instantly
Final Price: $1.51 or $0.13 per item

2. The "OYNO" Promo

Example: Spend $20, Save $5 on your next order (OYNO)

Your total before coupons is $20, then redeem any coupons and pay. With your receipt your cashier will hand you a long, receipt-like Catalina coupon worth $5.00 off your next order. These Catalinas can be rolled. This means you can do one transaction, receive the Catalina, do another identical transaction, pay with the first Catalina, and a new Catalina will still print.

H-E-B

Before you shop H-E-B with coupons, here's some information on the policy:

- H-E-B accepts manufacturer coupons from newspapers, online, and H-E-B Catalinas.
- H-E-B weekly ads run Wednesday to Tuesday. Also available is a monthly sale flier that alerts you to sales valid for that month and a free monthly magazine distributed in stores, featuring coupons redeemable in-store.
- H-E-B store coupons are available in store (typically colored yellow), via direct mail and Big Saving coupons found at HEB.com.
- You can stack up to one store-sponsored H-E-B coupon with one manufacturer coupon per item. Only one manufacturer coupon per item is permitted (including H-E-B issued manufacturer coupons).
- H-E-B does not accept competitor coupons or give cash back if the coupon value is greater than the item's purchase price.

THE SECRET

Stack H-E-B store coupons with manufacturer coupons on promotions
like the weekly Meal Deal or Combo Locos.

Example: Buy 2 Ball Park Franks at $3.50 each, Get Hormel Chili, French's Mustard and H-E-B shredded cheese Free.

Buy 2 Ball Park Franks $3.50 each
Buy 1 Hormel Chili
Buy 1 French's Mustard
Buy 1 H-E-B shredded cheese
Use 2 $0.75/1 Ball Park manufacturer coupons
Final Price: $5.50 for franks, chili, mustard, and cheese or $1.10 each

KMART

Before you shop Kmart with coupons, here's some information on its policy:

- Kmart's regular prices are fairly high, but they have weekly sales, and select regions occasionally double coupons!

- Kmart accepts newspaper, printable, and other manufacturer coupons.

- Kmart store coupons may print at the bottom of your receipt, or you may receive purchase- based coupons, such as $5 off $50 by signing up for Kmart emails.

- Kmart store coupons can also be found in the Kmart Storewide Savings Guide periodically available at the customer service desk. These booklets offer store "Super Coupons" and even "free item" coupons on occasion! Select Kmart locations allow stacking one Super Coupon and one manufacturer coupon per item.

- Kmart does offer some promotions such as Spend $15 on participating products, receive $3 off your next order.

- Kmart sales run Sunday to Saturday.

THE SECRET
Combine double coupon days with in-store promotions!

Kmart Double Coupon Days is advertised in select regions on a random basis. Double coupons run for an entire week: Sunday to Saturday. Manufacturer coupons up to a certain value are doubled automatically by the register. For example: when Kmart doubles coupons up to $2.00, present your $2.00 coupon and receive $4.00 off. Coupons valued at $2.01 will not be doubled. Kmart usually sets a limit on how many coupons may be doubled per day.

Combine Kmart Double Days with a Catalina Promotion.

Example: Buy 2 Dry Idea Deodorant, Earn a $2 Catalina to use on your next order

Buy 2 Dry Idea Deodorant $4.49 each
Use 2 $2.00/1 Dry Idea printable manufacturer coupons (each coupon will double to $4.00)
Pay $0.98, Receive a $2 Catalina to use on your next order
Final Price $1.02 Moneymaker! (after factoring in the $2 Catalina) or above

KROGER

Before you shop at Kroger with coupons, here's a little information about its policy:

- Kroger accepts both newspaper, printable, and other manufacturer coupons. Printable Coupons must have a scannable barcode, a "bill to:" or "send to:" address in the fine print, and a valid, future expiration date.

- Kroger has weekly sales and promos, including Catalina promotions.

- Kroger's weekly sales usually run Wednesday to Tuesday, but in some regions run Thursday to Wednesday or Sunday to Saturday.

- Kroger also accepts eCoupons. Load them directly to your Kroger card!

- You must use a Kroger card to get store savings. You can sign up at the store's customer service desk.

- In some areas Kroger stores double coupons. The value and amount of coupons they will double varies by region.

THE SECRET
Shop Kroger promotions with coupons, and double coupons where you can!

Kroger stores run "Save Instantly" promotions. The most common is called a Mega Event, where you Buy 10 items, Save $5 Instantly.

Example: Buy 10 Progresso soups, Save $5 instantly

Buy 10 Progresso Soup $1.50 each
Use 10 $0.50/1 Progresso manufacturer coupons (depending on your region, up to 10 will be doubled to $1.00)
Save $5 instantly
Final Price: Free!

MEIJER

Before you shop Meijer with coupons, here's some information on the policy:

- Meijer accepts both newspaper, printable, and other manufacturer coupons.

- Meijer has weekly sales and promos, including Catalina promotions.

- Meijer weekly sales usually run Sunday to Saturday but in some regions run Wednesday to Tuesday.

- Meijer has great store coupons found at Meijer Mealbox (printable coupons) and through mPerks (digital store coupons).

- Up to one manufacturer coupon and one store coupon may be used per item purchased.

- Select Meijer locations double coupons. Most double coupons up to $0.50 in value (limited to two like coupons), so a $0.35 coupon is worth $0.70 off, a $0.50 coupon is worth $1.00 off.

THE SECRET

Stack store coupons from Meijer Mealbox or mPerks, manufacturer coupons, and sale prices!
Plus, double your manufacturer coupon to save big!

Example:

Buy 2 Mt. Olive Pickles, $1.67
Use 2 $0.50/1 Mt. Olive Pickles manufacturer coupon (each coupon will double to $1.00)
And use $1.00/2 printable Meijer store coupons
Final Price: $0.17 each, when you buy 2

PUBLIX

Before you shop Publix with coupons, here's what you should know about its policy:

- Publix accepts newspaper, printable, and other manufacturer coupons.

- Publix has store coupons, which can be used with manufacturer coupons.

- Publix has a bi-monthly Advantage Buy flier. In these fliers, you will find manufacturer and store coupons.

- Publix accepts competitor coupons, such as grocery store issued coupons, like Super Target coupons. Typically, Publix will not accept drug store coupons from Walgreens or CVS, but you may ask your manager whether they are considered a competitor. Each Publix has a list posted of the stores they consider to be competitors. These vary by store.

- Select Publix stores distribute coupons found in the Sunday Publix circular for Penny or Mystery Items. Sometimes they may get sneaky and put the penny item coupon somewhere else in the Sunday paper. These coupons are valid on Sunday and Monday only and are for select items and sizes. Usually there is a limit of one offer per customer, and you must spend $10 on other purchases. The $10 purchase is the total before coupons, so use coupons to get your out-of pocket-expense down.

- Select Publix stores double coupons. Most of these participating stores will match the value of the coupon up to $0.50. This happens automatically at the register. Florida stores do not double.

THE SECRET
Combine a sale price with a manufacturer coupon that can be doubled and stack with a competitor's store coupon.

Example: Buy 1 Get 1 Free General Mills cereal

Buy 2 General Mills cereal $3.79
Use 2 $0.50/1 General Mills manufacturer coupon (each coupon will double to $1.00)
And use a $1.50/2 General Mills Super Target printable coupon
Final Price: $0.29 for 2 or $0.15 each

RITE AID

Before you shop Rite Aid with coupons, here's some information on the policy:

- Rite Aid accepts no more than one Rite Aid Valuable Coupon, one Rite Aid "manufacturer" (in-ad) coupon and one manufacturer coupon on a single item.

- The best deals at Rite Aid utilize the Single Check Rebate (SCR) system. Rite Aid sends you a monthly check for the total of all your rebates purchased during that month. You can cash it as you would any other check.

- Rite Aid also has a +Up Reward system. On qualifying purchases, you will receive a +Up Reward (Rite Aid cash) back to use on just about anything in the store. The +Up Reward prints on the bottom of your receipt. You can use +Up Rewards in conjunction with coupons.

- Rite Aid has a "Video Values" program, where you watch videos online and then print Rite Aid store coupons. With each new month there is a new batch of videos.

- Rite Aid accepts newspaper, printable, and other manufacturer coupons.

- Rite Aid sales run Sunday to Saturday, except in Southern California, where the ads run Friday – Thursday

- Rite Aid accepts only one coupon for the purchase of two items that are on a Buy One, Get One Free Promotion.

THE SECRET

Stack coupons with rebate items or +Up Reward items and get items for very cheap or free.
You can even "make money" at Rite Aid. Often Rite Aid advertises an item as "Free after Rebate"
in its Sunday ad; add a coupon on top of it and "make money".

Example: Rebate of $2.49 for Scotch packaging tape.

Buy 1 Scotch packaging tape on sale for $2.49
Use $1.00/1 Scotch product manufacturer coupon
Pay $1.49
Submit for the rebate and receive $2.49 at the end of the month.
Final Price: $1.00 Moneymaker!

Example: Motrin on sale for $2.99 with a $2.00 +Up Reward, Limit 2

Buy 1 Motrin $2.99
Use $2.00/1 Motrin manufacturer coupon.
Pay $0.99, Receive a $2.00 +Up Reward
Final Price: $1.01 Moneymaker! (after factoring in the +Up Reward)

Since there is a limit of 2 on this transaction, you could turn around and do it again, or if you choose to buy both items at the same time, you will receive 2 $2.00 +Up Rewards on the bottom of your receipt. At Rite Aid you CAN use your +Up Reward to pay for your next transaction of the same item, and receive another +Up Reward. You will not receive cash back when using a +Up Reward to pay for an item, so you will want to make sure you are purchasing enough to cover the amount of +Up Reward you're planning to use. Also, you cannot pay tax with your +Up Reward.

SAFEWAY

Before you shop Safeway (or Safeway affiliate stores which include: Carrs, Dominick's, Genuardi's, Pavilions, Randalls, Tom Thumb and Vons), here's some information on the policy:

- Safeway accepts newspaper, printable, and other manufacturer coupons.
- Safeway store sales run from Wednesday to Tuesday.
- Safeway has store coupons, in-ad "Super Coupons" and printable coupons from Safeway.com.
- Safeway allows both a store and manufacturer coupon to be used per item.
- Safeway requires a Store Loyalty card, so sign up at the register or customer service desk!
- Safeway also accepts eCoupons. Load them directly to your Safeway Club Card!
- Safeway runs promotions each week.
- Safeway doubles coupons in select regions, usually up to $0.50.

THE SECRET

Use coupons, both store and manufacturer, on these promotions to maximize savings!

Safeway runs two kinds of promotions, the "Save Instantly" promo and the "On Your Next Order" promo.

1. The "Save Instantly" Promo

Example: Buy 5, Save $5 Instantly.

The register instantly deducts $5 after you buy five participating products and scan your Safeway club card. You may take advantage of this promo multiple times in one transaction. Meaning, if you buy ten products, the register will deduct $10 (twice in $5 increments).

Example: Buy 5 Welch's Grape Juice, save $5 instantly

Buy 5 Welch's Grape Juice $3.49 each
Use 5 $2.00/1 Welch's manufacturer coupons
Save $5 instantly
Final Price: $2.45 or $0.49 each

2. The "On Your Next Order" Promo

Example: Spend $30, Save $15 on your next order (OYNO)

Your total before coupons is $30, then redeem any coupons and pay. With your receipt, your cashier will hand you a long, receipt-like Catalina coupon worth $15.00 off your next order. These Catalinas can be rolled. This means you can do one transaction, receive the Catalina, do another identical transaction, pay with the first Catalina, and a new Catalina will still print.

SHOPRITE

Before you go to ShopRite with coupons, here's some information on the policy:

- You will need to sign up for a Price Plus Club card to take advantage of savings and sale prices. You may load eCoupons to your card, although these cannot be stacked with a manufacturer coupon on the same item.

- ShopRite store Super Coupons are periodically printed in their weekly circulars. One manufacturer coupon and one store Super Coupon may be combined on one item.

- ShopRite accepts valid manufacturer and Internet printable coupons. You may also load electronic coupons to your club card online.

- Internet coupons for a "free product", "buy one get one free" offers, and those with a high value in relationship to the item's price are subject to refusal.

- ShopRite management reserves the right to limit total number of coupons or multiple identical coupons.

- Select ShopRite stores will double up to four identical coupons per household per day. See your location for their double coupon policy, as it varies by store.

- ShopRite offers store coupons available in their store circular. Each store may release slightly different coupons.

- ShopRite allows you to use both a manufacturer coupon and a store coupon together on one item.

THE SECRET
Stack a sale price or promotion with manufacturer and store coupons,
plus double up to 4 like manufacturer coupons per day!

Example:

Buy 5 Nabisco Snack Saks $1.00 each
Use 2 $0.75/2 Nabisco coupons (each coupon will double to $1.50)
Final Price: $0.40 each

STOP & SHOP

Before you shop Stop & Shop with coupons, here's what you should know about its policy:

- Stop & Shop accepts newspaper, printable, and other manufacturer coupons.
- At Stop & Shop, you can use one store coupon and one manufacturer coupon on one item. Many store locations allow the use of one eCoupon and one manufacturer coupon per item.
- Stop & Shop runs Catalina promotions.
- Price Guarantee: If any item scans higher than the price marked or advertised, customers are entitled to one unit of the item FREE.
- You will need a Stop & Shop customer card to get savings and sales. You can also load saving offers to your card online.
- Weekly sales run from Friday to Thursday.

Stop & Shop doubles coupons:

- Select Stop & Shop stores double coupons up to $0.99 in value.
- Catalina coupons cannot be doubled.
- You can only double four coupons for identical items and up to sixteen of the same coupon. For example, if you have twenty General Mills cereal coupons, only sixteen of them will be doubled, and you can only buy up to four identical cereals. You could buy four Trix, four Cocoa Puffs, four Kix and four Cheerios.

THE SECRET
Stack sale prices with manufacturer coupons, double coupons and promotions!

Example:

Buy 1 Reese's Peanut Butter Cups minis $1.25
Use $0.55/1 manufacturer coupon (coupon will double to $1.10)
Final Price: $0.15

Stop & Shop runs two kinds of promotions, the "Save Instantly" promo and the "On Your Next Order" promo.

1. The "Save Instantly" Promo

Example: Spend $25, Save $10 Instantly.

The register instantly deducts $10 after you spend $25 (total before coupons) on participating products and scan your Stop & Shop customer card. You may take advantage of this promo multiple times in one transaction. Meaning, if you spend $50 on participating products, the register will deduct $20 (twice in $10 increments).

2. The "On Your Next Order" Promo

Example: Spend $10, Save $3 on your next order (OYNO)

Your total before coupons is $10, then redeem any coupons and pay. With your receipt your cashier will hand you a long, receipt-like Catalina coupon worth $3.00 off your next order. These Catalinas can be rolled. This means you can do one transaction, receive the Catalina, do another identical transaction, pay with the first Catalina, and a new Catalina will still print.

Before you shop Target with coupons, here's some information on the policy:

- Target accepts newspaper, printable, and other manufacturer coupons. Internet coupons for free products are not accepted.

- Target price matches: bring in a competitor ad and Target will match the price of the product as long as it's an exact match.

- Target runs gift card promotions; an example is "Buy 5 Kashi items, receive a $5 Target gift card." You may use coupons on these items, and your result will be great savings! You do not have to separate your transactions. If you buy ten Kashi items, you'll receive two $5 gift cards, etc.

- Target has store coupons available at Target.com or occasionally available in your Sunday coupon inserts. Target printable store coupons read: Limit one per transaction. You may do separate transactions.

- Target allows one manufacturer coupon and one store coupon together on one item unless the coupon itself prohibits it.

- Target offers mobile coupons that can be downloaded straight to your phone.

- Target will reduce the value of the coupon if it exceeds the price of the product.

- Target sales run Sunday through Saturday.

- Target does not accept a second manufacturer coupon of any kind in combination with a BOGO manufacturer coupon. But you can use a store coupon in conjunction with a BOGO manufacturer coupon.

THE SECRET
Combine a gift card promotion with store and manufacturer coupons;
add a price match to the mix and now you're really krazy.

Example: Buy 5 Kashi products, Receive $5 gift card

Buy 5 Kashi products $2.88 each
Price Match: Take your local grocer ad that has Kashi products priced at $2.33
Use 5 $0.75/1 Kashi product manufacturer coupons
Pay $1.58 per item, or $7.90 total, Receive a $5 gift card
Final Price: $0.58 per item (after factoring in the gift card savings)

WALGREENS

Before you shop Walgreens with coupons, here's some information on the policy:

- Walgreens accepts newspaper, printable, and other manufacturer coupons.

- Walgreens has a great "Register Reward" Program. A Register Reward is a type of Catalina coupon that prints after you make a qualifying purchase. It is typically good for "X" amount off of your next purchase. When you purchase the qualifying item, you will receive a Register Reward to use on your next purchase.

- Register Rewards can not be "rolled", which means if you buy 1 Gillette Body Wash and receive a $1.00 Catalina, you can not buy another Gillete Body Wash, use the $1 Catalina and get a new $1.00 Catalina after you pay. You can however buy Suave Deodorant, use your $1.00 Catalina that you earned purchasing the Gillette, and you will get a new Suave Deodorant Catalina.

- Walgreens has store coupons available in its weekly ad.

- At Walgreens, you can use one manufacturer coupon and one store coupon on one item, as long as neither coupon prohibits it.

- Walgreens sales run Sunday to Saturday.

- Managers can limit the number of sale items that you buy in a shopping trip.

- When the store is running a Buy One, Get One Free promotion, up to 2 coupons can be used against the items as long as the net price does not go below zero.

- If the coupon being used exceeds the amount of the item, then the amount of the coupon will be adjusted down.

THE SECRET

Combine a Sale Price with a Register Reward and a manufacturer coupon to save big!

Example: Buy 1 True North Nut Crisp or Clusters, Earn a $2.00 Register Reward

Buy 1 True North Nut Crisps or Clusters $3.00
Use $1.00/1 True North product printable manufacturer coupon
Pay $2.00, Receive a $2.00 Register Reward
Final Price: Free! (after factoring in the $2.00 Register Reward)

WALMART

Before you shop Walmart with coupons, here's some information on its policy.

- Walmart accepts newspaper, printable, and other manufacturer coupons but will not accept printable Internet coupons that require no purchase.

- Walmart has everyday low prices as well as roll back prices.

- Walmart price matches: just mention the price match before your cashier rings up the items. You don't even need to carry the competitor ad with you!

- Walmart accepts competitor coupons: bring in competing store coupons to your store. Will not accept coupons from competitors involving dollar off or percentage off entire basket purchases. When using a competitor coupon, you cannot stack it with a manufacturer coupon.

- Walmart does not run many promotions or release a weekly grocery ad on any regular basis. Prices and sales tend to vary greatly by region.

- Walmart does not have consistent enforcement of any portion of its coupon policy. Some shoppers have a great experience at Walmart while others have quite the opposite.

- Walmart does not allow more than one coupon of any kind for one item. You may not use a store coupon and a manufacturer coupon together.

- Walmart will give you overage (in the form of cash back or applied towards other items in your cart) when the coupon value exceeds the value of the item.

THE SECRET
Combine coupons with Walmart rollback prices or price match with a competitor ad
and use manufacturer coupons to lower your out of pocket expense.
Also look for items that "pay" you and apply the overage to the rest of the items in your cart.

Examples:

Breyers Ice Cream 2 for $5.00 in Walgreens Drugstore weekly ad
Buy 1 Breyers Ice Cream $2.50
Use $1.00/1 Breyers product printable manufacturer coupon
Final Price at Walmart: $1.50 each

OR

Breyer's Ice Cream 2 for $5.00 in Walgreens Drugstore weekly ad
Buy 1 Breyer's Ice Cream, $2.50
Use $0.75/1 Breyers product store coupon from Albertsons grocery ad
Final Price at Walmart: $1.75 each

Similac Ready to Feed Formula $3.86
Pampers Wipes $2.00
Use $5.00/1 Similac manufacturer coupon
Use $1.00/1 Pampers manufacturer coupon
Final Price: $0.14 Moneymaker!

WHOLE FOODS

Before you shop Whole Foods with coupons, here's what you should know about its policy:

- Whole Foods accepts newspaper, printable, and other manufacturer coupons.
- Whole Foods has store coupons that you can stack with a manufacturer coupon.
- Sign up for its "Whole Deal" newsletter at wholefoodsmarket.com to receive additional store coupons bi-monthly.
- Keep your eyes peeled for all sorts of coupons in store aisles. You will find tearpads, booklets, and complimentary magazines loaded with coupons.
- Take your own reusable bag to checkout to save $.10 per bag.
- Consider buying in bulk the items you use most frequently. Whole Foods will offer a discount when you buy a large quantity. Ask your customer service for more details.
- Whole Foods ads run Wednesday through Tuesday.

Whole Foods is not your conventional grocery store. If you are committed to shopping organically, you may be thinking that you will be limited when it comes to shopping with coupons. Or you may be afraid your organic shopping days are over if you want to save money. While your savings will not be 70%, you can stay committed to shopping organically, all while becoming a Krazy Coupon Lady.

THE SECRET
Stack a sale or clearance markdown with manufacturer coupons and store coupons.

Example:

Buy 1 MaraNatha Roasted No Stir Almond Butter or Peanut Butter, 16 oz $3.99
Use $1.00/1 MaraNatha product manufacturer coupon
And Use $1.00/1 MaraNatha Nut Butter printable store coupon
Final Price: $1.99

WINCO

Before you shop WinCo with coupons, here's what you should know about its policy:

- WinCo accepts newspaper, printable, and other manufacturer coupons. Internet printable coupons may not exceed a $5 value and "free product" printables are not accepted.

- Customers are limited to one coupon per item. Coupons are not subject to doubling or tripling, nor are competitor coupons accepted.

- WinCo does not distribute a weekly ad or coupons on a regular basis.

- WinCo is the classic no-frills grocery store. Not a penny spent on advertising, just passing the savings on to the customer. Bag your own groceries in exchange for everyday low prices.

THE SECRET

Take your coupon binder with you whenever shopping at WinCo and
watch for low prices and coupons to pair together!

As you peruse the aisles, watch for WinCo's "Wall of Values", Price Shocker areas, and Extra Savings green price tags. They rarely do promotions—just sale and everyday low prices. Watch for things like BBQ sauce in the summer and baking goods during the holidays. As WinCo prices follow the categorical sales trends, you will be able to use coupons to achieve good savings.

You will not be able to achieve savings of 70% by only shopping at a no-frills store like WinCo, but you could save $50-$100 a month with their low everyday prices. Compare your WinCo shopping list with **TheKrazyCouponLady.com** Printable Coupon Database, and print your savings before heading to the store. WinCo is meticulous about checking your printable coupons. Expect a manager to be called over to verify their validity.

WinCo can be the best place to buy some items. Low prices are often found on dairy, meat, and in their extensive bulk section. It's a matter of keeping your eyes peeled. But do your big stockpile shopping (like special ordering twenty boxes of cereal for a quarter each) at a high-end store with big promotions.

Glossary

$1.00/1, $2.00/1, etc.: One dollar off one product, two dollars off one product, etc.

$1.00/2, $2.00/2, etc.: One dollar off two products, two dollars off two products, etc. You must buy two items to receive any savings; you cannot redeem the coupon on one product for half the value.

B1G1, B2G1: Another way to write "buy one, get one." The "B" stands for "buy," the "G" stands for "get." The numbers indicate how many of a product you must buy to qualify and the number of products you get when you redeem the coupon or offer. B1G1 = Buy one, get one. B2G1 = Buy two, get one. B2G2= Buy two, get two.

Blinkie: Manufacturer coupons dispensed by coupon machines found in grocery aisles next to products. Recognize them by the blinking red light. Dispenses coupons one at a time in intervals. Manufacturer blinkie coupons may be redeemed at any store, not necessarily the store in which you found them.

BOGO: Buy one, get one. Will usually end with "free" or "half off" meaning buy one, get one half off, or buy one, get one free.

Catalina: Sometimes abbreviated as "CAT," Catalina coupon machines, located at register, dispense long receipt-like coupons that may be used on a future purchase. Catalinas refer to the coupons themselves, which may be manufacturer or store coupons. Some Catalina coupons are advertised, and some are generated based on consumer behavior.

Coupon: A note from a store or manufacturer that entitles shopper to a discount on a specific product. Coupons may be clipped from the newspaper, printed from the Internet, or even downloaded to your store loyalty card.

Couponer: [koo-pon-er, kyoo-] (n.) A person who collects and saves coupons to redeem them on products, such as groceries.

Couponing: [koo-pon-ing, Kyoo-] (v.) The practice of redeeming discount coupons in order to save money.

Coupon Insert: Coupon circulars inserted into Sunday newspapers among the other advertisements. Smart Source (SS), Red Plum (RP), and Procter & Gamble (P&G) put out coupon inserts, sometimes just called "inserts." Coupon inserts are a valuable money-saving tool, and The Krazy Coupon Lady recommends buying multiple Sunday newspapers in order to have enough coupons to create a stockpile.

CRT: Cash Register Tape. Usually used when talking about CVS pharmacy, CRTs print at the bottom of your receipt and are generated based on your purchasing history (seemingly random). CRTs are specific to the store where they were printed. They are usually product specific coupons, example: $1.00 off any deodorant purchase.

Double Coupons: Select stores always double coupons up to a certain value, usually $0.50. If your store doubles coupons up to $0.50 off, any coupon $0.50 or under will be doubled in value. Coupons $0.51 or greater will be worth face value, no doubling. You do not need to present two coupons for one item. Each coupon will be worth twice the value. Other stores may double coupons on a particular week-day, usually a slower day like Tuesday. Other stores may offer physical store "twice-the-value" coupons. Even other stores may feature double coupons on a special promo week basis and will advertise this in their weekly ads.

ECB: Extra Care Buck CVS pharmacy program; now renamed Extra Bucks.

eCoupons: Electronic coupons may be downloaded onto your store loyalty card or cell phone. Download from your PC or go mobile and download to your loyalty card through your cell phone. Grocery coupons must be downloaded to your loyalty card and will be deducted automatically when you swipe your card at checkout. eCoupons may be downloaded to your cell phone for other retail items such as movie rentals. Download a coupon using the mobile ap and show your discount code to your cashier.

EXP: Expires or Expiration Date.

Extra Bucks: CVS rewards program, formerly called ECBs. Extra Bucks print according to the store's weekly or monthly advertised deals. When you make a qualifying purchase, you receive the coordinating Extra Bucks value as advertised. Extra Bucks are similar to Catalinas or Register Rewards, but they print directly onto the bottom of your receipt.

FAR: Free After Rebate. Drugstores often feature a product or two each week that are FAR. An example might be Crest TotalCare toothpaste $2.49. Submit for a rebate in the amount of $2.49. This item would be considered free after rebate. You will still be responsible for sales tax.

GS1 Databar: The latest and most accurate barcode for products and coupons. Databar symbols can carry more information than UPC bar codes, which reduces coupon fraud.

Handling Fee: Refers to an amount, usually $0.08, paid by the manufacturer to reimburse the store for the trouble of accepting a coupon. The handling fee is usually used to pay a clearinghouse to sort, organize, and bill the manufacturer. If a store chooses to sort its own coupons, it will keep the handling fee.

IP: Internet Printable coupons may be printed right from your home computer, usually limited to two prints per computer. Download quick and safe printing software to be able to print securely from home.

IVC: Instant Value Coupon. IVCs are store coupons found in the weekly Walgreens ad. IVCs may be stacked with a manufacturer coupon.

KCL: Krazy Coupon Lady, refers to TheKrazyCouponLady.com

Krazy: Intensely enthusiastic about or preoccupied with saving money by using coupons.

Limit Per Shopping Trip: Verbiage included on some coupons to indicate a specific number of coupons which the shopper may use per store location, per day.

Manufacturer: The company which produces the brand items: Dove soap manufacturer, Pace salsa manufacturer, etc.

Manufacturer Coupon: A coupon created by the manufacturer, or by a marketing company on the manufacturer's behalf. Manufacturer offers a discount to shoppers in order to entice them to buy their products. When a coupon is redeemed, the manufacturer reimburses the store for the entire value of the coupon, plus a handling fee, approximately $0.08.

MFR: Manufacturer abbreviation.

MIR: Mail in Rebate, refers to rebates which must be submitted by mail. These are the traditional rebates that require you to mail in both your receipt and proof of purchase in the form of UPC barcodes.

One Coupon per Purchase: Refers to your ability to use one coupon per item. Meant to enforce the point that you may not use two of the exact same coupon for one item.

One Coupon per Transaction: Limits you to using only one of this coupon per transaction. You may request to do separate transactions. Example: If you have five coupons that read "one coupon per transaction" you may request to separate into five transactions and pay five times.

OOP: Out-of-Pocket; refers to the amount of money you will pay a store to make your purchase. Does not include after-purchase savings, coupons, or rebates.

OYNO: On Your Next Order. Store promos such as "Spend $25, save $10 on your next shopping order." OYNO refers to savings that you will not see on your first transaction, but that may be applied to your next purchase. Most OYNO coupons have no minimum purchase. If you spend $25 and receive a coupon worth $10 off your next order, there is no minimum purchase on that next order. If you spend over $10, you may redeem your coupon. If you spend under $10, you may use your coupon but will forfeit the difference.

Peelie: Adhesive manufacturer coupons found on products in the store. A peelie is often good on a wider selection of products than the one to which it is stuck. Be sure to read the fine print on the peelie to discover whether the coupon may be used on a smaller size or different variety of the same product to allow you to maximize savings.

P&G: Procter & Gamble manufactures a wide range of consumer goods and is one of the largest corporations in the world. Procter & Gamble puts out monthly coupon inserts filled with coupons for a variety of Procter & Gamble produced brands, just a few of which include: Always, Bounty, Crest, Dawn, Gillette, Olay, Pampers, and Tide.

PSA: Prices starting at. When a group of items is on sale, such as Fiber One products 25% off, I might write "PSA $2.09" and list a group of Fiber One coupons. This means that the cheapest Fiber One product is $2.09 and prices go up from there.

Purchase: A purchase refers to buying any item. If I buy thirty items on a single shopping trip, I just made thirty purchases.

Purchase-Based Coupon: Purchase-based coupons specify a dollar amount off a minimum dollar future purchase. Some common values: $2 off $10, $3 off $15, $4 off $20. Purchase-based coupons may be used in addition to store and manufacturer coupons.

Q: Coupon abbreviation. (Not used on TheKrazyCouponLady.com).

Rain Check: A rain check is a written slip you can request from a store when a sale item is out of stock. When the store restocks the item, after the sale period is over, a rain check entitles you to purchase for the previous sale price. Store may include an expiration date as well as a quantity limit on your rain check. Rain checks are usually issued at the customer service desk.

Rebate: A rebate is a refund of part or all of the amount paid. The Krazy Coupon Lady refers to rebates as programs that offer you cash back for making a qualified purchase. Rebates are sponsored by a store or a manufacturer. Either clip and mail UPC barcodes or enter the receipt proof of purchase online; then wait for your rebate check in the mail.

Rolling Catalinas: Rolling refers to the practice of separating your purchase into multiple transactions in order to use register Catalina coupons from your first transaction to pay for your second transaction. Another Catalina prints from the second transaction that pays for the third transaction and so on.

RP: Red Plum. Formerly known as Valassis, Red Plum's coupon inserts and website feature coupons from a variety of manufacturers. Red Plum is part of Valassis Interactiv.

RR: Register Rewards. Walgreens drugstore rewards program, a version of the Catalina coupon. Look for the same machines located at register, dispensing long receipt-like coupons that may be used on a future purchase. RRs cannot be "rolled" like Catalinas.

SCR: Single Check Rebate, Rite Aid Drugstore monthly rebate program. Each month pick up your rebate booklet to see hundreds of dollars in possible rebate savings. Shop with coupons, save your receipts, and enter quick information online. The SCR system stores all your rebates and totals them each month. Request your monthly check be mailed to you and cash it like any other check! No clipping barcodes or UPCs, no mailing or stamping an envelope.

SS: Smart Source. A marketing company, like RP, Smart Source coupon inserts and website feature coupons from a variety of manufacturers. Smart Source is part of News America Marketing Co.

Stacking: Stacking may refer to using any two promotions together. When a coupon coincides with a promotion, I say, "stack the coupon with the sale or promotion."

Stacking Coupons: Stacking coupons refers to using both a store coupon and a manufacturer coupon on one product. Nearly all stores will allow you to "stack." Only one manufacturer coupon may be used per item.

Stockpile (n.): A food storage or stash of food and non-food items. Stockpiling is a key principle to The Krazy Coupon Lady methods. Buy items when they're on sale and you have a coupon. Buy products before you need them and build up a stockpile of food and toiletries. When you run out of an item, shop from your stockpile.

Stockpile (v.): To buy many items at a time in order to build your stockpile.

Store Coupon: A coupon created by the store to entice you to buy a certain product at that store. Stores receive no reimbursement from store coupons. Store coupons may be found in the weekly ad, printed online, or downloaded as e-coupons.

Store Loyalty Card: A free card that you present at checkout to receive additional savings. Fill out a short application to receive a loyalty card at your local grocer. If you don't want to carry the card, the cashier can look up your preferred card by entering your ten digit phone number.

Tear Pad: A pad of manufacturer coupons found near a product on shopping aisles. Tear pad manufacturer coupons may be used at any store, not just the one where you found the coupon.

Transaction: A transaction refers to your entire purchase, especially the payment you make for that purchase. If I buy thirty items and then pay the cashier, I just made one transaction.

UPC: Universal Product Code. Bar code printed on product packages that can be scanned electronically.

WAGS: Abbreviation for Walgreens Drugstore

WYB: When You Buy. Some sales or coupons require purchase of multiple items. When reporting a deal on The Krazy Coupon Lady.com, I always include a final price. Example: Buy 2 Mint Milano cookies $2.00 each, use 2 $1.00/2 coupons, Final Price: $1.50 each, WYB 2. You must buy two in order to use the $1.00/2 coupon, so the final price states "WYB 2."

YMMV: Your Mileage May Vary. A phrase used to describe that an experience one shopper has may differ from your experience. One store may allow you to stack additional promos and another location may not do the same. Some stores, such as that "one" supercenter that does not have a universally enforced coupon policy, will often let one customer do one thing and another do something completely different. If I receive an email from a reader with a great shopping scenario, I might report it and say, "YMMV until we see if stores nationwide are allowing the same scenario."

Index